Social Problems and Issues

Social Problems and Issues

A Canadian Perspective

Subhas Ramcharan
University of Windsor

NELSON CANADA

© Nelson Canada,
A Division of International Thomson Limited, 1989
Published in 1989 by
Nelson Canada
A Division of International Thomson Limited
1120 Birchmount Road
Scarborough, Ontario M1K 5G4

Canadian Cataloguing in Publication Data

Ramcharan, Subhas.
    Social problems and issues

Bibliography: p.
ISBN 0-17-603439-0

1. Canada - Social conditions - 1971-
2. Social problems. I. Title.

HN103.5.R35 1989   301   C89-093717-6

Printed and bound in Canada

4 5 6 7 8 9 WC 95 94 93

To Nigel, Chantele, Adele, and Margaret

Contents

List of Tables and Figures

Preface and Acknowledgements

This book provides under one cover an analysis of the diverse but interrelated social problems and issues facing Canadian society today. As an undergraduate text, it introduces students to the major theoretical approaches sociologists use to determine and interpret the causes of social problems, and to assess their impact on individuals, groups, and society as a whole. The social problems texts currently available to Canadian students deal almost exclusively with American society. Since I do not believe that the two countries are socially or culturally interchangeable, *Social Problems and Issues: A Canadian Perspective* is intended to fill a vacuum in the field of Canadian sociology.

No single book can adequately cover all the social problems encountered in Canadian society. The subject matter in this text has been carefully selected to reflect both manifest problems—whose analysis at this time in our history is critical—and latent problems, which have been growing in significance in recent years. The structure of the book is flexible enough to allow the instructor to alter the chronology of topics for lecture purposes. Each chapter concludes with a summary of the main points in the text. A general glossary provides quick reference to definitions.

Part 1, The Analysis of Social Problems (Chapter 1), begins with a definition of social problems. Following a discussion of the uniquely Canadian perspective on social problems, the student is introduced to the major sociological approaches to social problems. The section concludes with an examination of the basic research methods available to the sociologist.

Part II, Social Disorganization (Chapters 2 through 8), examines social problems that have arisen out of conflict and disorganization in Canada's social institutions. Each chapter proposes broad strategies for mitigating the problem under review.

Part III, Regional and Intergroup Conflict (Chapters 9 and 10), looks at problems associated with regionalism and visible minority groups. In Chapter 9, regional issues are studied within the context of Canada's historical and economic development. Chapter 10 explores the role and status of visible minority groups in Canadian society, with particular reference to immigration policy, racial discrimination, and majority–minority group relations.

Part IV, Deviance (Chapters 11 through 14), examines the causes and consequences of deviant behaviour, and suggests ways in which it might be alleviated. Of special emphasis in this section is the relationship between deviant behaviour and labelling.

I wish to acknowledge Peter Milroy of Methuen and Anita Miecznikowski of Nelson Canada for their support and enthusiasm. They believed in the project and saw it through. To the secretaries in the Sociology Department at the University of Windsor, Pierina Pittao, Sue McGilveary, and Andrea Turner, who spent many long hours typing the manuscript—my sincere appreciation. Finally, I would like to thank my wife Margaret, without whose boundless encouragement this book would not have seen the light of day. My debt to her is eternal.

PART 1

ISSUES AND PERSPECTIVES

1

The Analysis of Social Problems

INTRODUCTION

The definition of a social problem may appear, at first glance, to be a fairly straightforward matter. However, while there is general agreement among Canadians that some social issues (e.g., poverty or crime) are clearly social problems, on other issues there is far less consensus. This is mainly because of the difficulty we have in delineating the common characteristics of all social problems. Many people, for example, regard discrimination against minority groups as a problem, while others think of it as functional, that is, as serving an economic or social purpose. Similarly, some people define homosexuality per se as a problem, whereas others locate the problem in society's prejudicial attitude toward homosexuals. Public opinion is likewise split on such problems as drug use and addiction, child and wife abuse, alcoholism, mental illness, family disorganization, and urban problems.

For the purposes of this text, we will be using Fuller and Myers' (1981:100) classic definition of a social problem as "a condition which is defined by a considerable number of people as a deviation from some social norm." Other aspects of this definition include the belief that these conditions can be eliminated or reduced through group and societal action, as well as the understanding that people have to be aware that the problem exists and that it threatens their basic values before it can be labelled a social problem and targeted for remedial measures.

The social and economic inequality experienced by French Canadians is an example of a social issue that remained *latent* for over a hundred years. It was not until the 1960s, after the birth of several protest and radical movements in Quebec, including the FLQ terrorist group, that Anglophone Canada became conscious of the social conditions existing for the masses in Quebec—conditions that gave rise to the separatist movement and the election to power of the Parti Québécois in 1976. In other words, the social problem became *manifest* only when a sufficient number of people became aware of the threat to their basic values and to Canada as a nation. The resulting attempts at remedial action were clear examples of the strategies that can be instituted to resolve a major social issue.

A degree of subjectivity enters not only into the definition of a social problem, but also into discussions of all the phenomena it encompasses. For instance, large industrial organizations and members of the power elite might perceive the concept of work and alienation as meaningless in

3

4 / Issues and Perspectives

the context of a social problem. For, such groups, the work environment may bear little if any relationship to mental illness, absenteeism, drug addiction, alcoholism, or family disorganization, and they may also ascribe worker alienation to personal or psychological inadequacies. From the perspective of the sociologist, however, the work environment can be socially and psychologically harmful, leading to social break-downs.

SOCIAL PROBLEMS FROM A CANADIAN PERSPECTIVE

Most western industrialized societies exhibit broad similarities in terms of how they interpret the causes and consequences of social problems, and, in the long run, attempt to remedy them. However, there are structural differences between each of these societies, which account for variations in the causes of the social problem and its effects on the individual society. From a Canadian perspective, therefore, it is essential that our social problems be analyzed within the context of our own social, cultural, and economic organizations. For example, in the important areas of social disorganization, intergroup relations, and institutional breakdowns (which can give rise to social problems), Canada as a society can only be understood through an internal examination of its social structure. Explanations derived from another culture and society, in offering a false sense of causation, can lead to ineffectual remedial measures.

In the context of intergroup relations, the conflict in French Canada is an outgrowth of the social, economic, and cultural imbalances that developed over the two hundred years since the Conquest. As such, it is only through an analysis of the internal growth and development of Quebec nationalism, combined with concepts of social and economic inequality from a Canadian perspective, that we can suggest possible solutions to the problem. Finally, in the context of interracial conflict in Canada, no solution can be postulated in the absence of a historical and contemporary study of the factors that have contributed to it—e.g., immigration policy, concepts of cultural pluralism and multiculturalism, and the entrenchment of prejudice and discriminatory behaviour in our society.

That social problems in Canada are frequently perceived as simply an extension of American social problems is not surprising given that the analysis of social problems in Canadian sociology has been inextricably linked to developments in American sociology. The general approach has been to transpose the study of society and conclusions about it from one country to the other. The fallacy of such an approach is underlined by the fact that the institutional structures of the two societies, upon which social order and change are contingent, differ markedly. While both are democratic societies, they exhibit sharp differences in terms of their political, cultural, and legal systems, and although both are immigrant-receiving societies, their expectations concerning the eventual outcome of immigrant–work relationships vary. Canada's goal is the growth of a multicultural society with cultural institutional persistence in a "mosaic" pattern, while the American ideal is the total integration of its immigrants into a "melting pot," with the development of common values and institutions at all levels of the system. Thus, a definitive analysis of Canadian social problems must entail an examination of the causes of internal conflicts in the institutions of Canadian society.

SOCIOLOGICAL PERSPECTIVES ON SOCIAL PROBLEMS

As defined by Rubington and Weinberg (1981:9), a sociological perspective "includes a basic orienting idea from which one's conceptualization and analysis follow." This perspective, which normally reflects a particular set of ideas and assumptions regarding the nature of people and society, can resolve for the sociologist not only what social problems should be analyzed, or what method of analysis should be employed, but also what solutions to the problem can be postulated. Rubington and Weinberg (1981:10–11) cite five basic perspectives on social problems: social pathology, social disorganization, value conflict, deviant behaviour, and labelling. While in each perspective the basic definition of what constitutes a social problem remains constant, there are marked divergences between them with regard to the causes and consequences of the breakdown, and with regard to possible solutions to it. All five perspectives, according to Rubington and Weinberg, discuss violations of the norms and reactions to these violations, but each differs on the question of whether the problem has its base in the norms of the society, in the deviation from these norms, or in societal reaction to the violations.

Social Pathology

Early North American sociologists equated society with an organism, which was either healthy or sick depending on whether it was functioning normally or abnormally (Henshel and Henshel 1983:42). This *social pathological perspective* evaluated individuals in the system who were not able to operate within the normative structure as causing social problems. In the social and cultural environment of nineteenth-century North America, standards of normality were based on the assumption that the status quo was normal. Anyone who deviated from this frame of reference was labelled "sick."

In more recent interpretations of this perspective, society is viewed as pathological, while the nonconforming individual is seen as the victim of societal institutions that need to be changed. There is no doubt that, given these contrasting viewpoints as to what constitutes social pathology, the impact of this school in the study of social problems has waned significantly. Some writers, notably Kavolis (1981), have devised a framework for cross-cultural analysis of social problems, which attempts to distinguish between truly pathological behaviour and simple deviance from a set of norms that may or may not be causative of the pathology. However, few can agree as to what constitutes a "healthy" society. Furthermore, in the context of modern society, many of the phenomena previously seen as the *subject matter* of social pathology are now regarded as the *symptoms* of conflict, cultural value, and attitudinal change, and thus as relating to the processes of social disorganization.

Social Disorganization

The growth of urbanization, industrialization, and immigration produced in early twentieth-century North America social breakdowns that the social pathology model could not adequately explain. Mass immigration to the United States intensified cultural conflict in the society. In addition, rapid urbanization introduced problems that society was unable to cope with, leading to the formation of subcultures and non-normative coping mechanisms. Drug addiction, mental illness, crime, and delinquency increased as normlessness and rootlessness became a way of life for large segments of the population unable to adjust to new patterns of behaviour demanded by the new industrial world.

As a result of societal breakdowns, the *social disorganization model* was developed to, first, analyze the causes and consequences of inadequate social institutions and norms, and second, to suggest remedial measures. For society, disorganization could only be remedied if the cause of the breakdown was isolated, and institutional changes, in addition to a new set of rules and expectations, introduced to bring the society to a new base of equilibrium. The fundamental goals of the social disorganization school, then, were to promote the theoretical and empirical analysis of society, to isolate causative phenomena, to document negative consequences of the behaviour, and to provide solutions through changes in social and economic institutions. In this period sociology was most successful in developing its subject matter and in formulating a set of theoretical concepts outlining the perimeters of the discipline.

Unfortunately, later generations of sociologists generalized the concept of social disorganization to include *all* forms of behaviour that failed to conform to established norms. Clinard and Meier (1979:63–67) suggest that this school tended to confuse social disorganization with change, deviant behaviour, subcultures, and with human variation. Making the case for a more narrow definition of social disorganization, they suggest that the concept has merit only for the study of specific groups and institutions, and that broad generalizing analysis fails to explain, for example, why social change can be both disorganizing in some instances and integrative in others. Another problem with the social disorganization school, according to Clinard and Meier, is that it involves a value judgement on the part of the observer and the members of his or her social class. Finally, although deviant behaviour may be on the rise, it does not necessarily follow that there is a consequent threat to the basic values of our society, which shows a high degree of integration and consensus, despite increasing incidences of suicide, crime, alcoholism, and other forms of non-normative behaviour. In some instances, by creating a "we group," subcultural activities and membership can contribute to the integration, rather than the weakening, of society.

Value Conflict

Conflict theorists contend that social problems occur when groups with different, and often opposing, values compete and in so doing generate tension and sometimes violence. The major conceptualization of the *value conflict* approach to social problems was put forward by Fuller and Myers (1981), who suggested that social problems were the result of social conditions that were incompatible with the values or interests of competing groups in society, and that all social problems go through three stages: awareness, policy determination, and reform. In the first stage, groups see the situation as a threat to their values. In the second stage, they choose sides, redefine values, and offer proposals for action. In the third, or final, stage, they resolve the problem by translating formulated policy into public action, which is represented by the machinery of the government (legislative, executive, and judicial branches) enforcing changes on society, either by consensus or by the use of power. The value conflict perspective can be applied with particular success to such issues as interracial conflict and poverty.

In conclusion, there is no inherent reason why conflict between different interest groups should be perceived as ultimately negative for society. In fact, according to this approach, the resolution of value conflict between competing interest groups could lead to a state of renewed equilibrium and integration. For example, the resolution of racial and sexist discrimination in society would have the inevitable result of providing more opportunities for all to fulfil their aspirations, thus lessening societal conflict and tension.

8 / Issues and Perspectives

Deviance

While it is difficult to define deviance in terms that are generally acceptable, sociologists agree that certain kinds of social conduct can be classified as deviant (e.g., crime, drug addiction, juvenile delinquency, prostitution, homosexuality, suicide, and mental disorders). Hagan (1984:4)
argues that "the central themes of a culture are an important influence in
determining a society's conceptualization of deviance." In simple terms,
deviance, for Hagan, is variation from social norms. The many different
categories of deviance can be seen as a continuum ranging from mild to
very serious deviations from acceptable conduct.

A significant factor in how deviance is defined is the *societal evaluation* of the negative consequences of the non-normative behaviour. For
example, as Hagen (1984:13) sees it, acts such as drug abuse or gambling
are "victimless" in the sense that participation is voluntary. Regarding
other acts of deviance, such as crimes of violence, robberies, or even
white-collar crime, the social consequences are more apparent and the
perception of victimization more visible. The vast majority of Canadians
support strong action against such behaviours. However, public opinion
is more divided when it comes to noncriminal types of deviance (e.g.,
mental illness, suicide, drug and alcohol abuse, and homosexuality),
which, although more prevalent, are perceived as less harmful to society.

In discussing possible approaches to deviance, Henshel and
Henshel (1983:Chapter 3) suggest that social disorganization and conflict
theories are successful in delineating social situations that are likely to
create social problems, but they are basically inadequate in terms of
explaining what causes individual non-normative, or deviant, behaviour.
For example, while some persons in situations of conflict or social
disorganization choose to act out a pattern of negative behaviour, others
do not; hence the need for a theory that explains *individual* behaviour.

According to the *deviance perspective,* social problems develop
when a person acts in ways considered unacceptable by mainstream
society. In sociology, there are three basic theories of deviance. The
differential association theory expounded by Sutherland (1981), suggests
that deviance results from the learning processes, and that differences in
behaviour between individuals are due to the frequency, duration, and
intensity of their contacts with either deviant or law-abiding persons.
However, Henshel and Henshel (1983:50) note that "while this theory
can explain that kind of deviance which results from involuntary contacts,
it fails to consider that many social contacts are voluntary." This is in
contrast to Merton's *anomie theory* and Cohen's *delinquent subculture
theory,* both of which attempt to provide explanations of the structural
bases that lead to preferences in association between people.

Merton (1968:140–45) argues that anomie could develop for persons in certain segments of society when their cultural goals and their legitimate opportunities to achieve these goals are incompatible. He notes that this conflict can produce four types of deviant behaviour: (1) "Innovation," when people adopt new illicit means of achieving the goals; (2) "ritualism," when they renounce the goals, but tend to emphasize the means; (3) "retreatism," when they renounce both the goals and society's norms, and (4) "rebellion," when they attempt to replace both the goals and the means by another system. Merton's theory of deviant behaviour can be applied to many different social problems. For example, organized crime, pornography, or prostitution can reflect innovation, while drug addiction or mental illness can reflect retreatism on the part of the individual.

In his theory of the delinquent subculture, Cohen (1955:27) attempts to synthesize the anomie and differential association theories by postulating that boys from a working-class environment become anomic after exposure to the middle-class values of the school system. The result is the formation of a subculture that rejects the cultural values of the school and mainstream society. Through this process of differential association, they develop and transmit a set of normative behavioural patterns that provides status and roles within their gang subculture. According to this perspective, the main solution for deviant behaviour is resocialization through increased primary group contact with legitimate patterns of behaviour, and reduced contact with illegitimate primary groups. Cloward and Ohlin (1981:159–60) also note that increased economic opportunities must be created in order to alleviate the strains that motivate people to behave in unacceptable ways; if legitimate opportunities are opened up for these individuals, socially deviant forms of behaviour would decrease.

Labelling

We have already noted that sociologists involved in the study of social problems have developed different perspectives on the causes, consequences, and solving of social problems, as well as on the question of what societal dysfunctions should be examined in the first place. Let us now consider criticisms of, and responses to, the deviance perspective, which is basically concerned with the "whys" of deviancy.

Critics have noted that the deviance perspective fails to adequately define the *causes* of deviance. Thus a new school has developed which is more interested in knowing how people define situations or persons as problematic. Through *labelling theory*, sociologists have begun examining the negative consequences of formal social control agencies that have become part of modern industrial society. From the deviance perspective, agencies of social control were perceived as supportive units designed to alleviate social problems. However, sociologists are increasingly becoming aware that these agencies may be exacerbating the problems by stigmatizing the individuals or groups classified as deviant.

The labelling school, which is the latest approach in North American sociology to social problems vis-à-vis causation, attempts to answer questions left unanswered by the deviant behaviour perspective, and to observe society from the point of view of both those who have been defined as deviant and those who assign the definitions. In a multigroup society, conforming to the rules of one's own group sometimes requires violating another group's legal, moral, or social rules. Furthermore, violators of the norms are not classified or treated in the same way (Becker 1981:191–92). As a result, sociologists have begun to examine the conditions under which violations are sanctioned. While there are differences between the labelling and deviant schools in terms of their approaches to analysis, their positions are basically the same. The major difference is that labelling theory focuses on the effects of the labelling or stigmatization on the individual or group, while deviance theory emphasizes, as Henshel and Henshel (1983:52) note, the relationship between "cultural expectations and social reality."

The foundation of the labelling perspective was laid by Lemert (1972), who introduced a theory of deviant behaviour based on the premise that deviance is defined by social reactions. Becker (1981:189) crystallizes the focus of the school in his suggestion that "social groups create deviance by making the rules whose infraction constitutes deviance, and by applying those rules to particular people and labeling them as outsiders." In this regard, it is the *social response* to the behaviour that accounts for its negative status. Furthermore, labelling becomes something of a self-fulfilling prophecy as individuals begin to act out the labels applied to them. A major assumption behind labelling theory, as Hagan (1984:122) points out, is that much deviant behaviour could be mitigated if negative labels were eliminated. Becker's work suggests that the process toward deviancy is a dynamic, interactive one, that the enforcement of moral rules is essentially political, and, most importantly, that the meaning and measurement of a deviant act can change over time.

Serious criticism has been levelled against the labelling school. Nettler (1981) argues that labelling theory fails as both a predictive and explanatory theory, and is therefore an ineffectual tool in the analysis of deviant behaviour. Labelling theorists, Nettler suggests, emphasize definitions of deviance but show little concern for the acts of deviance, focusing instead on how others in society react to the behaviour. Labelling theory thus depends heavily on the idea that social relations are defined before they are reacted to. For example, as Nettler (ibid) notes, from the labelling perspective "crime" is word, not an act. Crime is socially defined and criminals are socially produced, in that the majority applies labels to minority groups, who in turn are provoked into fulfilling the roles assigned to them by mainstream society. While labelling theory is politically important because it challenges the status quo and enables sociologists to examine the effects of assigning deviant status to certain non-normative forms of behaviour, it never comes to grips with the need to explain *why* people behave differently. As Nettler (ibid) suggests, it slights the possibility that a label may correctly identify consistent differences in conduct, and fails to consider why society continues to apply a label once it has been used.

Conclusion

While each of these five perspectives differs in emphasis as to the causes of social problems, they are not mutually exclusive but can be seen as extensions of one another. From our point of view, some perspectives are more relevant to the analysis of Canadian social problems than others. For example, the social disorganization model best explains many of the institutional breakdowns in society that result from social, cultural, and technological changes. The problems of people in urban environments, of work and alienation, and of the aged all exemplify the inability of existing social institutions to cope with the impact of modernization and industrialization.

Similarly, in terms of intergroup relations in Canada, the value conflict perspective gives us clear answers as to the causes of social inequality, prejudice, and discrimination. Our language, native people, and visible minority problems show quite vividly that Canadians are in a state of group conflict between those with a collective interest in maintaining social and economic inequities and those interested in changing the system.

Finally, in this text neither the deviant behaviour nor labelling perspectives are viewed as singlehandedly providing all the answers to the causation of abnormal behaviour in Canada. In situations where there are clearly defined and uniformly supported norms, the deviant behaviour approach will be utilized (e.g., in our analysis of crime and delinquency, where there is universal support for the agencies of social control). However, in the case of "victimless" crimes (e.g., marijuana use or prostitution), the social processes leading to the societal reaction are best studied from the labelling perspective.

RESEARCH ISSUES AND METHODS

The main purpose of sociological research is to investigate and explain group behaviour in the social system. It is only through research that we can obtain a clear focus on phenomena that are perceived as social problems. Personal impressions cannot be generalized as reflecting those of the total society. Often our opinions are biased, our data base inaccurate, and our conclusions erroneous. Sociological research attempts to remove these factors in its incorporation of a number of clearly defined stages and methods.

Defining the Problem

This is the crucial initial stage in the research process. Often if the problem is defined improperly the results will be inaccurate and possible solutions difficult to formulate. In a single study of the causes of poverty, for example, it is often impossible to delineate and analyze all of the variables that contribute to the problem. Preferably the researcher should develop clear goals and limits, examining instead some of the major variables (e.g., changes in technology and its relationship to job obsolescence) that cause poverty.

Reviewing the Literature

After the initial problem has been defined, the researcher should review previous research on the topic. The purpose is to obtain a clear grasp of the findings of previous investigations, such that they can be amplified, refuted, or replicated. In some instances, a review of the literature can lead to the reformulation of the problem.

The Case Study

This method is especially useful when the objective is to study a particular phenomenon in considerable depth (e.g., a riot, residents in a neighbourhood, or inmates in a prison). The researcher carefully studies the subject, analyzes the data, and then draws conclusions that can be applied to comparable situations. Early research into the causes of deviant behaviour generally adopted this method (e.g., Thrasher's [1927] study of *The Gang* in Chicago, Chambliss's [1973] study of delinquent gangs, and Whyte's [1943] study *Street Corner Society*), which can provide clear insights into human behaviour that other methods may miss. However, depending on the skills of the researcher, distortions of the evidence can occur. Furthermore, because the findings are based on a particular group, the ability to generalize to other groups in the society is often limited. Still, when combined with other methods—particularly the sample survey—the utility of this approach is unquestioned in sociological research.

The Sample Survey

In this method, members of the public are sampled on their attitudes or opinions on a wide array of social issues. In terms of perimeters, the population sampled can be nationally based (as used in Gallup polls), or limited to a particular social category (e.g., working women). If the sample is reliable and representative of the category, the findings can be generalized to the total population. (This method of social research has been widely adopted by sociologists in analyzing attitudes toward poverty, racism, pornography, homosexuality, crime prevention, capital punishment, and other social issues.) The sociologist can then infer from the results various interpretations of human behaviour vis-à-vis race, education, age, sex, income, and other variables. For example, in a study of racism in Toronto, Henry (1978) demonstrated through a sample survey that different groups held markedly different opinions and attitudes about visible minorities in the city. Using her findings, policy makers could introduce ameliorative measures aimed at reducing intergroup conflict.

While the sample survey may not be as useful for in-depth analyses of social problems, it is a major source of information on social characteristics and public attitudes, as well as a tool for measuring attitudinal changes on social issues over time. For example, Gallup polls taken in Canada in 1968 and 1978 show that the public's attitude toward homosexuality has changed positively in the ten-year period, suggesting the efficacy of government legislation concerning nonpublic homosexual behaviour. However, the difficulties of obtaining an accurate sample must not be underestimated. The researcher must check for bias, erroneous or untruthful answers, and sampling errors before generalizing his or her findings to the total population.

Analysis

After collecting and organizing the data, the researcher arranges the information in a clear and coherent manner, interprets the findings, and if testing various hypotheses, either confirms, rejects, or modifies the hypotheses, reformulating, when necessary, theoretical and methodological concepts. In writing a report, the sociologist must deal with the problem of bias. From the point of view of objective science, value free sociology is the ideal goal. Unfortunately, in terms of human behavioural research, unconscious values and assumptions invariably do intrude into research and theory. To avoid this problem, researchers should make a determined effort to distinguish between fact and opinion in their research, to minimize personal bias in their research conclusions, and to publicize their research methods, data, and findings for critical comments by colleagues.

While it has not been widely discussed in the literature, Canadian sociological research in the analysis of social problems has been growing. In the chapters that follow, our task is to carefully analyze each problem under discussion and to integrate the research findings within a theoretical base. The interrelationship between theoretical concepts and research findings will be crucial to our analysis of the causes and consequences of societal breakdowns, and possible solutions to them.

SUMMARY

1. From the standpoint of the majority, a social problem may be defined as a deviation from some cherished norm. It is generally believed that social problems can be eliminated or mitigated through group or societal action.

2. Social problems can be either latent or manifest. The social and economic inequality experienced by French Canadians in Quebec is an example of a social problem that remained latent until the rise of political and separatist movements in the 1960s.

3. There is widespread agreement that crime and poverty, which cause deprivation and suffering, are social problems. In a pluralistic society like Canada, however, there is less concensus on whether other issues—e.g., soft drug use or prostitution—qualify as social problems.

4. Canadian social problems are often viewed as extensions of American social problems, despite fundamental differences between the two countries in terms of their institutions, goals, and values. From a sociological perspective, the study of Canadian social problems is most fruitfully explored in the context of Canadian social, cultural, and economic institutions.

5. The early social pathology perspective compared society to an organism whose health depended on the ability of its members to function normally. Social problems were caused by those individuals—labelled "sick"—who deviated from the status quo. In a more recent interpretation of this perspective, society is viewed as sick, while the nonconforming individual is seen as the victim of social institutions that need to be changed.

6. The social disorganization model views social problems as resulting from the failure of social rules and norms to explain the social disorganization precipitated by rapid social and cultural change. Social problems are remedied, therefore, through changes to social and economic institutions, and through the introduction of a new set of rules and expectations.

7. According to value conflict theory, social problems occur when the

values and interests of competing groups in society clash. All social problems go through three stages: awareness, policy determination, and reform.

8. There are three basic theories of deviance. According to Sutherland's *differential association* theory, deviance is a learned behaviour. In Merton's *anomie* theory, deviance is seen as occurring when individuals are frustrated in their attempts to reach their goals through legitimate means. Cohen's *subcultural* theory is an attempt to synthesize the anomie and differential association theories.

9. According to labelling theory, deviance is defined by social reactions. Rule-breakers are labelled "deviant" by certain groups in society. The effect of such labelling is to provoke individuals into acting out the labels attached to them. If negative labels were removed there would be a reduction in deviant behaviour.

10. The five basic perspectives on social problems are not mutually exclusive. Depending on the nature of the social problem under review, each perspective has its particular strengths and weaknesses.

11. The main purpose of sociological research is to investigate and explain occurrences in the social system. The five major stages of research utilized by the sociologist are: defining the problem, reviewing the literature, the case study, the sample survey, and analysis.

PART 2

SOCIAL DISORGANIZATION

2

Urbanization

INTRODUCTION

The proportion of Canadians residing in urban areas increased from 34.9 percent in 1901 to 76.2 percent in 1981 (see Table 2.1). Since the Second World War, Canada has experienced one of the largest urban growth rates in the industrialized world, and, together with the United States, comprises the most urbanized sector in the world. Almost 40 percent of our population resides in the three largest metropolitan areas—Toronto, Montreal, and Vancouver (see Table 2.2). For the average Canadian, the rise in urbanization has brought about an improved standard of living, rapid cultural change, and social progress. Accompanying positive changes, however, have been a deterioration in the quality of life of inner-city residents, racial and ethnic conflict, increased social disorganization, and the abandonment of competent and coherent city planning that places the needs of people first (Kennedy 1983:49).

The growth of metropolitan centres shows no signs of easing up. Kennedy (1983:152) predicts that by the year 2001 Canada will have a population of 34 million, with 90 percent resident in urban areas and 73 percent concentrated in twelve major centres, making cities like Montreal and Toronto as large—and perhaps as unmanageable—as New York, Chicago, and Los Angeles are today. The deterioration of the urban core, traffic congestion, urban sprawl, and the cycle of poverty so common in the large American cities may well reach untenable levels in Canada unless comprehensive urban development policies are implemented.

THEORETICAL PERSPECTIVES

For Canadians the consequences of urban deterioration are manifest and real; more difficult to determine are the causes of the problem and ways to alleviate it. Urban sociologists have developed two main perspectives in attempting to analyze the causes and consequences of urban problems.

The *disorganization perspective*, as expressed in the work of Park (1981), perceives the urban environment as a dehumanizing place in which secondary, impersonal relationships are the norm. This model, based on the growth of American industrial cities, sees social disruption (in the form of crime, delinquency, mental illness, and poverty) as the inevitable result of the drift of uneducated, unskilled, and immigrant groups into the cities. Unable to participate in the economic opportunities of mainstream society, such people were compelled to develop an

19

Table 2.1
Percentage of Urban Population for Canada and Provinces, 1901–1981

Region or Province	1901	1931	1961	1981
Canada	34.9	52.5	70.2	76.2
Maritimes	24.5	39.7	49.5	51.9
Prince Edward Island	14.5	19.5	32.4	36.3
Nova Scotia	27.7	46.6	54.3	55.1
New Brunswick	23.1	35.4	46.5	50.7
Quebec	36.1	59.5	74.3	77.6
Ontario	40.3	63.1	77.3	81.7
Prairies	19.3	31.3	57.6	71.4
Manitoba	24.9	45.2	63.9	71.2
Saskatchewan	6.1	20.3	43.0	58.2
Alberta	16.2	31.8	63.3	77.2
British Columbia	46.4	62.3	72.6	78.0

Note: Percentages for Canada exclude Newfoundland, Yukon, and Northwest Territories.
Sources: Census of Canada (1971, Bulletin 1.1-9: Table 10); Census of Canada (1981, Cat.
92-901: Table 6). Reprinted by permission.

alternative lifestyle based on socially unacceptable ways of acting and behaving. Congested urban neighbourhoods led to an increase in social disorganization and social problems—problems that, from this perspective, are an inevitable consequence of the growth of urbanization and industrialization.

The _conflict approach_, on the other hand, perceives the urban environment as composed of large numbers of interest groups competing against each other, with the most powerful ones controlling the decision-making process and deciding where resources can be allocated. By the inadequate allocation of resources to deprived groups in the city, the governing group creates the conditions of physical and emotional deprivation which lead to poverty, crime, and a psychological climate of alienation, apathy, and despair. In addition, according to this perspective, urban conditions are only considered as social problems when these powerful groups feel that their goals and status are affected.

URBAN BLIGHT

Central to the problems of the inner cities in Canada is the question of urban blight. Boyd and Mozersky (1975:402) define urban blight as "that part of the man-made environment which is deemed to be undesirable by a majority of urban residents." They suggest that "the main causes of urban blight are related to changes in the population organization, environment, and technology of a city" (ibid).

Cities like Toronto, Vancouver, and Montreal, which have seen the

Table 2.2
Census Metropolitan Areas in Decreasing Population Order for Canada 1986

National Population Rank	Census Metropolitan Area	Province	Population
1	Toronto	Ontario	3,427,168
2	Montreal	Quebec	2,921,357
3	Vancouver	British Columbia	1,380,729
4	Ottawa-Hull	Ontario-Quebec	819,263
5	Edmonton	Alberta	785,465
6	Calgary	Alberta	671,326
7	Winnipeg	Manitoba	625,304
8	Quebec	Quebec	603,267
9	Hamilton	Ontario	557,029
10	St. Catharines/Niagara	Ontario	343,258
11	London	Ontario	342,302
12	Kitchener	Ontario	311,195
13	Halifax	Nova Scotia	295,990
14	Victoria	British Columbia	255,547
15	Windsor	Ontario	253,988

Source: Statistics Canada, *Population: Census Metropolitan Areas for Canada, 1986.* Catalogue No. 92-104. Ottawa: Supply and Services Canada, 1987. Reprinted by permission.

largest increase in population growth, show the scars of urban blight most vividly. Outward expansion has left the less expensive inner-city housing in the hands of the poor, the unemployed, and the newer immigrants. According to Boyd and Mozersky (1975:405), "there is evidence that blighted areas contribute disproportionately to a city's problems." Citing an urban renewal study in Edmonton (ibid), they note that while the physical space comprises only 1.4 percent of the total city area, it accounts for 6 percent of the city's population, 17.9 percent of the city's physical assaults and sexual offenses, 13.3 percent of the city's juvenile problems, and 7.2 percent of the city's infant mortality. Clearly, a *slumlike*, deprived environment adversely affects the social environment and the quality of life of people living in these neighbourhoods. Urban renewal planners must take this relationship into account in their attempts at improving the physical environment of our deprived groups.

URBAN RENEWAL

Canada and the United States differ quite markedly in their attempts at *urban renewal*. In the United States urban renewal, which was intended to renew deteriorating city centres and provide reasonable quality housing, has generally failed. Local urban renewal agencies bought up slum properties, demolished them, and sold the land to private developers who concentrated their efforts not on subsidized low-income housing, but on profitable office towers and luxury apartment buildings. Under the urban renewal program, the housing problem for the poor simply intensified, since almost twice as many housing units were torn down than were built. In addition, the high-density apartments for the poor that *were* built created vertical slums, characterized by high crime rates, vandalism, and a lack of social services, the very conditions of social and personal disorganization the urban renewal program was supposed to remedy. Given this failure, the new thrust in inner-city renewal in the United States is to rebuild the central city by renovating existing residential and commercial buildings, constructing downtown shopping malls, and generally refurbishing the city core. This approach, however, has done little to solve the housing problems of the urban poor.

More fortunately, Canada's approach to urban renewal has from the beginning been more concerned with the needs of residents. Realizing the heavy social costs that could be created by allowing the inner cities to deteriorate into slums, municipal, provincial, and federal governments, aided by sophisticated planning departments, set about the task of obtaining the co-operation and support of residents in areas deemed to be in need of urban renewal. Citizen coalitions of concerned residents often had a direct input into programs under development. At the back of Canadian planners' minds was the failure of American urban renewal programs, and the high crime rates, decreased standards of health, reduced opportunities for mobility, and waste of human resources that accompany the growth of slums. Two major goals of the Canadian citizen coalitions were the renovation of existing neighbourhoods and the continuity of neighbourhood networks and friendship patterns.

The city of Toronto is a good example of the result of neighbourhood co-operation and involvement in the political process necessary for successful urban renewal. The inner city, home of the newer immigrant groups, has been largely refurbished and a quality of life maintained that has kept social problems at a level no higher than in the newer suburban areas of metropolitan Toronto. Despite the success of the program, conflict is ever present between the demands of the private developer seeking property as a site for a luxury office tower or highrise apartment, and the desire of citizen groups to maintain the residential character of their neighbourhoods. An example of the private developer winning out is Toronto's St. James Town highrise development, a conglomeration of densely populated highrise apartments that represents the worst aspects of urban renewal in Canada, and is the breeding ground for problems similar to those afflicting cities in the United States. It is to be hoped that social problems latent in this type of development have been recognized, and that cities will not allow the deterioration of their inner core. A mixed blessing for inner-city redevelopment in Toronto is the refurbishment of townhouses for the wealthy. While a sign of the positive quality of life in our cities, refurbishment reduces the availability of housing units for the poor and the elderly in the inner-city core.

The inner cities of Canada house the vast majority of economically disadvantaged groups, immigrants, and urban native peoples. The fact that the inner city remains disproportionately represented in incidences of deviant behaviour is to a large extent related to the poverty and lack of opportunity among its residents. Clinard and Meier (1979:145) note that the subculture of working-class urban areas prescribes normative codes, values, and social relationships that are more likely to be categorized as deviant than are their middle-class counterparts. Many conflict theorists argue that powerful interest groups in society maintain a set of legal norms that proscribe working-class behaviour while prescribing middle- and upper-class behaviour. From this perspective, economic deprivation leads people to commit criminal acts, while the psychological problems that result from living in a cycle of poverty are responsible for the high incidence of mental illness among the urban poor.

URBAN POLITICS

In Canada, organized action by urban groups to obtain grass-roots involvement in the political decision-making process began in the 1960s and gained momentum in the following decade. The aim of citizen coalitions, neighbourhood groups, and grass-roots political organizations was to decentralize the power structure so that many different interest groups would have identical amounts of power, or access to power.

Until the 1960s, citizens' groups were usually outmanoeuvred by powerful developers who could rely on the support of a majority of pro-development aldermen and city officials eager to replace tradition with expressways and modern apartment and office towers. The growing awareness of citizens' groups as to their role in community planning derived partly from the recognition that elected officials may not necessarily have been representing *their* interests in important planning decisions, and partly from the activism that pervaded all aspects of North American life in the 1960s.

Today, planning decisions are still made by the elected officials, but they are carried out under the watchful eyes of neighbourhood groups and pro-citizen politicians concerned with preserving the character of the inner cities. In Toronto, for example, notable challenges to development projects in the last dozen years include the halting of the Spadina Expressway—which would have divided numerous neighbourhoods—the prevention of the Trefann Court redevelopment project, and the preservation of the old Chinatown district. While, in the past, neighbourhood groups formed around particular issues often disintegrated once the issues were resolved, in the last twenty years, issues relating to neighbourhood policy—particularly urban renewal—have galvanized these relatively unstructured groups into cohesive organizations with clear and precise goals for neighbourhood improvements and the direction of city development. At present, citizens participate in municipal government as organized neighbourhood groups, as appointed civic leaders to special committees of the municipal councils, and, finally, as lobbying or special interest groups.

Along with greater citizen participation have occurred other changes to Canada's urban political system over the past two decades. In the inner cities, nonprofit housing corporations have been created to develop better quality housing. Self-help projects for deprived visible and ethnic minority group members have seen marked success in many of our large cities. In short, while there will always be conflicting interests in a heterogeneous society, there has been a shift in the balance of power between groups, which bodes well for the future of Canadian cities.

VISIBLE AND ETHNIC MINORITIES IN CITIES

The post-World War II period of industrial expansion and economic growth saw the immigration of millions of people to Canada, the vast majority of whom settled in our urban areas. Boyd and Mozersky (1975:406) note that "the most important type of physical movement with respect to changes in urbanization and urban form is *net migration*, or the difference between the numbers of people migrating to a city from another area and the number of people leaving the city for another area during the same time period." The growth of Canadian cities through migration has been the result of three types of movement: rural–urban, urban–urban, and movements of immigrants to Canada from other countries. More than 80 percent of all postwar immigrants to Canada reside in cities, and in 1986 the three largest metropolitan areas of Canada (Toronto, Montreal, and Vancouver) contained 3 million immigrants, or 80 percent of the total foreign-born population (Statistics Canada 1988).

The ethnic heterogeneity of Canada's large cities began with the immigration of ethnic groups from non-British or French sources in the post-1945 period, but it was not until after 1967 that the racial composition of our cities began to change drastically. At that time, revisions in immigration policy allowed visible minority groups equal opportunities for immigration, and hundreds of thousands of visible minority migrants were, like their ethnic counterparts earlier, drawn to the large urban centres of Canada. Toronto has by far attracted the largest number of visible and ethnic minorities to its boundaries. The 1986 Census of Canada estimates that 18 percent of metropolitan Toronto's population is nonwhite, while 30 percent are ethnic minorities from non-British/ French backgrounds. Almost one-half of Toronto's population, then, consists of visible or ethnic minorities who arrived in Canada over the last three decades. The consequences of this marked shift in the demographic and social structural profile of Canadian cities are profound. The urban problems of congestion, lack of occupational opportunities, insufficient housing for middle- and low-income earners, and social conflict have been exacerbated in large cities by the new complexities of culturally and racially different groups competing for scarce resources. The result has been an increase in racial and ethnic group tensions, and in the development of a climate of distrust between minority and majority groups.

Given Canada's support for the concept of multiculturalism, it is not surprising to find that the visible and ethnic minorities in our cities have created group-oriented communities within which many aspects of social and cultural life are completely self-contained. The racial or ethnic community has become a central aspect of life for minorities on the lower end of the socio-economic scale. Richmond (1972:62) notes that in cities like Toronto immigrant groups create partially separate ethnic neighbourhoods and social networks with a high degree of institutional self-sufficiency. These institutions include churches, clubs, welfare organizations, newspapers, radio programs, as well as specialty shops catering to the minority clientele.

The *residential concentration* of ethnic and visible minority groups in our cities is crucial to an understanding of their present role and status. Such concentrations also provide clues as to the future social and economic mobility of these groups, and to their eventual integration into mainstream society. Kalbach and McVey (1979:89–90) found that three-quarters of the Asiatic population and two-thirds of the population of Italian, Ukrainian, and Polish descent resided in the inner cities of our metropolitan areas, a pattern they associate with the low level of educational attainment that characterizes inner cities. In their respective studies of Toronto and Winnipeg, Darroch and Marston (1971:498) and Dreidger (1978:193) also note a high degree of ethnic residential segregation in these cities; they conclude, however, that the key variable is not education, income, or occupation, but rather the preference of ethnic group members to reside in neighbourhoods with other members of their ethnic group. Richmond (1972:47) further reports that high occupational status is no guarantee that a household will move away from an area of ethnic concentration, although it increases the probability of it doing so. Regarding visible minority immigrants to our cities, research suggests that newer, low-income immigrants are more likely to reside in the inner cities, while their more educated, professional counterparts are usually dispersed in the more affluent suburban areas. For the latter group, as Ramcharan (1982:35) suggests, the racial community and in-group networks have become secondary to the positive aspects of residing and integrating into areas of low racial concentration.

In the American experience, factors of ethnicity and racial background militated against the social integration of urban low-income visible and ethnic minority groups, resulting in social disorganization in the form of anomie and high rates of crime, delinquency, and mental illness. Many inner-city neighbourhoods in the United States became "zones of transition," as ethnic and racial groups tended to use them as a way station, with geographical mobility related to occupational mobility. This contributed to the rapid physical deterioration of inner-city neighbourhoods, which in the long run became slums and ghettos inhabited by newly arrived immigrants, transients, and social isolates.

In Canadian cities, an interesting alternative has developed. While our inner-city areas may have a high concentration of visible and ethnic minorities, research has shown a high degree of residential stability and neighbourhood integration in both Montreal and Toronto. That minorities reside in similar neighbourhoods is more suggestive of the need for social networks and community institutions than for any social policy of institutional segregation. Social disorganization in Canada's inner cities is related more to the culturally and economically deprived environment in which the lower class resides, than to the phenomenon of transition and segregation as experienced in many American cities. Frequently, recent immigrants to Canada who reside in these slumlike areas have strong loyalties to their neighbourhoods, which many seek actively to improve. At the same time, community organizations provide social and psychological support in helping immigrants adjust to their new society.

SUMMARY

1. The proportion of Canadians living in urban areas has more than doubled since 1901. Canada and the United States together comprise the most urbanized sector in the world.

2. While the growth of urbanism has improved the standard of living for the average Canadian, it has also been responsible for greater intergroup conflict and deterioration in the quality of life for inner-city residents.

3. From the disorganization (functionalist) perspective, social problems in cities are the inevitable consequence of the large-scale migration of uneducated, unskilled, and immigrant groups to urban areas.

4. According to conflict theory, urban problems are created by powerful interest groups that control the decision-making process and fail to allocate sufficient resources to deprived groups, thereby producing poverty, crime, and alienation.

5. Canadian urban renewal planners have generally met with more suc-

cess than their U.S. counterparts, avoiding the massive ghettoization, rampant crime, and severe deterioration that characterize many large American cities.

6. The high incidence of deviant behaviour in the inner city can be attributed to the poverty and lack of opportunity among its residents. Conflict theorists argue that the behaviour of inner-city residents is more likely to be labelled deviant than is middle- or upper-class behaviour.

7. Major changes to the urban political system have occurred over the last three decades. The 1970s saw the rise of citizens' coalitions, neighbourhood groups, and grass-roots political organizations intent on giving the average citizen a voice in decision making at the municipal level of government.

8. The residential concentration of ethnic and visible minority groups in cities provides important clues as to the future social and economic mobility of these groups. The high degree of inner-city ethnic and racial segregation can be correlated with low levels of education, income, and employment.

3

Population and the Environment

POPULATION AS A SOCIAL PROBLEM

The rapid expansion of the world's population in the last one hundred years has reached calamitous proportions, and can be considered to be one of humanity's most urgent social problems. According to the Population Reference Bureau (1983:23), in 1981 the world's population was 5 billion, double that of fifty years earlier. Should the present rate of increase remain unchanged, it is estimated that the world's population in 2010 will approximate 8 billion. Thus, while from the beginning of the Christian era it took over fifteen hundred years for the world's population to double, it will take only thirty-five years for our present population to almost double in size (see Table 3.1).

Why has this situation developed? Demographers ascribe the low rate of population growth in the world prior to the start of the Industrial Revolution in the eighteenth century to the high mortality rates that resulted from widespread disease and famine. With the advent of the Industrial Revolution, however, the demographic profile in Western Europe underwent a marked change. Industrialization brought improvements in agriculture and health care, and a resultant decline in the mortality rate. Since birth rates were still high, population growth continued. However, the social and cultural changes brought on by urbanization and industrialization in Western Europe and North America over the last century have led to a decline in birth and death rates and to the present low population growth rates, which anticipate an eventual *zero population growth* (or *stationary population*) in these societies. This scenario is in stark contrast to the continuing inability of the developing countries to contain their high population growth, a situation that has made population in many of these countries a major social problem.

PERSPECTIVES ON POPULATION

From the *functionalist perspective*, change in any one part of the system has marked effects on the total system. Changes in population size will thus affect all aspects of a society and its institutions, and negatively so if the equilibrium is upset. In this context, population growth can be perceived as a social problem when it produces conditions that threaten the smooth functioning of a society.

One of the earliest population analysts who saw population growth from the functional perspective was Thomas Malthus, who, writing at the

28

Table 3.1
Population Projections by Regions of the World

Region	Population 1985 (in millions)	Projection for 2020 (in millions)	Population Percentage Increase between 1985 and 2020
Asia	2,829	4,340	53
Africa	551	1,433	160
Latin America	406	752	85
Oceania	24	32	33
Europe	492	507	3
Soviet Union	278	364	31
United States and Canada	264	330	3
Total	4,845	7,760	60
Less Developed Areas (Asia excluding Japan, Africa, Latin America, Oceania)	3,671	6,409	75
More Developed Areas (Europe, Soviet Union, United States, Canada, Japan)	1,174	1,351	15
Total	4,845	7,760	60

Source: Population Reference Bureau, *World Population Data Sheet.* Washington, D.C.: U.S. Government Printing Office, 1983. Reprinted by permission.

turn of the nineteenth century, argued that population growth if left unchecked would lead to severe problems for society, including misery, vice, poverty, and labour surpluses. In his *Essay on the Principle of Population*, Malthus suggested that nature used two types of checks on population growth: "preventive checks," including late marriage and celibacy, and "positive checks" such as famine, war, and plagues. Morris (1969) notes that, despite criticisms levelled at the Malthusian doctrine by influential population theorists, the present population explosion tends to support it. Today, the number of people on the verge of falling victim to the ultimate check on population—famine—is estimated by Fisher (1972) at half a billion, twice the total world population when Malthus wrote his treatise. For functionalists like Malthus, population becomes a problem when we cease to recognize that unchecked population growth will lead to a depletion of the world's limited resources.

From the *conflict perspective*, population issues only become labelled as problems when powerful interest groups in the society see them as threatening their values and interests. Conflict theorists emphasize the struggle between groups for scarce and valued resources, with competing groups determining whether a population is too large or small in terms of their own interests. This view of population as a social problem, therefore, is based on the premise that it is not population per se, but rather the methods of production in the capitalistic economic system that outpace the available resources. According to Sullivan et al. (1980:108), population growth becomes a social problem when the economic system artificially limits the resources available in order to maximize the profit factor. Population exceeds resources when there is an inequitable distribution of resources. Many leaders of developing countries contend that the rich and powerful nations could, by sharing their resources, execute a more equitable distribution of the wealth of the world. With such a redistribution the growing populations of the developing world could be adequately fed. Supporting this argument are such examples as the present policy in the United States whereby farmers are paid *not* to grow grain so that the price can be kept artificially inflated.

Whether a society has a population problem depends to a large extent on how it defines overpopulation. A society's concept of acceptable standard of living and acceptable quality of life will, in turn, decide what action is taken on population growth and control. For example, any definition of the ideal standard of living in the developed countries of the Western world has no meaning or relevance to the peasant in Bangladesh, or to the slum-dweller in Brazil. Many leaders of overpopulated countries believe that the industrialization of their societies will lead to economic changes, a transformation of values, and a subsequent decline in fertility rates, as occurred in the West a hundred years ago. However, Third World overpopulation, coupled with lack of natural resources, capital, and skills, leaves little hope that many of these countries will repeat the demographic transition earlier achieved by Western societies.

VARIABLES AFFECTING POPULATION GROWTH

Fundamental to any classification of human populations are the variables of age, sex, rural or urban residence, and racial or ethnic origin. Other important variables that provide vital information on a country's population include marital status, occupation, educational status, and religious background. These variables can give us a comprehensive picture of a society's social structure, which examined in a worldwide context can lead to policy statements on global population issues and problems. Finally, any understanding of the problem of rapid population growth must involve an analysis of three processes that affect the size of a population: fertility, mortality, and migration.

Fertility

Fertility can be defined as the number of births to women of childbearing age. This is different from the biological capability of bearing children, which is referred to as "fecundity." All societies have socially and culturally regulated means of childbearing through which levels of fertility can be controlled. For example, in India where girls marry in their teens, fertility is higher than in societies where marriage and childbearing are postponed. Similarly, societies in which remarriage and premarital or extramarital intercourse are proscribed reflect lower fertility rates. In addition, in some societies, particularly those with extended or joint families, large families are welcomed while the childless couple is viewed as cursed. In industrialized nations like Canada, however, where the nuclear family is the norm, a large family is frequently an economic hardship. Furthermore, rising female labour force participation is accompanied by lower fertility. Finally, societies that condemn contraception as a means of family planning would be expected to exhibit higher birth rates.

Mortality

Mortality refers to the death rate in a society. Generally, it is related to economic rather than social factors. Improved health and sanitary conditions, housing and nutritional standards, and medical advances have all contributed to a worldwide decline in mortality rates. While the declining mortality rate has been met in developed countries with a corresponding decrease in fertility rates, thereby keeping population growth in balance, a comparable system of checks and balances has not occurred in the developing world.

Although the principal factors related to variations in the death rate are biological and medical, socio-cultural factors can influence death rates as well. For example, Kammeyer (1969:262) notes that, historically, rural people had a greater life expectancy than urban dwellers, a fact he attributes to the higher density of urban environments, and, in their early development, to unsanitary living conditions. Another interesting social relationship exists between death rates and marital status. Married persons have lower death rates than single persons, who, in turn, have lower rates than widowed or divorced people. This pattern holds true even when age is held constant.

While mortality rates for all groups have decreased over the last fifty years, in both the developed and developing countries of the world, the degree of decline varies markedly by race, ethnicity, and rural–urban/socio-economic status. In addition, the life-expectancy rates in North

America and Western Europe exceed those in developing countries by approximately 25 percent. It is to be expected, however, that as nutritional, medical, and educational improvements are made in developing countries, there will be a corresponding increase in life expectancy.

Migration

No discussion of population variables can underestimate the role of migration. Immigrants have had a dramatic impact on population growth in Canada since its foundation. In 1986, the foreign-born component accounted for 15 percent of the population (Statistics Canada 1988). The demographic profile of Canada's large immigrant groups has in the past differed greatly from that of the native-born population. For example, such variables as family, marriage, and educational attainment have had profound effects on fertility and mortality rates among immigrant groups.

In 1975, Canada embarked on a review of its immigration policy, which centred around issues of population growth. Since the major determinant in future population growth was immigration, the final Immigration Act legislated in 1978 set out new guidelines for the type, quality, and number of future immigrants to Canada. While Canada does not have an overpopulation problem and still needs immigrants, it was decided that they should be selected on the basis of education, skills, and adaptability. In periods of high unemployment, the economic system cannot bear the burden of large increases in the labour force, and therefore an annual global nondiscriminatory quota was established by the Minister of Employment and Immigration to take into account the needs of Canadian society for skilled and professional workers.

Public opinion on the issue of immigration is also divided. There are those who oppose the changing ethnic and racial character of society that has resulted from the influx of nonwhite immigrants to Canada in the last fifteen years. For this group, limiting immigration invariably means limiting nonwhite immigration. For others, the issue is not racial characteristics per se, but rather the growing concentrations of racial and ethnic communities in Canadian cities; faced with the immediate problems of inflation, unemployment, housing shortages, and environmental pollution, many Canadians believe that population increases should be minimized. While there is little public consensus on the crucial aspects of population growth—e.g., issues of size, rate of growth, distribution, and composition—the limits placed on immigration make explicit the government's position that our human resources should not be augmented too drastically from abroad.

Of crucial importance to the Canadian population situation are problems of family planning, imbalances in population distribution, an aging population, and fertility and mortality rates, which we shall turn to now.

CANADIAN POPULATION PROBLEMS

At the present time, Canada's annual population growth due to natural increase (births minus deaths) is less than .5 percent. In January 1983, the estimated population of Canada, including net immigration, was 24.5 million, an increase of 10 percent since 1973. The declining birth rate is reflected in the fact that between 1971 and 1981 the number of children 0–4 years of age decreased by over 15 percent. As Balakrishnan et al. (1985) note, Canadian fertility will remain low for the forseeable future.

While overpopulation is not a factor in Canadian society, the population variables of births, deaths, and migration are important indices of how Canada is evolving as a society and of how we will set about resolving many of our social issues. For example, the rapid decrease in Quebec's birth rate in the last three decades has convinced many Quebeckers that increased fertility is necessary if the province is to retain its political and social power. Thus, Quebec's decline in fertility, coupled with its inability to attract large numbers of immigrants to the province, has altered its role in Canada.

Of course, not just Quebec but Canada as a whole is reflecting low fertility rates. One of the consequences of an educated public and a new liberality in the laws relating to the dissemination of birth control information is an awareness in the public that decreases in family size can significantly improve one's standard of living. As a result, the Canadian family is barely reproducing itself, with an urban birth rate of 1.6 percent. McVey (1987) further notes that greater female labour force participation will be accompanied by an increase in birth control use. Also potentially contributing to the low birth rate is the Supreme Court of Canada's 1988 decision that the Abortion Law of 1968 infringes upon the rights of women under the Charter of Rights. The Supreme Court decision could result in the replacement of the old law with one that allows abortion on demand during the first trimester of pregnancy.

While fertility and its ramifications have attracted the lion's share of attention in the last decade, of further concern are mortality differentials between provinces, regions, and groups of people. Native peoples, for example, have had the highest mortality rates (particularly infant) of all groups in Canada (Kalbach and McVey 1979:82). In 1976, the life expectancy rate for the native person was approximately one-half that of the white Canadian. Finally, our native peoples, with their high fertility and mortality rates, exhibit many of the problems facing developing countries, particularly low levels of education, income, standard of living, and quality of life.

THE ENVIRONMENT AS A SOCIAL PROBLEM

In the past decade, North Americans have become aware that the deterioration in the quality of the physical environment is a serious social problem. There is a growing perception that unless urgent steps are taken to reduce the mismanagement of our environmental and physical resources, the quality of life in our society will be immeasurably affected. While pessimists claim that humanity has already lost the battle, the evidence suggests that concerted public awareness can lead to effective environmental programs. For example, marine life now thrives in the Thames in England, where five years ago no life existed, and the Great Lakes are slowly being regenerated as governments on both sides of the border have undertaken clean-ups of the sources of pollution. However, political dissension and nonco-operation threaten even that initial step in solving what is an international problem.

The basic cause of Canada's environmental problem lies in the inability of the physical environment to sustain our needs without deterioration. The production of goods and services dictated by an industrialized and consumer-oriented society means not only the eventual depletion of Canada's natural resources but also the devastation of our land, water, and air, all depositories for the waste products created in the mad rush to produce and consume. With less than 1 percent of the world's population, Canada consumes 5 percent of its natural resources, and together with the United States contributes more than half of its industrial pollution.

PERSPECTIVES ON THE ENVIRONMENT

From the *functionalist perspective*, the environmental crisis has its beginnings in industrial growth in North America, which brought affluence and a higher standard of living for its people, and at the same time sowed the seeds for the continuous increase in the use of natural resources. On a global scale, the pace of economic productivity created a greater demand for industrialized goods. In the race to produce manufactured goods, little serious thought was given to the negative consequences of industrial growth, and only lip service was paid to the development of methods for dealing with environmental pollution. Ecologists who in the 1960s predicted catastrophic results were scoffed at or branded as radicals. But as Robertson (1980:60) notes, "the delicate balance of nature has been upset to the point where population, industrialization, and pollution cannot continue to grow at their present rates without disastrous consequences."

From the *conflict perspective*, the values and interests of the economic and political elites direct the continued development of resources and are thus responsible for inevitable increases in environmental pollution levels. The production of raw materials into manufactured goods means economic growth and votes for politicians subsequent to a rise in the standard of living. To the corporations and industrial sector, pollution controls, while beneficial to the consumer, mean added costs for the product and possibly smaller profits. According to Davies et al. (1975:26), the clash in values between ecologists and private enterprise has intensified in recent times, with the power structure supporting business interests over environmentalists. In addition, federal and provincial governments have paid mere lip-service to environmental protection issues, by handing out minimal fines to industrial polluters, and by waffling when it comes to introducing legislation to combat the problem.

While it is not our purpose to dwell at length on individual aspects of the environmental crisis, no clear picture of the causes of the problem can be drawn without reference to the fact that Canadian society, by emphasizing modern technology, may have locked itself into a destructive path, for it is technology and industrialization that threaten the ecological environment and its stability. As Commoner (1971:10–16) has noted, while modern technology has achieved important benefits for human welfare, the accompanying pollution is not an unexpected by-product. It is the *success* of insecticides that threatens our wildlife. It was the *success* of the internal combustion engine that led to smog and air pollution. It is the *success* of modern fertilizers that pollutes our rivers and lakes. Technological and economic progress, therefore, will lead to increased health hazards and environmental deterioration unless we are willing to pay the higher costs associated with prevention of pollution hazards. A safe nuclear plant can be built, but additional costs may not make it competitive with other energy sources.

How issues of environmental safety are resolved will to a large extent depend on whether special interest groups representing the polluters can influence government decisions, or whether environmental groups can sway public and political opinion sufficiently for the enactment of effective anti-pollution laws, which conceivably could lead to large-scale economic dislocations. The question is whether society is, firstly, aware of the incompatibility between materialism and a healthy environment, and, secondly, whether for the long-term survival of human life we are prepared to alter our priorities.

ENVIRONMENTAL SOLUTIONS

In 1970, the Club of Rome, a private international group of scientific and business leaders, commissioned a study on the effects of industrial and population growth. The study, entitled *The Limits to Growth*, attracted immediate worldwide attention as it zeroed in on the problems of population growth, industrialization, depletion of resources, and pollution. Its authors, Meadows et al. (1972) conclude that humanity will collapse within a hundred years unless the nations of the world face the problems of overpopulation and find an equilibrium for industrial output. Rapid industrialization will inevitably lead to increased pollution, with devastating effects on public health and the ecosystem.

While the scientific community endorsed the Club of Rome report, business and political leaders of the developed world have at best reacted with half-hearted proposals for solving the problem. There are, of course, no easy solutions. One of the most difficult tasks is to mobilize the public against those interest groups that are opposed to environmental protection. It was not until the 1960s that Canadians became acutely aware of the environmental hazards surrounding them, a perception which led to the formation of large-scale environmental protection movements. Since that time some progress has been made. Air quality has improved—mainly due to the imposition of exhaust emission standards on automobiles—along with water quality in the Great Lakes region and in our oceans. Since 1970, a federal Minister of the Environment has been appointed to co-ordinate efforts at environmental improvement. Government legislation aimed at imposing fines on industrial polluters has been implemented, and occasionally serious violators have been prosecuted and ordered to introduce anti-pollution devices in their plants. Millions of dollars have been spent to build municipal sewage treatment plants and to provide grants for scientific study of environmental problems. However, these efforts are designed more to appease the public than to seriously attempt to eradicate the problem.

The tragic pollution of the Rainy River and Lake of the Woods area of Northern Ontario is a vivid illustration of the point. In this region, chemical effluent from pulp and paper industries has polluted the rivers, lakes, and streams to the extent that the fishery has been destroyed, the water made unsafe for drinking, and the recreation and tourist industries of the area totally erased—a case of deliberate contamination of the environment in the interests of industrial progress. In the face of a public outcry, rehabilitative measures have been introduced, with in-plant preventive action as well as municipal sewage treatment plants constructed. The quality of the water has improved, but whether the environment can be returned to its original form is highly questionable. Clean-up efforts in this and other areas have shown that preventive measures are always less expensive and less harmful than rehabilitation after the fact.

It must be stressed that our piecemeal, short-term approaches to industrial planning and natural resource uses have disastrously affected the ecological environment. Only by maintaining the natural balance between air, water, and soil will we achieve the healthy quality of life we desire. The fact that this balance slowly but surely is being irreparably upset should be widely communicated. As the Conservation Council of Ontario (1981:107) notes, people may recognize that their local beach is now unsafe for swimming, or that the air pollution in their neighbourhood is worsening, but in this "quiet crisis" they have to be made aware that their problems are not just local but international in their dimensions. Furthermore, it must be emphasized that industries forced to introduce anti-pollution devices do not by necessity collapse. For example, when the Inco mine in Sudbury, the source of almost half the acid rain produced in North America, was forced to introduce scrubbers on its smokestacks the resultant improvement in air quality was substantial, and while there was a monetary cost (a small price to save some of our lakes and rivers), the mine is still in operation.

One area of the environmental debate that has generated widespread public support and interest is the anti-nuclear lobby. In recent years, serious nuclear power plant accidents at Chernobyl in the Soviet Union, Three Mile Island in the United States, and Pickering, Ontario have made people dramatically aware of the potentially disastrous consequences of nuclear-generating plants, and of nuclear energy in general—an illustration of how a social condition threatening the values of a people can be translated into a social problem. Equally, there is an awareness of the conflict between personal security and society's need for economical sources of energy. Ecological disasters such as the contamination of the Rainy River area have taught us the high economic and social costs of environmental pollution. Should they choose to reverse the trend, Canadians will have to pay the costs in the form of higher prices for goods and services, and possibly social unrest as conflicting interest groups attempt to alter the distribution of power and resources for their own benefit. In the final analysis, the worst scenario that can develop is a complacent public that accepts environmental pollution—and, over time, higher levels of it—as a necessary evil.

SUMMARY

1. High population growth rates can be expected to continue for the developing countries. For western industrialized societies, declining

birth rates, which resulted from a variety of social and cultural changes, point to an eventual zero population growth.

2. From the functionalist perspective, population growth becomes a social problem when it produces conditions—e.g., famine—that threaten the smooth functioning of society.

3. According to conflict theory, population growth only becomes a social problem when the economic system, in order to maximize profit, imposes artificial constraints on the availability of resources.

4. Fertility, mortality, and migration are three major variables that determine population size. Canada as a whole reflects a low fertility rate. Mortality rates among our native peoples are disproportionately high.

5. Recent changes to Canadian immigration policy have limited immigration by introducing new criteria—e.g., education and skills—into the selection process.

6. With less than 1 percent of the world's population, Canada consumes 5 percent of its natural resources and together with the United States contributes more than half of its industrial pollution.

7. The functionalist perspective attributes the environmental crisis to industrial growth and inadequate checks on pollution levels.

8. Conflict theorists blame economic and political elites for encouraging, through their values and interests, technological and industrial development at the expense of the environment.

9. The environmental tragedy of Rainy River illustrates the need for long-term approaches to industrial planning (e.g., preventive measures designed to promote environmental safety).

4

The Power Structure

INTRODUCTION

We begin this chapter with a brief examination of the two fundamental theoretical approaches to the analysis of power in Canada. *Conflict theorists* emphasize that Canada is held together through the power and influence of a small number of people, to the disadvantage of individuals and groups who have little or no access to the power structure. The goal, as defined by this school of thought, is to change this unequal distribution of power. Until this occurs, Canadian society will remain marked by conflict between the powerful and the powerless.

The *functionalist perspective*, on the other hand, views social inequality and the existence of a power elite as arising inevitably from society's need for order. Porter's (1965) major criticism of the power structure in Canada was that it had remained relatively closed—hence his advocacy of open recruitment from all classes and ethnic groups to membership in the power elite. Clement (1975) shares Porter's belief that the power elite is narrow and unrepresentative of the population, but he differs from Porter in his view of the effects of this power structure on Canadian society. Porter's argument was that all interest groups could eventually obtain influence in the power structure through the development of political pluralism. Clement (1975:259), however, sees the unequal distribution of resources and power in society as inevitably leading to social class conflict.

For the remainder of the chapter, discussion will centre on the concentration of economic and social power in Canada, as well as on methods for achieving a more democratic form of power sharing among interest groups. In addition, the effects of big business and big government expansion on the lives of individual citizens will be analyzed.

THE CORPORATE STATE

According to the conflict perspective, the worst evil of any political system comes from the centralization of power in the hands of relatively few in the business and government sectors of society, which has created the long-standing sense among Canadians of powerlessness and a lack of control over their own destiny (Ryerson 1968:13). The seeds for the growth in the concentration of power date back to the pre-World War Two period when government began expanding its role in society, while at the same time business and manufacturing firms began to consolidate, leading to the national and multinational corporations of today. When national goals and social policies or priorities (whether political or economic) are established within this narrow sphere, the *corporate state* is created, for often those with political and economic power are one and the same. The overlapping of economic and political interests reflects not a conspiracy between the elites, but rather the methods of the corporate state, which emphasizes its own interests over the public interest. In such a system conflict of interest is commonplace.

What factors led to the deepening of the relationship between government and the corporate sector in the pre-Second World War period? Conflict theorists suggest that, as government became a major provider of social services and embarked on the role of setting up Crown corporations (ostensibly to protect the public interest), government and business developed common interests. To ensure favourable tax structures, tax credits, depreciation allowances etc., big business began to manipulate the political decision-making process. Regulatory agencies such as the Canadian Transport Commission and the Canadian Radio and Telecommunications Commission soon became closely allied to the corporations they were supposed to control, leaving the consumer unprotected. From the conflict perspective, therefore, the close link between government and corporations, coupled with the growth of the corporate state, impairs the operation of the nation state. Although specific interest groups benefit from the present arrangement, many groups, including the poor, the unemployed, minorities, and other powerless groups, have experienced the negative effects of decisions that do not reflect their best interests.

It can be suggested that the growth of corporate state power constitutes a social problem to the extent that the alignment of big business and big government adversely affects the life chances of Canadians. Recent movements for the formation of consumer and citizen advocacy groups across Canada are examples of the average citizen attempting to challenge the monolithic corporate state. To those who see the increasing concentration of power in fewer hands as evidence of the growing powerlessness of the majority, only a fundamental reversal of that trend can create opportunities for a wider distribution of power.

Unlike the conflict approach, advocates of the functionalist perspective see the corporate state as representing the best interests of the nation. Co-operation between business and government is moving society toward goals that are shared by all Canadians. The role of business is to provide goods and services that improve the national standard of living. If the alignment of government with business furthers this goal, through favourable legislation or other means, then the corporate state should be seen as functional to the well-being of society. This argument may at first appear to be valid. According to conflict theorists, however, a detailed

Table 4.1
Percentage Allocation of Corporate Taxable Income
for Industrial Sectors by Country of Control, 1981

	USA	UK	Other Foreign	Canada	Unclass-ified
Agriculture, Forestry, Fishing	3.4		1.6	75.4	19.6
Mining	66.3	.6	8.4	24.1	.6
Manufacturing	50.8	5.8	4.1	37.7	1.6
Construction	8.1	1.2	2.8	68.0	19.9
Utilities	12.3	.6	1.5	81.4	4.2
Wholesale Trade	18.3	2.8	9.4	63.4	6.1
Retail Trade	11.6	.5	.8	72.3	14.8
Services	23.4	.5	.4	50.4	25.4
Total	37.4	2.9	4.4	48.4	6.9

Source: Adapted from Statistics Canada Catalogue 61-210, Corporations And Labour
Unions Act, Report 1981, Part I Corporations, Table 8. Reprinted by permission.

examination of the corporate state structure reveals that large government bureaucracies and corporations have so overwhelmed individuals that the corporate state ends up serving not society but itself. Massive bureaucracy serves to diminish both individuality and equality. From the conflict perspective, the corporate state constitutes a social problem because it militates against basic egalitarian values.

BIG BUSINESS

Clement (1975:74) notes that the movement from small business to corporate capitalism in the post-World War II period was accomplished by two distinct social forces: (1) the movement of branch plants into manufacturing, with American corporate expansion into Canada, and (2) an internal movement to consolidate small factories and plants into big business operations. Canada thus now faces a double-edged sword in its economic organization. First, the increasing centralization of the economy has made the concentration of power in the hands of a few a *fait accompli*; and second, considerable financial power is concentrated in big business and corporations which are to a large extent foreign owned and controlled, making Canadians spectators rather than controllers of the economic system. As Hiller (1986:49) notes, while foreign ownership is not a phenomenon unique to Canada, we reflect a substantially higher proportion of such ownership, with 51.6 percent of our economy being under foreign control (see Table 4.1). Bronson (1979) further points out that 100 out of 29,812 companies in the manufacturing sector accounted for 46 percent of all business activity, the majority of which were foreign controlled.

According to Clement (1975:105), the multinational corporation began as an efficient way of accumulating and concentrating capital (i.e., through establishing "branch plants on site" to make use of resource locations, and through providing the urban centres with manufactured goods), but in the course of its development assumed many negative traits. The power of multinational corporations resides not only in the resources they control, but in the flexibility of their operations. In order to maximize their profits, they can shift operations out of one country and into another at will, with little concern for the repercussions of their policies on domestic economies. The negative ramifications of such an approach have been felt in Canada over the last decade—in, for example, the decision of Inco in 1977 to shift production to Central America, which resulted in hundreds of worker layoffs. Further, in the economic recession of the early 1980s, dozens of multinational corporations (e.g., Bendix, Du Pont, General Motors, Exxon, A & P, and General Electric) simply closed down all or part of their operations in Canada, devastating the economic life of many communities.

Besides the multinational corporation, big business has found other means with which to concentrate economic wealth and power. One prominent way is through *vertical expansion*, that is, obtaining control or ownership of firms that produce at different stages in the development of a product. A supermarket chain, for example, might own meat and fish, packaging, transportation, and food processing companies. The advantage to the company is that it is ensured an efficient and uninterrupted flow of foodstuffs to the main operation at a set price, allowing for a stable and profitable operation. This approach, however, can spell financial disaster for the small company attempting to obtain markets for its products. Furthermore, the concentration of economic power diminishes the role of the marketplace in setting competitive prices for goods and services, thereby markedly reducing the consumer's power.

Another type of corporate expansion, the *conglomerate*, emerged in Canada during the late 1950s. A conglomerate is a large holding company that controls various companies in different areas of production and manufacture. Capital accumulation enhances the overall profitability of the corporation because financial loss in one company is compensated by the corporation's more profitable operations. In the last decade there has been a growing trend toward the establishment of conglomerates. Examples of large conglomerates in Canada are the Argus Corporation, George Weston Corporation, Power Corporation, Brascan Ltd., and the Safeway Corporation.

For the competitive marketplace, the growth of corporate power has been a negative development, in that large companies can set a price for their product based on what the market can bear, rather than on a fair profit margin. In addition, a conglomerate can effectively eliminate competition by setting unfair low prices for products from one of its companies, secure in the knowledge that its other companies will operate profitably; with minimal competition, it can then raise the prices exhorbitantly. Monopolistic companies also dominate key consumer product areas today. Is it mere coincidence that an increase in the price of automobiles and gasoline by one major company is almost always followed by identical increases by the others?

Finally, the powerlessness of the citizen over market conditions has been augmented in the last two decades through the mass manipulation of real or perceived needs by the advertising media. When the cost of this manipulation is added on to the product cost, consumers end up either paying more for a product they would have bought anyway, or else purchasing products they do not need. In this regard, advertising strengthens the control of big business over the decision-making capacity of the consumer. Big business, then, might be said to be a social problem in the sense that it has deprived the marketplace/consumer of the power to influence prices. In the present noncompetitive environment, moreover, the general public is at the mercy of the corporation in terms of product *quality* as well as price. This is in direct contrast to the capitalism of an earlier time when business was controlled by the consumer.

BIG GOVERNMENT

Prior to the Second World War, government bureaucracies were minimal in size. The rise of big government in Canada can be directly linked to industrial and technological development, population growth, and the perceived need by governments to establish centralized structures to maintain order, collect revenues, and administer social policies. To put the immense growth of government bureaucracies in perspective, in 1901 the federal government employed only 3,000 people. At present it has 530,000 employees—535,000, if one includes the various Crown corporations (Statistics Canada:1988). The number of federal, provincial, and municipal government employees has almost doubled in the last three decades to the current total of over 1.5 million. Why has this growth occurred? What are the repercussions of big government bureaucracy on people's lives? We might say that government has expanded (1) because people have demanded more government services, and (2) because the complexity of the modern industrial state requires the establishment of myriad regulatory agencies and a large staff to supervise and enforce rules and regulations.

Big government bureaucracy and intrusion in the lives of citizens has provoked vocal criticism from many groups. Big business and corporations see government bureaucracies as wasteful spenders of tax revenue, and as a threat to the capitalistic system. Public interest groups see proliferating government agencies as self-perpetuating, self-serving, and inefficient groups of overpaid workers who have little or no interest in serving the public. The number of Canadians who believe that government is wasteful and inefficient rose from 40 percent in 1961 to 78 percent in 1981 (Gallup polls 1984), a clear indication that the public has lost confidence in those government agencies that are supposed to protect their interests.

The crux of the problem is twofold. Firstly, government departments have multiplied at *the request of* public or powerful interest groups. In the last decade, for example, more than a dozen government regulatory agencies have either been established or else have had their services expanded. These agencies, which include the Consumer Protection Bureau, the Occupational Health and Safety Commission, the Food and Drug Agency, the Environmental Protection Commission, and the Canadian Railway and Transit Commission, provide important services for the public, and, while we may chafe under bureaucratic proliferation, we insist at the same time that our expanding needs be served. Although prospects for a general consensus on which government agencies or departments to relinquish are doubtful, the Tory government under Brian Mulroney is insistent that some Crown corporations be divested.

A second barrier to the streamlining of big government lies in the extreme difficulty of closing a government department, even if it has outlived its mandate. Cardinal (1977:222) notes, for example, that native leaders have argued for years that the Department of Indian and Northern Affairs is anachronistic and irrelevant in terms of meeting the needs of Canada's native peoples. However, entrenched bureaucrats in the Department have a vested interest in perpetuating their roles and increasing their budgets, and so Indian Affairs lives on, despite increasing evidence that it may be serving only itself rather than the people it was originally mandated to serve.

In conclusion, it can be said that the distate the average person feels toward big government is directly related to the growth in the concentration of power in the hands of a bureaucratic elite, which has no interest in communicating with the public as to its needs, believing instead that public opinion is irrelevant to the political decision-making process.

THE POWER ELITE

Public dissatisfaction with big government and big business largely stems from the fact that, while the theory of public sovereignty is the hallmark of the democratic process, our system of government is one of elitism. A privileged group controls the decision-making process in both the private and public sectors. The public is assumed to be ignorant of the intricacies of government (and is, as a consequence, left out of the political process), while those who clamour for involvement are treated like recalcitrant children, to be humoured but not taken seriously.

Mills (1956:4) defines the *power elite* as those whose positions in the society allow them to transcend the ordinary environment of average men and women. They make the decisions which affect all of our lives, and are in command of the major institutions and organizations of the society. They rule the corporations, run the machinery of the state, and occupy the strategic command posts of the social structure.

How has the power elite changed over time? In 1965, John Porter, who portrayed the economic elite as the most powerful of the groups, described its membership as being drawn from a narrow establishment base—white, Anglo-Saxon, male, clannish, and virtually closed to recruitment from outside. Members were closely allied to both the Liberal and Conservative parties, and were overrepresented in government boards, university boards of governors, and social agencies. Other important elite groups included the political and bureaucratic elites. Lawyers were overrepresented in the political elite, and had a distinct upper-middle-class origin. Co-option from business was also common, further contributing to the alliance between the business and political elite.

Darroch (1980), in analyzing the Canadian power structure in the past two decades, has suggested, firstly, that our elite structure has been expanded to include more ethnic representation, and, secondly, that the effects of intergenerational mobility is slowly permeating the traditional recruitment pattern of membership in the power structure. Cuneo and Curtis (1975) also note a decrease in the correlation between ascription and membership in the power elite. According to Olsen (1980:27), however, unless power is distributed more equitably among all interest groups, imbalance in decision making and elitism in Canada will persist. On the other hand, Berkowitz (1984:258) suggests not only that economic, political, and bureaucratic elites today are more ethnically heterogeneous, but that corporate power has become less concentrated since Porter's (1965) study.

An alternative to the power elite analysis of society is that of "balanced veto groups," by which Reisman (1969) describes the power structure in the United States. He suggests that no one group dominates the power structure, as strong interest groups (e.g., business and labour) block efforts on the part of others to encroach on their interests. Far from being dominated, the unorganized public in fact holds the balance of power, as the powerful interest groups attempt to win its support for their policies. In Canada, however, labour's lack of power in relation to business, combined with our history of government and business cooperation, suggests that we have a long way to go before achieving a balanced form of power sharing. Furthermore, even when widely influential interest groups do attain access to power, more often than not the ordinary citizen is still left out of the power sharing. For example, both the Canadian Medical Association and the Canadian Association of Small Business, to name two special interest groups, have had considerable influence on government legislation—but can we say that such major interest groups represent public opinion?

FUTURE PROSPECTS

There is little doubt that societal conflict has intensified as a result of the concentration of power in Canadian society. The subversion of the democratic process and the manipulation of the public by a small concentration of powerful people in government and business has served an influential minority at the expense of the majority of Canadians, many of whom feel powerless in the face of the status quo. Others, however, still believe that changes in the power structure are possible. Serving as watchdogs over governments and corporations, *citizens' groups* have begun to press for increased social responsibility in the corporate world. In addition, advocacy groups represent the public before regulatory agencies and legislative hearings on important social legislation. The central goals of these movements are the same—returning the decision-making process to the people and introducing fairer rules in the game of interest-group politics. Some of the more successful citizen-advocacy groups in Canada include the Environmental Law Association, the Consumers' Association of Canada, the Automobile Protection Association, the Canadian Civil Liberties Association, and the Greenpeace Movement. As national organizations established to protect the interests of the public, they have joined forces with local citizens' groups in lobbying against unfair corporate practices and government legislation.

Although progress is being made, the road to equality of power sharing is a long way off. Both politicians and the general public seem to agree that government in Canada has become too large, but it may be unrealistic to expect any drastic change in government structure and its bureaucracies in the very near future. A basic problem, as we mentioned earlier in the chapter, is that no two citizens' groups can agree on *what* government programs and staff should be eliminated or reduced, for the public has come to regard government services in health, welfare, environmental protection, consumer products, law enforcement, and education as basic rights. Rather than reduce such services, a more realistic goal might be to eliminate government inefficiency. Each year, federal and provincial auditor generals outline the horrendous waste of public funds. Accordingly, government must be reorganized to eliminate duplication of services, to consolidate its programs, and to introduce internal safeguards against bureaucracies becoming self-serving empires. Finally, corporate practices need to be scrutinized more closely and regulatory agencies given greater punitive power to deal with malpractices such as environmental pollution, false advertising, and consumer fraud.

SUMMARY

1. The deepening relationship between government and the corporate sector began in the pre-World War Two period, as government began to expand its role in society by setting up Crown corporations and becoming a major provider of social services, developing, in the process, common interests with the corporate sector.
2. From the funtionalist perspective, the corporate sector is a natural evolution of society's need for order. The alliance between government and big business represents the best interests of the nation because it facilitates the role of business, which is to provide the goods and services that improve the national standard of living.
3. For conflict theorists, the concentration of power in the hands of government and big business represents the worst evil of our political system in that it has deprived citizens of an effective voice in the decision-making process, and has had its most negative impact on deprived groups in society.
4. The multinational corporation, which began as an efficient way of accumulating and concentrating capital, has developed into a monolithic operation, shifting from one country to another at will and displaying little concern for the repercussions of its policies—e.g., layoffs—on domestic economies.
5. The last decade has seen a rise in the establishment of conglomerates which can manipulate prices for products and drive out competition, thereby taking away from consumers their ability to influence prices.
6. The number of federal, provincial, and municipal employees has almost doubled over the past three decades. Over the same period, public disenchantment with government has climbed sharply, due in large part to government inefficiency, waste, and bureaucracy, and a feeling that the elite has no interest in bringing citizens into the decision-making process.
7. The composition of the power elite has changed over the past two decades. Today, it reflects more ethnic representation, and is less rigid in terms of its criteria for membership.
8. The power structure in the United States is characterized by balanced veto groups. In this structure, competing interest groups wield roughly the same amount of power; it is up to the public to break the deadlock by supporting one group over the other. A balanced form of power sharing is less feasible in Canada, where groups such as labour

lack the power to hold their own with government and business groups.

9. Despite widespread public apathy, public-interest and citizen-advocacy groups, which are designed to combat the negative impacts of government and corporate concentration of power, have flourished in recent years.

5

Work and Alienation

INTRODUCTION

Prior to the Industrial Revolution, self-employment was the norm, as most people worked on the land, in their homes, or in small shops. Today, however, the majority of individuals work for large organizations. From adulthood to retirement, work demands the dominant part of our time, and penetrates to the core of our existence, affecting even our nonwork activities (Rinehart 1987:1). For the vast majority of Canadians, work is the means to economic well-being, social status, self-esteem, psychological fulfilment, and personal/professional networks.

According to Ritzer and Walczak (1986:3–4), work has become a social problem for two primary reasons. First, while every society defines work as a central obligation for most of the population, unemployment or underemployment is a continuing source of tension and conflict in Canadian society. A second issue is the persistence of worker alienation and job dissatisfaction. We will examine both issues as social problems later in the chapter. But first let us analyze the meaning of work in terms of the cultural values, norms, and beliefs of our society.

THE MEANING OF WORK AND LEISURE

In his classic study, *The Protestant Ethic and the Spirit of Capitalism*, Weber (1958) notes that in most traditional pre-industrial societies labour was not highly valued. The ancient Greeks, for example, viewed work as a curse and felt that human activity was best expended through the constructive use of leisure time. Slavery, therefore, was seen as freeing the citizenry for cultural enrichment. With the rise of Protestantism in Europe, however, there was a shift in the definition of work as a divinely imposed duty. Work was seen as both a service to God and a moral obligation. Moreover, the successful life could only be achieved through work and a subsequent accumulation of profits and capital. However, since the *Protestant work ethic* of Luther and Calvin regarded the consumption of luxury goods and services as sinful, profits were reinvested, thus giving rise to the era of capitalism.

One aspect of the old Protestant work ethic that has carried over into Canadian society today is this: most of us still equate work with virtue and unemployment with laziness. How central a role work plays in our lives is often indicated in meetings between strangers. "What do you do for a living?" is usually the first question asked on either side. This, in fact, reflects the prevailing attitude in society as to the significance of work per se. Ranking occupations is another matter. If you have a high-status job, your chances are better for developing a positive self-image, high prestige in the community, and sense of self-fulfilment. Conversely, given the close correlation between jobs and status, the unemployed, or people trapped in boring and meaningless low- status occupations, must bear the social stigmatization generally inflicted on those who are not fulfilling their expected roles.

Turning now to the role of leisure in today's society, it has long been felt that the individual more readily adjusts to the social environment if he or she is satisfied in both the realms of work and play. The reality, however, is that the majority of jobs are not personally satisfying, nor is the relationship between work and leisure time a particularly healthy one. People sell their labour to the firm or factory each day, and at nights and on weekends try to buy it back through fun and play. Increasingly, the literature suggests that we are trying to insulate ourselves from the alienating aspects of our work by seeking out *leisure* activities that we hope can lead to the development of a more favourable self-image. In other words, the pursual of leisure activities is an attempt to fill the vacuum created by an unsatisfactory work environment.

But can we expect to achieve psychic satisfaction through our leisure activities? Rinehart (1987:164) thinks not for two reasons. First, because work dominates our lives so much more thoroughly than leisure time, it may be a poor tradeoff; and second, people may be unable to psychologically compartmentalize their work and leisure activities, with the result that job dissatisfaction spills over into leisure time. The search for meaning and fulfilment through the pursuit of leisure, therefore, may be a futile one, not because leisure cannot be a positive force on the psyche, but because of what leisure in industrial society has become.

Finally, in our discussion of the role of leisure in modern society, let us consider the findings of Meissner (1971:362) regarding a sample of workers in Vancouver, which suggest a correlation between the type of work and the kind of leisure activities pursued. For example, workers with jobs that allowed for little initiative and innovation were unlikely to involve themselves in leisure activities that entailed serious and deliberate planning; in a similar vein, people in socially isolating jobs often pursued their leisure activities alone. Clearly, no matter how much we try to divorce ourselves from the negative effects of our workplace, they usually spill over into our social life. Perhaps, therefore, instead of depending on alternative structures such as leisure to compensate for the failure of the workplace, we should concentrate on making work more fulfilling, and hence complementary to leisure.

UNEMPLOYMENT

According to the National Council of Welfare (1984), more Canadians were out of work in the period 1981–1983 than in any comparable period in the last forty years. Rates of unemployment that would have been unthinkable only a few years ago have now become commonplace. According to Statistics Canada (1983), the average unemployment rate in Canada in July of 1983 was 12 percent (1,460,000 Canadians unemployed). In addition, while average unemployment levels hover at the 10–12 percent range, the rate for youth unemployment is closer to 25 percent (National Council of Welfare 1984). Along with younger people, more women are entering the labour force, and these two groups account for over 50 percent of the unemployed in Canada.

The disorganizational effects of unemployment include family dissolution and the growth of a culture of poverty, in which new generations are prevented from achieving their true potential. The inevitable social cost of chronic unemployment is the creation of a disfranchised group of people whose low self-image and sense of frustration and alienation can lead to antisocial and deviant behaviour. What is needed to alleviate the problem of unemployment is more government planning and involvement in the economic system, for example, in setting labour force participation rates, or in offsetting the impact of recessional unemployment. In addition, technological change in the workplace, which over the next decade will displace many workers by making their jobs obsolete, must be met with large-scale retraining programs. Finally, it is crucial that labour, business, and government develop a co-ordinated industrial strategy for the coming decades that will alleviate the ruinous effects of unemployment and underemployment in our society.

PERSPECTIVES ON WORKER ALIENATION AND JOB DISSATISFACTION

In sociology, *alienation* refers to the worker's lack of control over the organization and conditions of the workplace (Rinehart 1987:17). From the *functionalist perspective*, worker alienation has its roots in the growth of social disorganization caused by the rapid social and technological changes in society in the last four decades. As society became increasingly industrialized, the nature and organization of work underwent major changes. It was primarily through the *rationalization* of the workplace that issues concerning conditions of work became secondary. From the functionalist point of view, the rationalization of the productive process—exemplified by the assembly line of a modern factory—has enhanced efficiency and thus contributed to the higher standard of living enjoyed by Canadians. However, the growth of industrialization has become dysfunctional to the extent that it has turned many workers into extensions of the machine, thereby robbing them of the opportunity to express individual autonomy, creativity, and innovation in the workplace. Further exacerbating the problem are our cultural attitudes and values, which emphasize the idea of work as both fulfilling and important to the common good of society.

From the *conflict perspective*, worker alienation results from a conflict of interest between workers and employers. While workers are concerned with such things as pay, job security, and job satisfaction, employers stress efficiency and profits, often at the expense of craftsmanship and worker involvement in the decision-making process. For conflict theorists, positive change in the workplace can occur only if the worker is empowered to affect working conditions. If government, in alliance with the corporation, has no interest in realigning the power distribution in the workplace, then it is up to unions to instigate change through the collective bargaining process.

Karl Marx was the first conflict theorist to discuss the concept of alienation as it relates to the problem of workers in modern industrial societies. Worker alienation, according to Marx (1965) stemmed from *industrialization* and, specifically, the *division of labour* process, which, in creating specialized activities, separated (alienated) the worker from the end product. Marx further noted that, in the industrial society, work would become an increasingly involuntary activity, and one inimical to the creativity necessary to social and personal development. In Canada, with the advent of industrial capitalism came the system that formalized the control of the worker by the owners of the means of production (Rinehart 1987:35). By co-ordinating, supervising, and disciplining the workforce, employers could control their employees, thus making the factory a more productive environment than other less rationalized workplaces. In the early stages of industrialization, workers were exposed to intolerable working and living conditions, but it was not until the beginning of the twentieth century that workers' associations and the trade union movement directly challenged the factory owners, attempting, through the collective bargaining process, to attain some control over the production process.

Much discussion of worker alienation has been focused on the blue-collar worker. Analysts have attributed the alienation of the factory worker in particular to the boredom and frustration common to assembly-line work, and to a management out of touch with the realities of the workplace. Such negative conditions were commonly regarded as the inevitable price of increased productivity, and a subsequent higher standard of living. Strikes, absenteeism, and other symptoms of worker dissatisfaction were either dismissed by employers as efforts by malcontents to

Table 5.1
Percent of People in Occupational Groups
Who Would Choose Similar Work Again

Professional and Lower White-Collar Occupations		Working-Class Occupations	
Urban university professors	93	Skilled printers	52
Mathematicians	91	Paper workers	42
Physicists	89	Skilled autoworkers	41
Biologists	89	Skilled steelworkers	41
Chemists	86	Textile workers	31
Firm lawyers	85	BLUE-COLLAR WORKERS,	
Lawyers	83	CROSS SECTION	24
Journalists (Washington		Unskilled steelworkers	21
correspondents)	82	Unskilled steelworkers	21
Church university professors	77		
WHITE-COLLAR WORKERS,			
CROSS SECTION	43		

Source: *Work in America: Report of a Special Task Force to the Secretary of Health, Education, and Welfare:* Cambridge, Mass: The M.I.T. Press, 1973), p.16. Reprinted by permission.

disrupt the production process, or as manifestations of power plays by militant trade union leaders. Finally, plant automation, which was supposed to give workers a measure of control over the production process, has instead created a class of semiskilled operators who control neither their product, nor their time, as their work is dictated by a computer (Susman 1972).

In the last two decades, a new phenomenon has developed which adds another dimension to the issue of worker alienation and job dissatisfaction. A 1973 study done by the U.S. Department of Health, Education and Welfare found that 57 percent of *white-collar* workers expressed some degree of dissatisfaction with their work. While lower than the 76 percent of blue-collar workers who disliked their occupations, the figure is a bleak commentary on the structure of the workplace. The Department study also showed the close correlation between job dissatisfaction and other social problems. For example, both blue- and white-collar dissatisfied workers were more likely to reflect a higher incidence of alcoholism, drug addiction, and mental and physical health problems, in addition to family breakdowns and family violence. Furthermore, as Campbell et al. (1976:182) observe, there appears to be a close correlation between job satisfaction and occupational ranking in the stratification system (see Table 5.1).

Marked variations in levels of dissatisfaction have been noted, as well, among different groups of workers. According to Sullivan et al.

(1980:312), women and visible minorities express a higher than average degree of unhappiness with their jobs, reflecting their more menial occupational positions in the society, while younger workers generally express dissatisfaction with their jobs regardless of whether they are in white- or blue-collar positions. Rinehart (1987:83) locates the key sector of white-collar discontent among low-level office and sales employees in both public bureaucracies and private corporations. With the introduction of specialized services and mass production, the office, in terms of efficiency, has come to resemble the assembly line. Increased *automation* has turned office and sales clerks—the majority women—into extensions of the machine, like their counterparts in the factory. It is unlikely that the introduction of office computers will change this situation. The transformation of office work into semiskilled positions has widened the lines of demarcation between office clerk and management, with the removal of opportunities for promotion and advancement into middle-management positions, which had been the norm in earlier times.

Even high-ranking professional and technical workers are not immune to the problems associated with bureaucratic organizations. The separation of management from the professional role has led to conflict between bureaucratic authority and professional authority (Scott 1966:265). The autonomy that professionals should enjoy has been usurped by bureaucratic control over working conditions and the nature of the work itself. For this group, dissatisfaction is often related not so much to poor salaries or unpleasant working conditions, as it is to a low sense of occupational achievement, responsibility, and challenge. In many instances, the education and qualifications of the professional are underemployed. In the post-industrial world, it has been suggested that technicians, unable to apply their training, limited in their autonomy, and faced with a contradiction between sophisticated expertise and a subordinate role in the workplace, will become the major catalyst for the democratization of the production process.

WORKPLACE REFORM

Worker discontent and alienation, we have seen, are universal problems affecting both blue- and white-collar workers, from the unskilled labourer to the professional bureaucrat. The question that remains is, can this alienation be reduced, bringing to workers emotional satisfaction and a sense of responsibility toward the workplace?

At the present time we lack a coherent societal strategy for alleviating alienation in the society. Groups representing labour unions and the unemployed advocate a major restructuring of the social, economic, and political structure of society. Marxist theorists, for example, believe that alienation is the inevitable result of capitalism and will only disappear with the introduction of a socialistic economic system in which the needs of people are given priority over the profit motive. However, we have seen that government bureaucracies are no panacea for worker aliena-tion, as in most instances the structure of large organizations—private or public—creates the very conditions that give rise to worker dissatisfac-tion. Furthermore, there is little support in Canadian society, which traditionally has supported the free-enterprise system, for state socialism or state control of the economic system.

Langdon (1980) notes that in nineteenth-century Canada worker organizations tried through collective bargaining to improve wages, job security, pensions, and the quality of the work environment. However, in the course of its development, the collective bargaining process legitim-ized the right of management to control the workplace. Furthermore, the trade union movement, while ensuring workers better incomes, has not been overly successful in reducing worker alienation and job dissatisfac-tion, and in this regard we can ask whether it has relinquished a major role to management in its approach to collective bargaining. Despite their importance, income and job security are no guarantees against worker alienation and job dissatisfaction.

Knight (1979) suggests that workers today are just as concerned with intrinsic factors, which relate to the nature of the job, as they are with extrinsic motivations such as pay and job security. In a study of both blue-and white-collar workers, Locke (1973) found a number of variables perceived by workers as important to job satisfaction. These included workload and smoothness of work flow, achievement, enjoyment, promo-tion, responsibility, recognition, money, interpersonal atmosphere, and working conditions. Given the importance of human factors to job satis-faction, it is clear that solutions to the problem of worker alienation depend to a large extent on making the workplace a more humane environment. Referring to studies on the effects of the work environment on worker productivity and efficiency, which were conducted at the Western Electric Company between 1927 and 1932, the human relations theorist, Elton Mayo (1945:158), suggested that industrialization and urbanization had led to a breakdown in social control mechanisms. As microcosms of the wider society, workers were simply reproducing the normlessness of their lives in the factory. Mayo felt that only a science of human relations could succeed in producing worker–management co-operation, and hence a more satisfying work environment.

White (1984) discusses some of the techniques used by management to improve working conditions, as well as methods for psychic gratifica-tion in the workplace. Porter (1979:113) believes that the manipulation of both extrinsic and intrinsic reward structures can improve worker pro-ductivity and satisfaction. *Behaviour modification* departs from the tradi-tional management approach (motivating the employee through higher wages and better fringe benefits) in its attempt to introduce psychological variables, such as more recognition, greater social interaction among workers, greater participation in the total production process, and the creation of opportunities for personal growth and skills. In recent years, quality of working life (QWL) programs have been widely introduced in an attempt to make the workplace a more humane and fulfilling environment. In addition, programs aimed at bringing organizational improvements to both factory and office environments have met with some success. In the larger assembly-line operations of General Motors, General Foods, and other large corporations, work has been redesigned to make it more challenging, with, for example, routine jobs being rotated among all members. As well, attempts at involving workers in the decision-making process (e.g., in designing their work tasks) and at reducing status differences between workers and management have often resulted in reduced absenteeism, greater productivity and efficiency, and increased worker satisfaction.

SUMMARY

1. In most traditional pre-industrial societies, labour was not highly valued. With the ascension of the Protestant work ethic, however, it came to be seen as a moral obligation. Most Canadians today view work as a source of economic well-being, social status, self-esteem, psychological fulfilment, and personal/professional networks.
2. Many workers try to insulate themselves from the alienating aspects of their work by pursuing leisure activities. Research suggests that it is difficult to separate work activities from leisure activities. Frequently job dissatisfaction spills over into leisure time.
3. According to the functionalist perspective, worker alienation is the result of social disorganization brought on by rapid social and technological change. Automation, the rationalization of the factory or office, the growth of specialization, and the expansion of conglomerates are the inevitable price that society pays for a higher standard of living.
4. For conflict theorists, worker alienation is an outgrowth of social and economic inequality. In the conflict of interest generated between the powerful minority of employers—government and big business—and the powerless majority of workers, the former group invariably triumphs.
5. While worker alienation has traditionally been associated with the blue-collar worker, the last two decades have seen the emergence of white-collar job dissatisfaction.
6. Studies of both blue- and white-collar workers have shown a close correlation between job dissatisfaction and other social problems,

including alcoholism, drug addiction, mental and physical health problems, family breakdowns, and family violence.

7. Traditionally, labour was primarily concerned with extrinsic motivations such as pay and job security. Today's worker has become increasingly concerned with intrinsic motivations, including autonomy, creativity, shared decision making, and innovation.

8. Employers have responded to changing employee concerns by introducing quality of life (QWL) programs, which, in contrast to traditional management approaches, address both extrinsic and intrinsic reward structures.

6

The Aging Canadian

INTRODUCTION

In recent years, the field of *gerontology* has gained importance in Canada, particularly because the elderly population is undergoing rapid and dramatic growth. Of particular consequence are policies regarding health and income security. In 1966, the Canadian Special Senate Committee on Poverty found that two-thirds of senior citizens (people 65 years and older) lived in poverty, with 28 percent being supported by the Old Age Security Allowance alone. Myles and Boyd (1988) further show that, in 1977, 55 percent of all old age pensioners qualified for the federal government's means-tested Guaranteed Income Supplement, while Gee and Kimball (1987: 54) note that elderly female-headed households reflect the highest rate of poverty (see Table 6.1).

Why has Canada, one of the wealthiest societies on earth, disregarded the needs and concerns of the elderly? This chapter will address this as well as other questions concerning the current status of the elderly vis-à-vis health care, housing conditions, social participation, and institutionalization.

Table 6.1
Incidence of Poverty for Families and Unattached Individuals,
by Sex, Population Aged 65+, 1982

	Poor[a]		Not Poor	
	Number	%	Number	%
Families				
Female head	21,000	24.6	64,366	75.4
Male head	77,000	10.2	677,902	89.8
Total	98,000	11.7	742,268	88.3
Unattached Individuals[b]				
Female	337,000	60.4	220,947	39.6
Male	85,000	48.9	88,824	51.1
Total	422,000	57.7	309,369	42.3

[a] Statistics Canada definition of poverty (1978 base).
[b] Individuals who live alone or in households with unrelated persons.
Source: National Council of Welfare 1984b.

Table 6.2
Canadian Population Projections by Age
(in thousands)

Year	Total Population	0–17	%	18–59	%	60–64	%	65 +	%
1981	22,993	6,933	28	14,134	58	963	4	2,310	10
1986	25,713	6,833	26	15,919	59	1,110	4	2,615	11
1996	27,993	6,993	25	16,640	59	1,115	4	3,248	12
2001	28,794	6,805	23	17,401	60	1,165	4	3,425	13
2011	30,068	6,411	21	17,968	59	1,764	6	3,924	14
2021	30,877	6,378	20	17,255	55	2,151	7	5,093	18

Source: Victor Marshall, ed, *Aging in Canada*, 2nd ed (Toronto: Fitzhenry and Whiteside, 1987), p.24

AGING AS A SOCIAL PROBLEM

Traditionally, Canada has considered itself to be a young nation, with high birth rates and a high proportion of young immigrants. In reality, as Marshall (1987:1) suggests, the older population has grown as birth rates and immigration have declined. Forecasts indicate that in the next forty years the proportion of people in the over-65-year age group will double and, in absolute numbers, triple (see Table 6.2). The two major tasks we face as a society are (1) to provide the societal and structural adjustments necessary to satisfy the needs of this growing segment of the population, and (2) to redefine and assimilate to our value system the role and status of the elderly.

To understand why aging has become a social problem in Canada, let us consider three factors related to the *social role* and status of older people. First, social status and prestige are largely determined by a person's ability to contribute economically, politically, and socially to the society's well-being. The rapidly changing, youth-oriented Canada of the last forty years, with its emphasis on industrial and technological innovation, has left many older people economically and socially redundant. Their skills outmoded, and the learning and education process now almost exclusively the responsibility of educational institutions, the elderly have lost their traditional role as the transmitters and keepers of knowledge that is essential to social progress.

Second, the type of family and kinship relations that a society exhibits has direct bearing on the status of the elderly (Ward 1984:59). In societies where the status of the family is high (e.g., India and China), older people are respected and usually play an important role in the family. In contemporary Canadian society, however, the family farm or business has largely given way to the large corporation. With young family members earning their living outside the family environment, and usually provided by the state with the skills and knowledge necessary for survival, parents and children have lost their interdependence. Finally, the break-up of the extended family has left aged parents with no role or place in society.

Third, in most societies the status of the old is usually linked to the degree of acceptability in the *socialization process*, that is, the conferring of a new role and status on the aged person. Through resocialization the older person is directed into a newly defined role and position in the society after the cessation of the formal occupational role. Our society, however, having removed the individual abruptly from the world of work (and the role which he or she has played throughout most of adulthood), then places the retired person into a vacuum. With little sympathy or understanding from the general public, and with no clear opportunity to find a meaningful identity, many of our elderly spend their final years viewing the world with frustration, disillusionment, and increasing pessimism (Ward 1984:96).

Theoretical Perspectives

From the *functionalist perspective*, aging as a social problem is caused by rapid social, cultural, and technological change, which has depleted the value of the elderly and rendered them functionally inconsequential. The status and power of each group in society is directly related to its ability to contribute to the maintenance of the total unit. Longer lifespans, coupled with decreasing availability of roles in the economy, the family, and in other social institutions, has created a serious imbalance between the expectations of the aged and what society offers. Both technology and compulsory retirement have deprived many seniors of their occupational roles. The functionalist would argue that if individuals were allowed to remain integrated in the society at advanced stages of life, the problem of role deprivation would never develop. Therefore, to avoid the social disorganization and dysfunctions caused by an imbalance between the age and role structures, we must create a social and economic environment in which old age becomes a period of emotional and financial security, with the elderly remaining integrated in the social system through the adoption of useful and responsible social roles.

The *conflict perspective*, on the other hand, emphasizes the conflict between interest groups for valued resources. Discrimination against the aged is a direct result of their loss of economic and political dominance in modern, industrial Canada, and their subsequent loss of prestige and status. In losing control over social rewards, the elderly have become a subordinate group. Like other forms of discrimination, age discrimination discounts individual differences in abilities or potential by labelling all people over a certain age as inferior and useless. For the conflict theorist, social awareness of the injustices experienced by the elderly must precede changes to their role and status in our society.

PROBLEMS OF THE AGED

Myles and Boyd (1988:192) note that, as the Canadian population ages, there is increasingly an imbalance between the institutional infrastructure and the population it serves. Our institutions, which have been designed to serve a younger population, fail to meet the needs of a growing elderly population. The growing crisis in health care and pension funding for the elderly are just two examples of strains being felt in society as it faces the issue of reallocation of resources. Other difficulties that seniors confront include the psychological and social consequences of retirement, the problem of housing and institutionalization, isolation, negative stereotyping, and learning a new role.

Health Care

The predicted rise in Canada's elderly population (from 8 percent in 1971 to 11 percent in 2001) will generate a 30 percent increase in the demand for hospital care (Rombout 1975:23). The problem is not so much that the health care system may not be able to provide adequate services for the elderly, but that our health services emphasize resources in acute or short duration illnesses, while the needs of the elderly lie in the chronic care of long-term incurable illnesses. According to Myles and Boyd (1988:195), there is a bias in our present health care system toward *curative medicine*, which is designed to restore the individual to a normal level of functioning. While such health care makes sense for the younger population, *preventive* and *prosthetic health care* is more essential to the elderly.

Preventive health care involves nutritional guidance, public health nurse visitation, and other methods geared to prevent the occurrence of an illness, while prosthetic health care involves activities designed to reduce long-term or permanent disability, including counselling and the redesigning of housing and other facilities to accommodate seniors' needs. Health care budgets show decided preference for acute care hospitals over the chronic care hospitals required by the elderly. But as Myles and Boyd (1988:196) note, hospitals geared toward sophisticated and expensive technology are of little use in treating the diseases that affect the majority of the elderly population.

While the quality of senior health care has always been problematic, for the last three decades Canada has prided itself on the universality of its health care, which compares favourably with the situation in the United

States, where poverty often precludes adequate health care. In the last few years, however, a growing threat to the provision of universal health care has risen in some provinces, in the form of extra billing by medical practitioners and user fees in hospitals. While the federal government has banned these practices, given the higher rates of illness among the elderly, there is no doubt that this group—particularly the elderly poor— will suffer should current restraints on extra billing be relaxed in the future.

Income Security

One of the most critical issues facing senior citizens is inadequate retirement income. As we can deduce from Table 6.3, the median income of the over-65 population is approximately $10,000 for men, and $7,000 for women. A variety of private and public pension programs currently provide income security for seniors. Government pensions include the universal Old Age Security (OAS) plan, which provides a pension for all Canadians over age 65, and the Canada and Quebec Pension plans, which provide pensions based on contributory years in the workforce. Finally, there is the Guaranteed Income Supplement (GIS) program, which provides supplementary income to the poorest seniors. However, despite all of these important social security programs, 50 percent of all old age pensioners qualified in 1981 for the federal government's means-tested Guaranteed Income Supplement for people living below the poverty line (National Council of Welfare 1984).

Matthews (1980) notes the plight of many married elderly women who, while not currently living below the poverty line, stand a good chance of getting there on the death of their husbands and subsequent loss of pension income. Further exacerbating the problem, as Nishio and Lauk (1987) point out, is the fact that only 50 percent of the Canadian labour force is covered by private pension plans, leaving the vast majority to depend on government payments and whatever savings they may have accrued during their working lives. In 1980, it was estimated that 81 percent of unattached women over age 65 had no private pension at all (Roadburg 1985:34).

According to the National Council of Welfare's (1984) report *Sixty Five and Over*, 25 percent of all persons over 65 live below the poverty line, which, as established by Statistics Canada for 1984, is $9,000 annually for an unattached individual, and $12,000 for a two-person family. Clearly, then, retirement income does not provide an adequate standard of living for all seniors, who, as it is, spend a far greater percentage of their incomes on food and shelter than does the rest of the population. The NCW report also notes that people 65 years and over spent 49 percent of their incomes on food and shelter, compared to 36 percent for other age

Table 6.3
Average 1981 Income of the Elderly and Other Adult Population (25–64 yrs) by
Highest Level of Schooling, Age and Sex, Canada, 1981

Highest level of schooling and sex	Age group				
	25–64	65+	65–74	75–84	85+
	$	$	$	$	$
Men					
Total	20,700	11,500	12,600	9,100	8,400
Less than Grade 9	15,300	8,400	9,200	7,200	6,900
Grades 9–13	19,300	12,600	13,500	10,200	9,100
Some university or other non-university (with or without certificate)	21,100	14,900	16,000	11,500	12,500
University certificate or degree	30,300	25,900	27,900	20,800	18,700
Women					
Total	9,800	7,000	7,100	7,000	6,900
Less than Grade 9	6,400	5,700	5,500	5,900	6,100
Grades 9–13	8,600	7,200	7,100	7,400	7,400
Some university or other non-university (with or without certificate)	10,700	9,300	9,500	9,000	8,800
University certificate or degree	16,000	14,000	14,500	12,900	10,800

Source: Statistics Canada, *The Elderly in Canada*. Ottawa: Supply and Services Canada, 1984. Reprinted by permission.

groups. In addition, while the majority of seniors reside in their own homes or private apartments, the quality of living accommodations is often substandard. As a final blow, the elderly are unable to escape poverty because of mandatory retirement laws which deprive them of their employment and income at 65.

Mandatory Retirement

As Chapter 5 suggested, Canada is a work-oriented society, in which one's occupation provides not only economic rewards, but also social esteem, status, group interaction, friendship networks, and intrinsic personal satisfaction. Since becoming an industrial society, Canada has established mandatory retirement from the workforce at the age of 65. While 33 percent of Canada's senior citizens were in the labour force in 1921, by 1986 senior participation had declined to 14 percent (Statistics Canada 1988), which suggests that most employers in the private sector are following the public sector plan of mandatory retirement at age 65. At the same time, the span between retirement and death has lengthened over the last fifty years. Between 1931 and 1981, life expectancy at birth increased by 12 years for men (60–72) and 17 years for women (62–79) (Novak 1988:53). This means that a large proportion of Canadians over 65 are retired even though they may be physically and mentally capable of working. While senior citizens' groups continue to lobby against mandatory retirement in Canada, with the Supreme Court of Canada having the final decision, immense financial, psychological, and emotional strains are being imposed on those seniors who would prefer to remain in the labour force.

Two major problems face the retired. First, there is the question of economic security. Many people are reluctant to retire if it means a substantial reduction in their standard of living (Statistics Canada [1988] puts income for over 60 percent of the retired at less than the average for all members of the labour force). Second, many workers fear the loss of their social identity after they depart from the labour force, and may, in the absence of any clear new role allocation give in to feelings of meaninglessness and despair. Blau (1973:29) points out that the social expectation that older people must relinquish their jobs at a fixed age has a dislocating effect upon individuals, particularly men, the traditional "breadwinners" (with more women entering the workforce, we can expect a less pronounced gender gap in terms of the demoralization that often results from mandatory retirement). Many Canadians are simply unclear as to what is expected of them in retirement. The absence of the clearly defined social roles and relationships that characterized the world of work is often a source of emotional and psychological distress for senior citizens. Of course, not all seniors react negatively to retirement. Many seniors who are financially and emotionally prepared for the change gladly exchange the routine of work for a more leisurely lifestyle. But for those less financially secure, the sharp drop in income accompanying retirement can become an intolerable burden.

Stereotyping

Simone de Beauvoir (1973:57) once noted that the major problem was not old age per se, but rather its popular association with worthlessness and unattractiveness. Pervading our society are common *stereotypes* about seniors as infirm in body and mind, indifferent to sexual activity, and helpless without the support of nursing or retirement homes. In fact, Neugarten (1976) shows that over 89 percent of all men and women over 65 are self-sufficient and live in the community. Furthermore, Rubin (1976), while ascribing low levels of sexual activity among seniors to social expectations, suggests that most married couples remain sexually active up to age 75.

The mass media have also served to perpetuate stereotypes of the elderly. Literature, movies, television, and advertisements can all be indicted for portraying seniors as frustrated, bitter, and disillusioned people. Advertising, and in particular the cosmetic industry, cajoles the public into disguising all signs of physical aging. As a result, society has developed an irrational fear of growing old, which is manifested in *ageism*, or discrimination against the elderly.

Institutionalization

Concern about the plight of the aged often centres on those who are institutionalized in nursing homes, rooming and lodging houses, mental hospitals, and senior citizens' homes. While less than 10 percent of seniors live in collective housing, 25 percent of all deaths in the over-65-year category occur in nursing homes and other homes for the aged (Statistics Canada 1982). According to Marshall (1987), over 40 percent of Canada's population over age 80—the majority women—can be found in some type of institution.

While the need for institutionalization of the physically and the mentally ill is undisputable, most seniors in Canadian institutions are there because they lack the social and financial independence—due, perhaps, to loss of spouse or home—necessary for them to function on their own in the community. Historically, health care services were biased toward providing financial support for hospital and institutional care, rather than home care. Instead of relying on social support, we have provided seniors with an abundance of nursing homes and other forms of institutional care (Schwenger and Gross 1980). This has been done at the expense of alternative approaches (e.g., home and community care), which remain undeveloped, firstly, because financial resources to implement alternative health care services are in short supply, and secondly, because hospital administrators and owners of homes for the aged have a vested interest in keeping their beds filled and the industry operating at optimum capacity.

Much has been written about the *effects* of institutions on the aged. Brody (1973) argues that institutionalization makes a resident totally powerless (the admission procedure alone serves to transfer an individual's control over his or her own life to the personnel of the institution). In addition to generalized experiences of dependency, depersonalization, low self-esteem, and boredom, residents in institutions exert little control over even the most rudimentary aspects of their personal lives—food, clothing, leisure activities. On the other hand, Connidis (1987) points out that, while depersonalization does occur in institutions for the aged, in many instances the individual's quality of life would have been even worse outside, given the lack of alternatives provided by society to the poor, the widowed, and the sick. Furthermore, old age homes are capable of becoming pleasant and humane environments if only their residents are given more control over their lives.

AGING IN MINORITY COMMUNITIES

In a multicultural society such as Canada, differences among ethnic groups are of critical importance. According to Ujimoto (1987), previous studies of ethnic relations in Canada, which tended to homogenize ethnic groups and to disregard intergenerational differences, have done a disservice to minority communities. First- or second-generation Japanese Canadians, for example, greatly differ from third- or fourth-generation Japanese in terms of social adaptability, socio-economic status, and relations with the majority group.

While Canada has developed an extensive social welfare and health care system, practitioners in the field have observed an underemployment of these services among seniors in the minority communities. Difficulties with language, cultural barriers, and an absence of social networks deny many aged immigrants ready access to available social and economic support services (Ujimoto 1987). Chan (1983) notes that Chinese senior citizens in Montreal are aware of in-group health and community services, but have little knowledge of services for the elderly at agencies and institutions outside the Chinese community.

Of further importance is the question of long-term care for the senior ethnic minorities. Maclean and Bonar (1985:52) describe the problems associated with placing this group in institutional environments established for the majority group. Unable to converse in the majority language, and receiving little empathy from staff members, they become unhappy and disillusioned with their setting. Related to the problem of noncommunication between institutional staff and senior minority patients, both Ujimoto (1987) and Naidoo (1981) have analyzed how cultural values among aging Japanese and South Asians differ from those of mainstream Canada. Ujimoto (1987) found among the Japanese a strong tendency not to question authority figures—e.g., doctors—or to express feelings of pain or suffering (for many, suffering means strength, while requesting assistance means weakness). Thus it is only through nonverbal clues that a true picture can be obtained, an area of research that is only beginning to be explored in the relationship between ethnicity/aging and institutional care. Similarly, Naidoo (1981:84) observes that, while in the traditional South Asian family, elderly persons enjoy respect, status, prestige, and control, in Canada the loss of traditional family values has led many seniors to fear either abandonment by their relatives, or institutionalization.

FUTURE PROSPECTS

The degree to which the problems facing seniors are solved will to a large extent depend on the power and influence seniors can wield as lobbyists. Given that seniors represent the fastest growing segment of the population—a potentially huge voting bloc—it is quite feasible that governments will become increasingly responsive to seniors' demands. For this to occur, however, the organization of seniors into pressure groups (e.g., the Grey Panthers) is essential. The ongoing debate on the abolition of *mandatory retirement* at age 65 is the direct result of political pressure by seniors. In 1983, the Manitoba Supreme Court ruled that mandatory retirement for public service workers was unconstitutional. The Federal Supreme Court is currently being asked to rule on whether mandatory retirement contravenes the Charter of Rights. We can expect that more provinces will begin reviewing their policies on this issue in the near future.

Alternatives to mandatory retirement are, of course, highly problematic. In times of high unemployment, particularly, many would argue that the young workers who are trained and qualified deserve a chance to establish themselves in the labour force. Whether seniors in the labour force do, in fact, adversely affect the chances of younger workers depends on many factors, including the number of older people who choose to continue working, the type of jobs and skills that they hold, as well as on the pressures or financial inducements offered for voluntary retirement. The essential problem is that mandatory retirement at a set chronological age is discriminatory because it takes no account of the physical and mental capabilities of people in suggesting that they can work productively until—but not after—their 65th birthday. Having a set age for retirement is an administrative convenience for employers and government bureaucracies, but the alternative of individually reviewing each worker's performance, while more time-consuming and problematic, would be fairer.

Given the failure of the *pension system* to eradicate poverty for Canada's seniors, the introduction in the last decade of Registered Retirement Savings Plans augurs well for future retirees. As well, the recent expansion of pension schemes in the private sector, which includes about 50 percent of the labour force, suggests that in the next decade the majority of retirees will have supplementary pensions to the government's programs (Messinger and Powell 1988). In the short run, however, only public pressure can lead to increases in Old Age Security and other government-funded pension plans to alleviate the financial hardships of those without supplementary pensions. Since Canada has the resources to ensure its seniors a decent standard of living, government policy must insist on the provision of a retirement income above the poverty line.

In terms of *health care*, our medical system must shift some of the emphasis from acute type diseases to the chronic disorders that afflict seniors. Unfortunately, until *geriatrics* becomes as well-funded as some other medical specialties, the problem (in addition to the general short-age of chronic care hospitals) will remain. With regard to our visible minorities, we must further analyze the impact of the aging process on these groups, and move away from the holistic approach of treating all groups as homogeneous.

The question of the *integration* of seniors into the community can be seen in the context of the debate concerning the effects of special *institutions* established exclusively to care for the elderly. These institutions can take the form of homes for the aged, nursing homes, or retirement communities. Of the three, the planned community, which offers self-contained shopping, in addition to health and recreational facilities, has drawn the least criticism. However, Rose and Peterson (1965:181) argue that keeping the elderly segregated in planned communities isolates them from other groups, which gives rise to ageism. Thus, as long as is physically possible, seniors should be encouraged to remain in their neighborhoods and communities. Unfortunately, despite the success of such programs as foster grandparents, little government funding has been committed to providing efficient home and community care services for the elderly.

Finally, even if the financial, housing, and health care problems of seniors can be ameliorated, their status in society will remain low unless social attitudes (largely based on stereotypes and prejudice) toward them also change. There is a need for public education programs that not only provide a clearer picture of the social and biological aspects of the aging process, but at the same time encourage policies for social change, to ensure that, in Canada, retirement and old age will become a fulfilling and rewarding period of life, eagerly anticipated instead of feared.

SUMMARY

1. The dramatic growth of Canada's older population in recent years has given added prominence to the field of gerontology.
2. According to the funtionalist perspective, the loss of prestige, status, and influence experienced by the aged is the result of rapid social, cultural, and technological change, which made seniors' roles obsolete in terms of contributing to the smooth functioning of the system.
3. Conflict theorists link the declining role of seniors to their inability to command financial power. The powerlessness of the elderly in

modern industrialized societies has, moreover, given rise to age discrimination.

4. Seniors have been the victims of a health care system that emphasizes acute care at the expense of chronic care, which is essential to the needs of the aged. Extra billing poses an additional threat to seniors, particularly among the economically disadvantaged.

5. Despite the availability of private and public pension programs, significant numbers of seniors—particularly women—live below the poverty line. Government pension payments should be increased to keep seniors who lack supplementary benefits above the poverty line.

6. Mandatory retirement at age 65 lowers the standard of living for seniors, while at the same time depriving them of intrinsic job satisfactions such as group interaction and self-esteem. Loss of morale and feelings of depression and anxiety are common responses to forced retirement.

7. Ageism, or discrimination against the elderly, is reinforced by common stereotypes about seniors as mentally and physically infirm people. The mass media, with its bias toward youth, plays a major role in perpetuating negative attitudes about the aged.

8. While institutionalization can benefit the physically or mentally ill, many seniors are institutionalized because they lack the social and financial resources to survive in the community. Dependency, depersonalization, and low self-esteem are among the factors commonly associated with institutionalization.

9. Aging ethnic visible minorities face language and cultural barriers in their dealings with social and economic support services. These barriers often prevent such groups from getting help at all, or, in the case of those who require long-term care, only enhance the negative effects of institutionalization.

10. As an alternative to institutionalization, seniors should be encouraged to remain in the community as long as possible. This could be achieved, in part, by increasing government funding to home and community care services.

7

Poverty in Canada

INTRODUCTION

Canada is one of the most affluent countries in the world, with abundant natural resources, sophisticated technology, and a standard of living surpassed by few other countries. Yet in the midst of all of our wealth and affluence, 12 percent of all Canadian families live in *poverty*. According to the Statistics Canada (1988), 639,000 families live in poverty, while 31 percent of all single persons live at, or below, the *poverty line*. The National Council of Welfare (1984) estimates the number of persons living in poverty in Canada at four million, while according to Statistics Canada (1984), one out of eight Canadians lives below the poverty line.

DEFINITIONS OF POVERTY

Before discussing general explanations of poverty from both the functionalist and conflict perspectives, let us attempt a definition of poverty. The most widely employed method for calculating poverty lines in Canada is the *low-income cut-offs* used by Statistics Canada to produce profiles of the low-income population. The low-income cut-offs are based on a *subsistence conception of poverty*. In 1982, it was estimated that Canadian households spent on average 42 percent of their income on food, clothing, and shelter. Since economically disadvantaged families must devote an above-average proportion of their income to basic necessities, the cut-offs were set at 62 percent of income. Any family or individual with an income at or below the relevant low-income cut-off is considered poor. Also taken into account in the final calculations of the poverty line are family size and urban–rural variations in living costs (see Table 7.1).

While the Statistics Canada approach defines family units as poor if they spend 62 percent of their income on essentials, the Canadian Council on Social Development's (CCSD) poverty lines are based on a measure of *income inequality*. Taking into account family size, families and individuals are considered poor if they live on less than half of the national average income. The figures in Table 7.1 are based on an average family income of $32,000 for 1982. The final set of poverty lines can be determined using a method established by the Special Senate Committee on Poverty. This approach blends elements from both the Statistics Canada and CCSD methods. It takes into account both expenditures and income, as well as using National Health and Welfare monthly budget

Table 7.1
Comparison of Statistics Canada, CCSD* and Senate Committee Poverty Lines, 1982
Estimates

Family Size	Statistics Canada range	mid-range	CCSD	Senate Committee
1	$ 5,307– 7,303	$ 6,640	$ 6,857	$ 7,680
2	7,702–10,585	9,626	11,429	12,800
3	9,825–13,506	12,278	13,714	15,360
4	11,681–16,065	14,601	16,000	17,920
5	13,062–17,958	16,325	18,286	20,480
6	14,336–19,714	17,921	20,571	23,040
7 or more	15,717–21,615	19,649	22,857	25,600

* Canadian Council on Social Development.
Source: National Council of Welfare, *Measuring Poverty: 1982 Poverty Lines* (Ottawa: Supply and Services Canada, 1983), p.4. Reprinted by permission.

standards, adjusted for family size. As seen in Table 7.1, of the three methodologies utilized for arriving at a poverty line for Canadians, the Senate Committee's approach is the most generous.

Finally, poverty can be defined in terms of *relative deprivation*, meaning a denial of basic living standards common and expected in the society. While the poor in Canada can be said to be living in luxury compared to the poor in Bangladesh or Somalia, in terms of the affluence that surrounds them, their standard of living is one of deprivation. As Miller (1968:165) notes, people evaluate their poverty not only in relation to their basic needs (the absence of which constitutes *absolute deprivation*), but also in relation to the affluence of those around them. Defining poverty in Canada in relative terms, therefore, relates to the inability of certain groups to achieve the higher standard of living enjoyed by groups with higher incomes. Gillespie (1980:23) suggests that improvement in the income and status of the poor, in relative terms, has not altered significantly in the last thirty years. For example, in 1951 the poorest one-fifth of Canadians had 4.4 percent of money income, and 4.2 percent in 1981 (see Table 7.2). At the same time, the richest one-fifth obtained 42.8 percent of money income in 1951 and 42.3 percent in 1981.

THEORETICAL PERSPECTIVES

Much of the concern about poverty in Canada stems from its serious and undesirable social, political, and economic consequences. While few would deny that all Canadians should have an equal opportunity to improve their social and economic status, the fact remains that a large minority of our citizens live permanently outside the opportunity structure for self-improvement. Both the functionalist and conflict schools

Table 7.2
Percentage Distribution of Total Incomes of Families and Unattached Individuals
1951–1981, Canada

All Units %	1951	1961	1971	1981
Lowest 20%	4.4	4.2	3.6	4.2
Second lowest 20%	11.2	11.9	10.6	10.7
Middle 20%	18.3	18.3	17.6	17.7
Second highest 20%	23.3	24.5	24.9	25.1
Highest 20%	42.8	41.1	43.3	42.3
Total	100.0	100.0	100.0	100.0

Source: Statistics Canada, *Census of Canada, 1951–1981*. Reprinted by permission.

agree that the problem of poverty in Canada is related to *social stratifica-tion*. However, they disagree as to the necessity and consequences of social and economic inequality.

From the *functionalist perspective*, social stratification is integral to the maintenance of society. According to Davis and Moore (1945), in every society some occupational roles require special skills and training. Since people will not perform these specialized roles (e.g., physicians, scientists, or business executives) unless they are rewarded, society compensates them usually—but not exclusively—in the form of high income. On the other hand, people in jobs that do not require special talents (e.g., labourers or clerks) receive fewer financial rewards. From this perspective, social stratification, in fact, allows for the efficient functioning of society by permitting those most qualified to find their most effective positions in the economic system.

Roach (1965) further notes that the poverty that results from social stratification can serve to motivate people to improve their social and economic position and hence contribute positively to society. Poverty becomes a social problem only when it ceases to perform a motivating role, that is, when it no longer encourages people to be more productive. Theoretically, this situation could occur if the majority of the poor, while productive, were confined to their poverty status because of society's inability to reward them. Similarly, if the system was closed to upward *social mobility*, productive and ambitious people could be prevented from improving their status in the stratification system. In conclusion, functionalists see poverty as an inevitable condition growing out of social and economic stratification. Poverty exists, they argue, because society is overstratified with unequally distributed wealth and income. To the extent that certain groups are denied access to the reward and opportu-nity structure, the inequalities in the system have become dysfunctional.

From the *conflict perspective*, on the other hand, not only is social stratification the root cause of poverty, but social inequality is neither beneficial nor functional to society. Tumin (1953) believes that equality of opportunity in a class system is impossible, given the passing down of social status from generation to generation. Poverty is a consequence of some groups having greater access than others to the means of attaining social rewards and status. Conflict theorists further argue that privileged groups, in order to retain their monopoly over the highest socio-economic positions in society, use their power to ensure that groups in poverty remain in economically unrewarding positions over generations. Forcese (1975:57) notes that social stratification, instead of ensuring that the most qualified people fill the most important roles, simply allows for the perpetuation of a system of inequality. From the conflict perspective, equality of opportunity is a myth which, among other things, has fuelled public hostility toward welfare recipients. (According to the National Council of Welfare [1982], the vast majority of people on welfare either cannot work—e.g., the physically/mentally handicapped, or single mothers without access to day care—or else are excluded from employment because they lack the proper skills and educational background.) Arguing against the belief that the poor are content to adjust to their deprived conditions, conflict theorists maintain that the *culture of poverty* argument, which assumes that shared cultural characteristics have prevented the poor from transcending their status, has been used by the dominant groups to maintain their superior positions. Such institutions as welfare, for example, have allowed elite groups to keep the poor in a state of dependence.

WHO ARE CANADA'S POOR?

According to Caskie (1979:27–43), the incidence of poverty increases when one or more of the following characteristics are present: no member of the family worked during the year, the family resides in the Atlantic provinces, and the head of the family is 50 years of age or over /a woman/outside the labour force/ and not educated beyond the elementary level. We turn now to an examination of those groups that constitute the most economically disadvantaged in Canadian society today.

Women and Poverty

According to Gee and Kimball (1987:54), three out of every five poor elderly adults in Canada are women. Saunders (1988:172) notes that working women earn less than 60 percent of the male salary, while the National Council of Welfare (1985) estimates that 25 percent of women work for wages at or below the poverty line. In addition, a woman's chances of being poor are strongly related to her family status. Almost half a million wives live in poor two-spouse families, with poorly educated wives inheriting the status of their husbands (Statistics Canada 1980).

Finally, the public perception of single-parent mothers as being the largest group of female poor, is erroneous, since, according to the National Council of Welfare (1985), they comprise only 14 percent of Canada's poor women.

That poverty in Canada is so overwhelmingly a female phenomenon calls into question many popular notions as to why some people are poor and others are not. The widely held view that people are poor because they are lazy, for example, is contradicted by the fact that the poorest group in society are elderly widows—54 percent with incomes below the poverty line—who worked hard all of their lives without an income or a pension plan. There is little doubt that inequality of opportunity is a major contributory factor to the widespread poverty among women. Sex discrimination, while being reduced, is still a reality in education and the workplace, with the majority of working women still to be found in dead-end, low-paying jobs.

Poverty Among Native Peoples

The life of our native peoples is generally one of poverty. The average family income of Indians on reserves is about 45 percent of that of the majority society (Price 1978:92), and the plight of the Inuit is just as alarming. Kellough (1980) documents the despair found on reserves where the majority of native peoples live in homes devoid of basic sanitary services. Frideres (1983:see chapter 6) notes on some reserves unemployment as high as 70 percent, an average level of education no higher than Grade 5, and pre-school mortality three times the national average.

Statistics, of course, cannot begin to describe the alienation, disillusionment, and degradation experienced by this minority group, which have led to exceedingly high rates of alcoholism, suicide, mental illness, and criminal behaviour among the group's members (Frideres 1983: see Chapter 8). For those living off the reserve, the problem of poverty is no less severe. Unskilled and uneducated, and faced with widespread discrimination by a prejudiced majority, they soon become marginal figures living in the slums and tenements of our large cities. While the majority of urban Indians are unemployed, those employed are in part-time, unskilled jobs (Frideres 1983:191). In this hostile environment, most young, urban Indians, among whom a high degree of alienation and frustration is common, eke out an existence of poverty and deprivation on welfare payments. (For a fuller discussion of Canada's native peoples, see Chapter 10.)

Poverty and the Child

According to Statistics Canada (1983), in 1981 approximately 28 percent of all children under age 16 were classified as poor. On a regional basis, 38 percent of the children in the Maritime provinces were classified as poor, with the least poverty being found in Ontario, Alberta, and British Columbia. However, even in these provinces one child in six was living in a family with an income below the poverty line. In terms of family characteristics, 69 percent of children in female-headed single-parent families were living in poverty, as compared to 21 percent in two-parent families. Ryan (1972:36) notes a higher incidence of malnutrition, stunted growth, and physical or mental retardation among children from poor families. In addition, this group experiences socio-cultural handicaps, including deficient parental care, adverse physical environment, and inadequate health care.

Research suggests that there is a direct correlation between family income and educational intentions, with students from economically disadvantaged backgrounds reflecting lower educational aspirations than their higher-income counterparts. Why is the poor child an underachiever in the school systems of our nation? According to the National Council of Welfare (1985), the economically disadvantaged child is more likely to come to school underfed and hungry—a barrier to learning—to be absent from school more often, and to face a negative home environment. It is not uncommon for poor children with low grades to be channeled into dead-end slow-learner or special education classes. A study undertaken by the Canadian Teachers' Federation (1970) revealed that inner-city poor children were 25 times more likely to be assigned the label of "slow learner" than were affluent suburban children. In addition, many inner-city high schools lacked academic programs that would lead to university-level education, and the school environment of teachers and other children was generally more hostile to poor children. Given these conditions, it is not surprising that dropout rates for this group are so high. Unfortunately, by dropping out of the system, the child from a low-income environment only perpetuates the cycle of poverty for another generation.

The Regional Poor

The relationship between regional economic inequalities and poverty is very strong. While certain regions in Canada produce poverty, other regions produce affluence (Clement 1980:275). One is more likely to be poor in the Maritimes than in Ontario, Alberta, or British Columbia. A comparison of the average personal income—including all welfare pay-

Table 7.3
Average Earnings as a Percent of National Average Income, Canada and Provinces,
1946–1981

Province	1946	1951	1956	1961	1966	1971	1981
Newfoundland	—	93.0	81.4	85.7	77.5	79.5	74.9
Prince Edward Island	90.0	78.9	77.8	75.9	69.0	66.7	70.6
Nova Scotia	91.2	85.0	84.3	84.3	81.3	83.4	89.8
New Brunswick	88.9	83.1	82.5	79.4	79.5	78.5	77.7
Quebec	96.7	97.8	97.2	97.1	99.0	97.4	93.7
Ontario	104.4	104.8	106.2	106.1	105.7	107.6	102.9
Manitoba	93.0	93.9	91.3	93.7	98.7	89.1	93.6
Saskatchewan	103.1	92.5	85.7	88.7	90.4	79.6	101.3
Alberta	92.5	97.9	96.0	97.2	96.0	96.8	112.6
British Columbia	99.8	105.5	108.5	105.5	107.7	106.5	107.6
CANADA	100.0	100.0	100.0	100.0	100.0	100.0	100.0

Source: D. Forcese and S. Richer, eds., *Social Issues*, 2nd ed. (Scarborough: Prentice-Hall, 1988), p.75. Reprinted by permission.

ments, unemployment insurance benefits, old age pensions and other transfer payments—for each province reveals that personal income for the Maritime provinces is approximately 80 percent of that of Alberta and British Columbia. Furthermore, as Table 7.3 suggests, even though Canada has established programs to eliminate them, regional economic disparities have not changed over the past five decades. Jobs still pay less in depressed regions, and unemployment rates in the Maritimes and Quebec are consistently higher than in the other regions of Canada (Adams et al. 1971:59–60).

The basic problem is that industry and high employment have been traditionally located in the central provinces, with manufacturing centred in Ontario and primary extractive industries located in the western provinces. Depressed economies have starved education, health, and other social services in the poorer regions. Yet education and training are desperately needed to get the labour force into better-paying jobs and out of poverty. One solution has been out-migration, with mainly the young, skilled, and ambitious moving to provinces with the best job opportunities. However, in the absence of a national economic policy that alters the established trend of economic development of the centre at the expense of the periphery, the problem of regional economic disparities (see Chapter 9 for a fuller discussion) will persist.

The Working Poor

In the early 1970s, the Special Senate Committee on Poverty reported that the working poor were the most "invisible" of all low-income Canadians.

A decade later, the National Council of Welfare (1981) noted that over a million men, women, and children were living in 426,000 working-poor households. Today, almost one-half of Canada's poor work, yet remain below the poverty line.

Let us define the working poor as a family or single person whose income is below Statistics Canada's low-income cut-off definition of the poverty line. From our discussion of regional disparities in poverty, it is not surprising that Atlantic Canada is overrepresented in the number of working poor. The majority of Canada's working poor live in large cities of more than 100,000, with only 16 percent residing in small towns and rural areas. According to the National Council of Welfare (1984), one out of eight unattached individuals forms part of the working poor. Of the total working poor, unattached individuals comprise 31 percent and families with children 59 percent. Of further interest, family heads under age 25 form 17 percent of the working poor, three times the total for the all ages category. Not surprisingly, the education level of the working poor is low, with 60 percent of people in this category having less than a Grade 8 education. Finally, Statistics Canada (1983) notes that single women run a greater risk of poverty than single men. Three out of every ten are poor, and 25 percent are working poor. Women who head families are even worse off. According to the National Council of Welfare (1983), 46 percent of female single parents are poor, with 20 percent among the working poor.

CAUSES OF POVERTY

According to the functionalist school of thought, as we have seen, the poverty that derives from social stratification is functional to the total system insofar as it motivates people to work in order to improve their social and economic position. (This view, of course, fails to take into account the struggling pensioner who has worked all of his or her life, but who because of inadequate public and private pension programs must survive in old age on a minimal income.) On a more cynical note, Gans (1972:275) argues the poverty, while it may not be inevitable, is beneficial to social welfare agencies, criminologists, and others whose theoretical function it is to service the needs of the poor. In making themselves available for low-paying and unpleasant jobs, Gans further suggests, the poor are useful to the higher-status members of the society, who because they benefit from the status quo naturally resist any attempts to redistribute wealth and power.

Thus conflict theorists, who view poverty as caused by influential and powerful groups, argue that the so called "functions" of poverty are simply a ruse to legitimize the existing social order and to prevent necessary changes in the socio-economic structure. Adams (1971:35–47) sees the corporations as the controllers of the economy, exploiting the workers and consumers with the compliance of a government controlled by special interest groups. Richer (1980) contends that groups which control the opportunity structure in society hinder the education and training of deprived groups, thereby preventing them from achieving upward mobility. The exclusion of the poor from the limited high-status, high-income occupations sustains not only the cycle of poverty, but also the privileged position of the minority. As Harp (1980:231) observes, "[A]n individual's family background continues to be an important predictor of both educational aspirations and attainment in our society."

In addition, poverty in Canada can be attributed to the growth of "structural unemployment," the result of economic and technological change over the last few decades. Automation in the industrial heartland of Quebec and Ontario has made obsolete the skills and training of thousands of workers, many of whom have become unemployable and poor. As well, marginal farms in the last twenty years have become financially nonviable, resulting in the migration of thousands of rural people without marketable skills to the cities. Finally, the failure of government programs to provide adequate regional economic expansion to the Maritimes has brought unemployment and poverty in this region to crisis proportions. Add on to these groups the hundreds of thousands of employed poor who work for minimum wage, and we arrive at a picture of an economic underclass whose lives are characterized by chronic unemployment, underemployment, and poverty.

Much has been written about the so-called *culture of poverty* that develops among deprived peoples. Originally developed by Lewis (1980), the theory has taken on renewed importance with the work of Gans (1972). In essence, the theory builds on the cultural characteristics of a unique pattern of beliefs, attitudes, values, and behaviour commonly observed among the poor, which, the suggestion is, effectively separates the poor from the non-poor. In addition, the culture of poverty creates a social, psychological, and emotional attitudinal frame that makes it difficult for members to escape from their deprived environment. According to Lewis (1980:138), this distinct cultural pattern, which limits options available to the poor (creating despair, alienation, and fatalism), transcends ethnic, racial, national, and regional boundaries.

However, traits commonly attributed to the poor are more apparent than real, according to Coward et al. (1974), with less than one-half of the poor reflecting such cultural characteristics. But perhaps the most disturbing feature of the culture of poverty theory is that it rationalizes away poverty, and by blaming the victim removes the onus of responsibility from the state. Arguments that the poor pass on their attitudes of failure and disillusionment to successive generations, thereby ensuring their continued deprivation, fly in the face of the many research studies that correlate poverty with the discrimination and lack of educational and economic opportunity experienced by disadvantaged groups in this society. No sociological or social psychological profile of the poor can rationalize the structural causes of social and economic inequality in Canada. Feelings of fatalism, helplessness, dependence, and inferiority among the poor can be directly linked to their experience of social and economic repression.

Finally, it can be argued that the powerful interest groups which benefit from structural inequalities in society have been successful in resisting meaningful change in the redistribution of wealth and income in Canada. In 1980, the Canadian Council on Social Development (CCSD) noted that the evidence of the last twenty years contradicts the public's perception that governments have been successful in augmenting the degree of redistribution from rich to poor. In fact, the share of the pie controlled by the rich increased in the 1970s, and, as Johnson (1979) shows, welfare policies have failed to redistribute incomes.

Regarding tax reform, Horner (1980) argues that an effective tax transfer of 4 billion dollars to the income of poor families could lift them all above the poverty line. However valid this suggestion may be, income redistribution alone will not strike at the root cause of poverty in Canada. In this context, the argument put forward by Gans (1972), that the existence of an impoverished, underprivileged group in society serves to maintain the privileges of other groups, bears closer scrutiny. According to Gans, poverty is allowed to persist because it provides jobs for the non-poor and facilitates the lifestyle of the affluent by providing a ready pool of low-wage workers. Furthermore, by consuming shoddy and inferior goods, the poor increase profits to business and corporations (Adams et al. 1971:74–78). The removal of the structural inequalities that give rise to poverty appears, unfortunately, to be a remote prospect. In Canada, the legislative process is strongly influenced by lobbies representing privileged groups and strata. The poor, however, as a powerless and nonhomogeneous group with a negative public image, lack the opportunities for effecting legislation that could bring about positive structural change.

FUTURE PROSPECTS

A multidimensional approach to the problem is essential if the fight against poverty is to be successful. First, there must be a concerted governmental program to provide incentives in the educational and economic system for women, seniors, native peoples, and visible and ethnic minorities. While governments cannot legislate attitudinal change on an unwilling public, "laws with teeth" can act as catalysts in prodding employers to eliminate discriminatory hiring practices. Second, in light of the tremendous technological innovations taking place in the industrial and manufacturing sectors, there is an urgent need for comprehensive and up-to-date retraining programs for the unskilled and uneducated.

Third, efforts must be made toward weath and income redistribution. As noted earlier in this chapter, governments have been unwilling or unable, while vocalizing on the need for change, to introduce any meaningful restructuring of the Income Tax Act that would increase personal income among the poor. As St. Laurent (1980:430) notes, "the multi-million dollar social security system has not significantly reduced income inequality." In 1971, the Senate Committee on Poverty (the Croll Commission) concluded that the welfare system was inadequate, inequitable, and served to keep groups in poverty for a lifetime. The Committee recommended the implementation of a *guaranteed national income* program, which would incorporate already existing income programs such as Family and Youth allowances and the Old Age Security payments. The poor would be guaranteed an income above the poverty line, and would not have to choose between work or social assistance. Earnings would be taxed negatively, so that individuals who worked would always be financially better off. In essence, this system, in which each individual or family is entitled to a basic income or support level, "is a universal non-discretionary income-conditioned transfer mechanism that attempts to minimize any work disincentive" (Gilbert 1980:448). (Basically a program for the millions of working poor, a guaranteed national income would not be particularly useful in relation to the disabled or the aged.) In 1976, despite positive results from feasibility studies the program was shelved, and there is no current interest on the part of the federal government in resurrecting it. In this respect, it appears to have fallen victim to the economic and class factors that almost certainly will ensure that poverty and inequality remain part of our social environment in the foreseeable future. Hence the urgent need for the poor to become politically active and attempt not only to influence the political decision-making process, but also to alter negative public attitudes about deprived groups in our society.

SUMMARY

1. Poverty can be defined in terms of either absolute or relative deprivation. Absolute deprivation refers to the absence of basic necessities. Relative deprivation relates to the inability of certain groups to attain a standard of living as high as that enjoyed be other groups.
2. From the functionalist perspective, social stratification is integral to the smooth functioning of society. The poverty that inevitably results from social stratification motivates people to improve their social and economic positions. Poverty only becomes a social problem when it ceases to perform this motivating role.
3. According to conflict theory, the root cause of poverty is social stratification, which is neither beneficial nor functional to society. The low

rate of upward social mobility in Canada suggests that equality of opportunity is a myth.

4. The culture of poverty refers to a value system—involving an attitude of hopelessness, despair, and apathy—that prevents the poor from breaking out of the cycle of poverty. Conflict theorists argue that dominant groups in society use the culture of poverty argument to maintain their superior positions, and to keep economically disadvantaged groups in a state of dependence.

5. Women, native peoples, children, the elderly, and the regionally disadvantaged are among the most economically deprived groups in Canadian society. Despite their large numbers, the working poor are the most invisible of all low-income Canadians.

6. Those who blame poverty on its victims by adopting the culture of poverty argument fail to take into account the structural realities that encourage poverty. These include regional disparities; the failure of the economic system to accommodate or assist the unskilled and uneducated; low minimum wages; discrimination in the educational system against economically disadvantaged children; and, finally, a political system easily swayed by powerful lobbies concerned with maintaining gross inequities in the distribution of wealth and income.

7. In terms of mitigating poverty, strategies, goals, and policies must include

- legislation designed to protect minority groups, seniors, and women against discrimination;
- large-scale job retraining programs;
- a guaranteed national income;
- concerted efforts at income and wealth redistribution;
- the political mobilization of the poor;
- the changing of negative public attitudes toward the poor.

8

The Family in Canada

INTRODUCTION

Schlesinger (1979:1) notes that no other social institution holds such a sense of immediacy to our lives as the family. It is the cradle of existence, the source of biological inheritance, and the transmitter of culture. In short, one can say that the family is one of the key institutions in the social system, exerting a profound influence on other social institutions. Despite this, statistical evidence suggests that traditional legal marriage and the nuclear family are undergoing a period of disorganization. The marriage rate, according to Statistics Canada (1983) dropped 25 percent in the 1970s, while 40 percent of Canadian marriages ended in divorce. In addition, marriages ending in divorce today last an average of nine years, in comparison to fourteen years a decade ago. Of further importance, in the last ten years over half a million children have been affected by divorce. However, before we fall prey to the opinion that a higher divorce rate signals the breakdown of the institution, we should note that the rate of remarriages is also on the rise; in 1976, 13 percent of marriages involved at least one partner who had been previously married (Schlesinger 1983:2).

In this chapter, we focus on the impact of societal change on the family. But before turning to the causes and consequences of family disorganization, and to future prospects for the modern family, let us first examine the forms, functions, and roles of the family in Canada.

THE EMERGENCE OF THE NUCLEAR FAMILY

For most Canadians, the word "family" brings to mind a married couple and their children, in other words, the *nuclear family*. Many societies exhibit more than one form of family with one type predominant (Larson 1976:43). In Canada, however, the nuclear family of parents and children—comprising 77 percent of Canadians (Nett 1983)—is the normal pattern, though one-parent and three-generation families are also common. In addition, while traditional marriage is the norm, 25 percent of Canadians are living in common-law heterosexual unions, homosexual unions, or communal relationships.

One of the issues facing the family as an institution is that we still tend to idealize the nuclear family, and to perceive departures from this norm as threatening, such that alternative family patterns become characterized as family disorganization and conflict. Yet the nuclear family is a relatively recent phenomenon. In pre-industrial Canada, the majority of people lived in *extended family* systems, in which parents, children, grand-children, as well as other relatives, all shared the same household. The three- or four-generation family unit was functional to the social and economic needs of a rural (and often isolated) people. In addition to being a social unit, the family also served as an economic base, with most production and consumption occurring within the unit. Economic interdependence among family members fostered the growth of close-knit groups, and allowed for the maintenance of social order among groups of families. In this sense, the wide group of relatives formed a kin network, which served as the social, political, and economic basis of society.

However, as industrialization progressed in Canada, the social and economic organization of society was drastically altered. The growth of cities and large-scale business organizations made the family farm or business obsolete. As people moved to the urban centres in search of jobs and social and economic mobility, the economic functions of the extended family also became less relevant. The assembly line, the separation of the productive and consumptive roles of the family, and the geographical separation of its members all sounded the death knell for the extended family. What replaced it was the nuclear family—husband, wife, and children—residing in a separate household. As family loyalty crumbled, individualism replaced the group integration of family members, and the tight-knit social and economic organization of the extended family gradually disintegrated.

The pattern of life in the nuclear family differs markedly from that of the extended family. Marriage has become an individual rather than family-centred institution, and is often based on the concept of romantic love, with people choosing their partners for personal rather than economic reasons. Courtship and dating patterns have been liberalized. Furthermore, the entry of women into the labour force has necessitated a more egalitarian decision-making process in the family unit.

The emergence of the nuclear family as an independent unit and the social norm has not, however, been without negative consequences. The social independence of the nuclear family has resulted in the loss of economic and social security once provided by members of the extended family. The loss of family social supports has necessitated the introduction of formal counselling procedures in times of marital conflict. Financial, social, emotional, and psychological problems in the family now have to be handled by immediate family members, who lack the extended family safety valve to lean on during periods of crisis.

THEORETICAL PERSPECTIVES

According to the functionalist perspective, the fact that the functions of the modern family have changed immeasurably can be largely ascribed to the effects of industrialization and urbanization. Family economic, religious, protective, and educational roles, for example, have been minimized with the growth of other social institutions. The former self-sufficiency of the family unit has given way to what is primarily a consumption-oriented role. Formal social institutions such as schools, day care centres, hospitals, and senior citizens' homes cater to the needs of the young and the old more fully than do family members. And people generally depend on their own achievements to achieve status, rather than on family networks. Regardless of the form that the post-industrial family takes, however, its procreative, nurturing, and early socialization functions are irreplaceable.

Yet as we have already noted, the modern family has been showing increasing signs of disorganization. Rising divorce and legal separation statistics, violence within the family, and the decline in traditional marriage (and increase in other types of living arrangements) are all indices of an institution in a state of flux. From the *functionalist* point of view, the collapse of the extended family system, and its replacement with the nuclear family, has put an untenable degree of stress on the family unit. Until recently, the economic well-being of the nuclear family depended largely on the male breadwinner whose illness, death, desertion, or unemployment often spelt financial disaster for the family. Today, changing sexual and economic roles have also affected the traditional equilibrium of the family. The advent of the working wife and increasing egalitarianism in the family unit has meant that many of the traditional roles of the male head—e.g., breadwinner and decision maker—have been threatened, resulting in often irreconcilable family conflict. Finally, widespread changing social values (e.g., greater tolerance toward divorce and separation) have also contributed to family disorganization in Canada today. From the functionalist perspective, then, the modern family has become a social problem because it is no longer able to perform its social functions.

By contrast, *conflict theorists* see family disorganization as the result of the traditional dominance of one group over the other. They dismiss the functionality of sex-role discrimination as simply a convenient justification for traditional male authoritarianism. Changing women's roles, however, are placing inevitable strains on established family patterns, as women traditionally socialized into accepting an inferior role and status within the family unit, have come to expect their increased education and work skills to translate into a more important and equal role (Dotson 1974). In addition, conflict theorists believe that, since the integration of the family depends on coerciveness to obtain compliance among its members, a degree of conflict is inevitable. In an environment where social and cultural change is endemic, it is not necessarily a bad thing that a new family pattern, one that allows for greater power sharing among family members, may be developing. Ferguson (1988) suggests that we might get a clearer perspective of the problem of the modern family if we view it as an *adaptive* institution, characterized by a constantly shifting relationship between families and economic, political, and social forces—e.g., jobs, social service agencies, and the law.

In the *reciprocal exchange model*, the family is perceived as a unit ideally in equilibrium, based on a sexual division of labour. According to Scanzoni (1976:200), balanced marital decision making can be jeopardized by the current social emphasis on occupational achievement and success. In the struggle for material success, the family unit loses its immediacy as a haven for emotional gratification, with a consequent imbalance in the reciprocity of roles and responsibilities. While, in the traditional arrangement, the husband's role of breadwinner was balanced by the wife's role as homemaker, the increasing entry of wives into the labour force today, either to supplement the household income or to fulfil personal and career goals, has affected the balance of the unit, creating strains and conflicts, which sometimes lead to separation or divorce. While some married couples are able to adjust to a new division of labour, others find a new equilibrium impossible to attain.

We conclude this section with a brief examination of the *theory of interpersonal relations*, which delineates three components through which marriage can be analyzed: (1) internal sources of gratification, including sexual fulfilment, companionship, and self-esteem; (2) constraining factors impinging on the unit, including children, economic dependence, and family networks; and (3) external sources of gratification, including independent income, friends, and sexual relationships outside the unit. According to McKie et al. (1983:77), the probability of marital dissolution can be gauged on the basis of how these factors interact (e.g., low marital attraction, weak constraints, and excessive outside attractions increase the likelihood of marital breakup). We should note, however, that while certain conditions within the family unit favour dissolution, a couple may for personal and practical reasons prefer to remain in a conflict relationship rather than fracture it.

MARRIAGE AND DIVORCE

As we have suggested, the increase in family disorganization resulting from social change has been interpreted as evidence that the institution is endangered. Since most Canadian families begin with marriage, the

Table 8.1
Number of Marriages and Divorces and Marriage and Divorce rates per 100,000
Population for Canada, 1921–1984

Year	Marriages		Divorces	
	Number	Rate	Number	Rate
1921	71,254	790	558	6.4
1931	68,239	640	700	6.8
1941	124,644	1060	2,462	21.4
1946	137,398	1090	7,757	63.1
1951	128,408	920	5,270	37.6
1956	132,713	830	6,002	37.3
1961	128,475	700	6,563	36.0
1968	167,538	790	11,343	54.7
1969	179,413	920	26,079	123.8
1971	191,324	890	29,672	137.6
1976	193,343	840	54,207	235.8
1980	191,069	800	62,019	259.1
1981	190,082	780	67,671	278.0
1982	188,360	760	70,436	285.9
1983	184,675	740	68,567	275.5
1984	185,592	740	65,172	259.4

Source: Statistics Canada, Yearbooks 1941 to 1975 and Catalogue No. 84-205. Vital
Statistics, Vol. II. Marriages and Divorces, 1978. Catalogue No. 84-205; 1980,
1981, Table 10, 16-17; 1982, 1983, 1984, Catalogue No. 84-205. Vital Statistics,
Vol. II. Marriages and Divorces, 1984. Reprinted by permission.

issues facing the institution of marriage are central to an understanding of
the problems confronting the family.

As shown in Table 8.1, marriages peaked in 1969, with a rate of 9.2 per
1,000, and declined to 7.4 per 1,000 by 1984. While the marriage rate has
declined since the 1968 changes in divorce legislation, there has been a
marked increase in remarriages, with the percentage of persons who
remarried doubling between 1968 and 1981.

Although Lupri (1986:268) notes that three out of five Canadians over
15 are married (suggesting that the concept of legal marriage has not lost
its relevance to the vast majority of Canadians of marriageable age), the
evidence suggests that the cultural trait of romantic love on which many
marriages are based is a poor precursor for a lasting bond. (The idea of
marriage based on romantic love is, in fact, unknown in many cultures
and societies, including India, China, and Africa, where marriage is seen
instead in terms of sealing a bond between families and providing for
economic, social, and kinship alliances.) The evidence suggests that not
only is the institution of legal marriage unable to fulfil the aspirations and

needs of the modern family, but that its disadvantages are increasingly perceived as outweighing its advantages.

Cadwallader (1966) calls contemporary marriage "a wretched institution which stifles voluntary affection and transforms a beautiful love affair into a constrictive, corrosive, and destructive relationship." The problem, he believes, derives from the unreal expectations people have about marriage. The difficulty of meeting such marital goals as honesty, trust, fulfilment, and commitment discourages many unmarried individuals from embracing the institution, while provoking married couples into seeking alternatives. The traditional family, regardless of marital conflict, lack of intimacy and communication, and alienation, was expected to stay together, particularly if children were involved. In this family, where interaction was at best only instrumental, the unhappily married couple remained painfully knitted together, in part to avoid publicly admitting that their marriage had failed. The 1970s, however, saw in Canada a dramatic shift away from the unhappy marriage to a formal dissolution of the unit. While the undesirability of a rising divorce rate is debatable, in terms of both public perception and the academic and popular press, divorce represents a serious form of family disorganization.

According to McKie et al. (1983:59), the divorce rate took a momentous jump between 1969 and 1982. As shown in Table 8.1, in 1969, immediately after the passage of the New Divorce Act, it stood at 123.8 (per 100,000 population). Subsequently, the rate soared to 235.8 in 1976, and to 285.9 in 1982, a radical departure from 1921, when the divorce rate was 6.4 (per 100,000 population). The single-year probability of divorce is highest at age 27 for females and age 30 for males, and declines steadily thereafter, the divorce rate dropping to below 5 percent for people over 55. There is no reason to expect that the increased trend in divorce that began in the 1970s will be reversed in the 1990s. What may occur, however, is a gradual levelling off of the divorce rate, with a slight reduction in the percentage increase in each subsequent year.

What general conclusions can be drawn from these trends in Canadian society? That the nuclear family is disintegrating, according to one viewpoint. From another perspective, however, the high rate of remarriage in society can be taken as evidence that the nuclear family is still a popular goal, despite the high rate of first-time failures. But in the final analysis, we may have no alternative but to accept divorce as an inevitable part of modern society. Given a marriage lacking in affective and emotional bonding, does society have the right to coerce people to remain in such a union? One could argue that allowing both partners the opportunity to obtain fulfilment in other relationships would be the most functional solution to the problem of the unfulfilling marriage.

ALTERNATIVE FAMILY FORMS

The view that only a return to traditional norms and values can stabilize the institutions of marriage and family is not a realistic one, given the indelible mark that social and cultural change has left on traditional marriage patterns. Alternatives to legal marriage and the nuclear family need not be seen as replacements for the norm, but rather as options for those who find legal marriage unsatisfactory to their needs. According to Ramey (1976), alternative family forms represent for the majority of their participants a profound and sincere effort at meeting human needs in a more fulfilling way. While some of the alternatives outlined below may develop into little more than passing experiments, the success of others may mean that in future a greater choice of nontraditional family forms will be available to Canadians.

Cohabitation

The common-law relationship, or cohabitation, is becoming the most popular alternative to legal marriage, with the number of unmarried people sharing a household doubling between 1970 and 1979 from 65,000 to 125,000 (Statistics Canada 1982). While partners choose to live together for many reasons, fear of a legal marriage failing appears to be the major factor. According to Hobart (1975), most couples who cohabit share a genuine feeling of love and respect for their partners, and sexual fidelity is the norm. Whitehurst (1975) suggests that most people who cohabit expect to get married eventually, and view their living together as a trial period, preparing them better to cope with the problems of a legal union. Finally, it should be noted that in Canada the courts recognize property agreements in cohabitation relationships, providing a level of *de jure* social support for unions of this type.

Single Parenthood

While most people associate marriage with children, there is growing trend in society toward single parenthood, with 10 percent of families containing one parent (Nett 1983). *Single parenthood* can occur through divorce or death of a spouse, adoption of a child by a single person, or—an increasing trend—the decision of an unmarried pregnant woman to keep her child after birth. In 1973, 9 percent of births were to single mothers, 80 percent of whom, Schlesinger (1979:26) estimates, opted to keep the child. Today, much of the stigma formerly attached to single motherhood has been eroded. Further, high divorce rates have brought about a reevaluation of the societal bias toward two-parent families. Finally, while role conflict in the form of financial and family problems may confront the unmarried or divorced mother, increased government support for day care and other social services has made this alternative more feasible.

Communal and Group Marriage

Whitehurst (1975) predicts that *group marriages* (two or more couples living together as one marriage unit) will not become a popular option in Canada given the negative reaction to them in the mainstream population. Since we are not socialized to accept collective forms of intimate behaviour, these experimental alternatives will probably remain of marginal importance (although Whitehurst [1975] suggests that urban communes may become increasingly popular as a means of solving social isolation and economic problems). While sexual practices in the communes often range from "pairing off" to looser sexual relationships, unless the members of the commune are open-minded and willing to share in the responsibilities of organization of the unit, the experience will almost certainly lead to failure. Rural communes, popularized in the counterculture literature, are also prone to failure. People seeking the tranquillity and casual pace popularly associated with rural communal life are often ill-equipped when it comes to coping with a harsh physical environment. As Whitehurst (1975) notes, while communes theoretically represent a solution to the alienating and depressing aspects of the automated post-industrial society, their more utopian features are seldom translated into reality.

Open Marriage

Open marriage involves an explicit adoption by the spouses of a flexible marital pattern, often including the right of the partners to seek out extramarital sexual relationships (Knapp 1976). Participants in this form of marriage seem committed to the union and are willing to selectively retain some of the traditional role expectations, while avoiding those they consider either restrictive or irrelevant. Of course, not all marriages are able to adjust to a relationship that frequently involves the alteration of traditional gender-role stereotypes (Whitehurst 1975). Nonetheless, should social attitudes become positive enough to allow for greater equality of participation in all spheres of marriage, this alternative family form could gain popularity, for open marriage directly challenges the sexual double standard that prevails in many marriages.

VIOLENCE IN THE FAMILY

The social norm is for relationships within the family unit to be based on love, affection, and mutual respect; for parents to cherish and protect their children; and for spouses to solve their problems through verbal communication. Unfortunately, this ideal picture does not reflect those families which, in reality, are virtual battlegrounds. Two major forms of violence—against children and spouses—have received little public attention and scrutiny until very recently. This has been due, in part, to the traditional belief that what goes on in the family is not of public concern. Yet the myth of the happy, cohesive family, in covering up the seriousness of violence within it, can only damage the family, and, by extension, society as a whole. Let us now examine child and spouse abuse in terms of causes, consequences, and solutions.

Child Abuse

Child abuse, or the battered child syndrome, has been a longstanding latent social problem. In recent years, however, public concern regarding the effects of child abuse has resulted in societal intervention in what was previously considered a private domain. While child abuse can take various forms, its three main categories are physical, emotional, and sexual (Schlesinger 1979:92). Child neglect is usually considered child abuse, given the fact that the emotional and psychological scars created by the absence of love and affection can oftentimes be as damaging as physical abuse, which will be the focus of this section.

Statistics concerning child abuse cases in Canada are highly problematic. Schlesinger (1979:93), while noting that for Ontario alone the number of cases rose from 407 in 1970 to 1,045 in 1977, believes that the actual numbers are significantly higher, since the statistics only reflect verified physical abuse reported by Children's Aid Societies. Nett (1983) estimates that at least 60,000 children are physically abused in Canada, and furthermore suggests that more children die from injuries inflicted by parents and guardians than from all childhood illnesses combined.

The *battered child syndrome* takes its name from the fact that the child's injuries are the result of twisting, throwing, knocking about, or some other form of battering by the abusive person. These injuries often include bites, bruises, and combinations of arm, leg, rib or skull fractures. According to Van Stolk (1972:16), the helping professions have been reluctant to come to terms with the realities surrounding the battered child, often confusing neglect with battering, although the symptoms can be easily differentiated. Neglect involves failure to nourish, provide adequate living conditions, or to seek medical attention for one's children, while child battering involves the inflicting of physical injuries on a child by his or her caretaker.

Reported cases of child battering in Canada graphically illustrate the depth of the tragedy. Children have been punched, kicked, bitten, scratched, and hurled across the room. They have been beaten with whips, electric cords and belts, garden tools and furniture. They have been stabbed, burned, locked for days in closets, chained to bedposts, placed in scalding baths, and shut out of the house in their night clothes to brave subzero temperatures. The actual attacks on a child are usually carried out by one parent, with the other aware of the abuse but condoning it. Schlesinger (1979:96) notes that child abuse in Canada cuts across racial, social, and economic lines, occurring in both rich and poor families, one- and multiple-child families, one- and two-parent families, and among both the employed and unemployed. The tragedy of the battered child syndrome is that emotional and psychological scars return to haunt the battered child, who usually becomes a battering parent.

Why do parents abuse their children? According to Schlesinger (1979:97), abusing parents lack the confidence and trust to develop satisfying relationships with others largely because they did not receive adequate parenting as infants. As a result of negative early socialization experiences, they tend to lead alienated, asocial, and isolated lives, dominated by feelings of rejection, inadequacy, and loneliness. While most abusing parents claim to love their children, research suggests that they are primarily concerned with their own feelings and pleasures, reacting with cruelty whenever they feel threatened or frustrated by children's demands. It is this deep-seated feeling of hate and anger, stemming from their negative childhood experiences, that provokes a parent into become a child abuser. Van Stolk (1972:24) suggests that when abusing parents internalize the belief that physical punishment is an acceptable means of discipline (the child must be taught to "behave" and "obey," regardless of the consequences), it is quite easy for them to rationalize violence against their children.

Finally, it is the inability of the battering parent to perceive their offspring as children that separates them from nonabusive parents. They expect their children to be like adults in distinguishing right from wrong, and to be, in times of stress, "good" and "loving" and "obedient." When the child is not forthcoming with the "good" behaviour, an abusive situation often develops. It is this psychological inability, then, to identify with the child as a human being, with limited capabilities, control, and comprehension, that is at the root of the problem.

Taking into account the aforementioned factors, how best might we prevent child abuse from ever taking place? The punishment of parents through criminal prosecution, according to Schlesinger (1979:99) does not eliminate the cause of the problem. Nor, given the mental, physical, and emotional inadequacies of abusive parents, does punishment in itself alter their behaviour. What they need is guidance and counselling geared toward training them to accept their parental responsibilities, as well as social services (e.g., day care) that can provide assistance when the tensions and stresses of everyday living set off the mechanism of physical violence. Furthermore, rehabilitative programs must include not only family-oriented programs aimed at psychological and psychiatric rebuilding—they must also be co-ordinated with protective and legal services. The present societal concern for the plight of the battered child is commendable, but more than a lip-service recognition of the problem is necessary. Parent and public education programs emphasizing parental responsibilities must be entrenched, while professional schools that train the helping professions should offer mandatory courses on the problems of child abuse.

Wife Abuse

While our knowledge of physical violence between spouses is still limited, increasingly victims of family violence are bringing into the open this formerly private crime. Because, as Lewis (1982) notes, 72 percent of spousal violence is husband-perpetrated, our discussion will centre on the issue of wife abuse in Canada. Although statistics as to the magnitude of the problem are unreliable, MacLeod (1980) suggests that 10 percent of wives are physically abused. Gelles (1974:49) estimates that 20 percent of all wives in the United States are abused or battered to some degree, with 8 percent reporting incidents of violence ranging in frequency from once a month to every day. In one sample of low-income women, 34 percent reported some violence in their relationships (Whitehurst 1978). In addition, Lupri (1986:277) estimates that 20 percent of all homicides in Canada are spouse-related, in almost every case wives murdered by husbands. Wife abuse can occur among all ages, socio-economic, racial, and educational backgrounds.

Why do men abuse their wives? Schlesinger (1979:103) suggests that profiles of battering husbands show that they often use violence to demonstrate "power" and masculine aggressiveness, a pattern they may have acquired in childhood and through their parental lifestyle. Job dissatisfaction is another factor that can contribute to wife abuse, as can any frustration or failure in the outside world when projected onto wives. As well, alcohol or drug abuse may remove the inhibitions men have about battering their wives. Whitehurst (1978) notes that, in his sample, alcohol abuse played a prominent role in the original onset of the abuse, which increasingly became a regular occurrence. Finally, male power exercised through violence in the family is reinforced by our male-dominated legal, economic, and political institutions (Ferguson 1988).

Why so many wives tolerate battering, often for years on end, is a question that has fascinated specialists in the field. The research suggests that the vast majority of these women, far from exhibiting masochistic tendencies, are emotionally and/or financially dependent on their husbands, unaware of their options, and cowed by threats of further violence, against either themselves or their children, from their abusive spouses. Whitehurst (1978) links a pattern of socialization that reinforces male dominance and female subordination to questions of why husbands continue to hit and why wives stay. In terms of this pattern, husbands can rationalize their behaviour by blaming the victim. That wives remain in an abusive situation is related to their submissive roles in society. Should the husband proclaim his love in calmer moments, the wife forgives and hopes for his long-term reformation. Lack of family members' support, coupled with an often irrational sense of guilt and shame at having failed, may also keep a woman in an abusive relationship.

According to Ferguson (1988), if the situation of battered wives in Canada is to improve, women must lose their sense of powerlessness and develop the self-will to leave their abusive husbands. In addition, the helping professions and the state must provide active intervention and support, e.g., through the family crisis centre whose services should include advisory specialists in both law and family guidance. In the short run, more transition homes with qualified staff are needed, in addition to training programs for the helping professions that deal with battered women. In the long run, however, real solutions to the problem of wife abuse will occur only with radical changes to the current social relationship between men and women in our society.

CHANGING GENDER ROLES

In course of their development, all societies give rise to expectations, roles, responsibilities, and even personality traits based on gender. In Canada, as in other societies, stereotyped gender roles have developed over the years and have led to both blatant and subtle forms of gender discrimination in many spheres of life. The literature on gender roles tends to suggest that socio-cultural factors, not physiological differences, are the main determinants of gender traits. MacKie (1979) notes that without the customs and sex-role stereotypings demanded by the laws of society, in most instances behaviour would be unrelated to gender, and Canada, for example, would not have developed as a gender-polarized society. The rationalization for gender roles in traditional societies, where men were allocated the more physically demanding role of hunter and women the tasks associated with nurturing and family care, does not apply to technologically advanced societies such as Canada, where sexual division of labour is largely unnecessary, and where women no longer spend most of their adult lives in pregnancy and childrearing.

However, in terms of gender-role stereotypes, children are still being socialized into believing that males must be dominant and aggressive and that male jobs should be more prestigious, better paid, and more highly skilled. (According to Ishwaran [1986], children from working-class backgrounds tend to be more traditional in terms of sex-role stereotyping.) The mass media still reflect the dominant/submissive gender-role allocations. Images of the happy housewife persist. Chafetz (1974:46) notes that a content analysis of newspapers and magazines directed at women showed an emphasis on parties, beauty hints, recipes, and child care matters, to the virtual exclusion of legal, political, and economic matters. Popular songs, television, and the movies can also be indicted for portraying males as aggressive, decisive, independent, and emotionally strong (with women possessing the opposite traits), as can the advertising industry for exploiting and reinforcing myths about a woman's place and role in today's society. According to Komisar (1971), advertising is an insidious propaganda machine for a male supremacist society, which promotes an image of the ideal woman as sex mate, mother, or menial worker. While this may, in fact, be a true reflection of the current status of the majority of women in society, the image makes it extremely difficult for women to transcend sexist stereotypes in concrete terms. (This goal is further complicated by the emergence of such groups as REAL Women.)

Most damaging to women's aspirations has been institutionally sanctioned discrimination in employment. An examination of occupational status and income shows quite clearly that menial and low-paying jobs traditionally have been ascribed to women, and that laws designed to penalize employers who discriminate in their hiring practices are generally ineffective (Saunders 1988). The systematic attempt to exclude women from jobs requiring leadership and advanced levels of education is clearly dysfunctional, since, as Robertson (1980:326) notes, to be fully efficient an industrialized economy must allow social mobility on the grounds of merit, rather than gender. Increased educational opportunities for women since World War II, in addition to decreases in family size, greater female participation rates in the labour force, and the Women's Liberation Movement of the 1960s have all been catalysts for changing gender roles in the society. Nevertheless, even though sexist laws have been removed and sex discrimination is now prosecutable under the Canadian Human Rights Commission, egalitarianism between the sexes is still a distant prospect.

In terms of conflict theory, Carisse (1976:391–92) believes that since the female role is still defined as complementary to the male role, any attempt at change will involve conflict. To escape from their affective role, women must devise adaptive strategies that can minimize the conflict which nevertheless is essential, as conflict theorists see it, to the desegregation of gender roles. From the functionalist perspective, the social structure has led to the problem of sex inequality, and therefore changes to the offending institutions must be encouraged.

FUTURE PROSPECTS

As we have seen, the nuclear family has undergone radical changes in the past two decades. As Schlesinger (1979:170) notes, the nature of the family life cycle has been altered profoundly. A combination of demographic and social trends has raised the proportion of the married population, together with marriage and childbearing ages, and has universalized family planning techniques. In addition, changing gender roles have brought a greater degree of egalitarianism to the family unit.

While the future family in Canada will probably never regain many of the functions it formerly held, there is no doubt that its role of providing emotional security in an increasingly impersonal and anonymous world will become paramount. And despite the loss of its utilitarian functions, it would appear that the nuclear family will remain the norm for the foreseeable future, with alternative lifestyles experimented with, or adopted, by a minority. We can anticipate, too, a rise in the number of common-law relationships and single-parent households, reflecting increasing public acceptance. To conclude, the evolution of the family unit from a homogeneous to a pluralistic form should not be interpreted as evidence of the institution's imminent death. As Nass (1978:516) observes, the view that the growing cultural emphasis on self-actualization, individual autonomy, and mobility is weakening family bonds is unnecessarily pessimistic. The future family may, in fact, incorporate, enrich, and strengthen traditional family values of loyalty, duty, warmth, understanding, and supportiveness.

SUMMARY

1. In pre-industrial Canada, the extended family system was the norm. With the growth of industrialization and urbanization, the extended family gave way to the nuclear family, which has had both positive and negative impacts.
2. According to the functionalist perspective, the family has become a social problem because it has failed to adapt to social change. The family's economic, religious, and educative roles have largely been taken over by social institutions.
3. Conflict theorists see family disorganization as the result of recent challenges to the traditional patriarchal family unit. Changing women's roles have introduced into the institution conflict which may lead to a greater power sharing among members.
4. According to the reciprocal exchange model, the equilibrium of the family unit is based on a sexual division of labour. This balance may

be jeopardized by changing gender roles, in particular greater female labour force participation.

5. The theory of interpersonal relations examines marriage in terms of internal and external sources of gratification, and constraining factors. The relative health of a marriage can be gauged on the basis of how these factors interact.

6. The divorce rate has risen dramatically in the last two decades, partly because of the liberalization of divorce laws in 1968, and partly because of the unrealistic expectations people have about marriage. The recent growth in the remarriage rate suggests, however, that marriage and the nuclear family are still popular goals in society.

7. The common-law relationship, or cohabitation, is the most popular alternative to legal marriage. Most people who cohabit use their living together as a trial period before committing to marriage. In Canada, the courts recognize property agreements in cohabitation relationships.

8. Single parenthood is a growing trend in Canadian society. Much of the stigma attached to it has been removed, and the increased availability of government and social support has made it a more economically feasible alternative.

9. Communal or group marriage will probably remain of marginal importance in Canadian society given negative public attitudes toward collective forms of intimate behaviour. The open marriage has a greater chance of achieving popularity as an alternative family form.

10. Until recently, child abuse was an invisible problem in Canadian society. While statistics concerning child abuse are problematic, it is estimated that at least 60,000 children are physically abused in Canada.

11. Child abuse—like wife abuse—cuts across racial, social, and economic lines. Battered children often grow up to become abusing parents. Rehabilitation of the abusive parent is a more desirable approach to the problem than criminal prosecution.

12. Research suggests that 72 percent of spousal violence is husband-perpetrated, and that 10 percent of wives are physically abused. Growing numbers of women are leaving their abusive spouses.

13. Wife abuse can be linked to traditional patterns of male dominance and female subordination. Men often use violence to demonstrate masculine "power." Women are often compelled by their submissive roles to stay in an abusive situation. Frustration with the outside world and alcohol/drug abuse may prompt husbands to batter, while financial and emotional dependence on their husbands, coupled with threats of future violence, may prevent battered wives from taking positive action.

14. Social services must be expanded to deal with the immediate problems associated with wife abuse. Long-term solutions, however, will necessitate major changes to the dynamics of the male/female social relationship.

15. Gender discrimination in Canada is related to stereotyped gender roles that have developed in the course of its history. The literature suggests that socio-cultural factors, and not physiological differences, are the main determinants of gender traits.

16. Despite positive changes, such as making discrimination by employers on the basis of gender a prosecutable offence, egalitarianism between the sexes in Canada remains a distant prospect.

PART 3

REGIONAL AND INTERGROUP CONFLICT

9

Regionalism

INTRODUCTION

In the last decade, the question of Canadian unity has occupied many social scientists. As Bell (1987:629) notes, "regionalism shows two aspects: the smile of harmony and the tragic frown of hostility." For Woodcock (1981:21), the special character of Canada is expressed through its "symbiotic union of regions," while for Schwutz (1974:5), regionalism in Canada implies a sense of regional identity, attachment to one's own region, as well as an awareness of the region's distinctive interests. According to Bell (1987:629), however, this awareness translates into a belief by regions that they are being victimized by other regions, or by the centre. Interprovincial conflict is the result. Albertans, for example, regarded high oil prices, which became an issue in the federal elections of 1979 and 1980, as essential to the improvement of their socio-economic status, while to Ontarians they signified greed and selfishness on the part of Westerners. To a large extent, the nature of our federal system encourages provincial governments to lobby on behalf of their own regional interests, which necessarily pits them against the central government. Bell (1987:632–34) suggests that because our federal political institutions have often failed to provide equal representation for all the regions, the political party system has developed around regional supports, with the result that it is possible now for a governing party to exhibit no political representation from certain regions.

THEORETICAL PERSPECTIVES

In his analysis of regional disparities in Canada, Matthews (1983:Chapter 2) examines a series of sociological formulations purporting to explain, firstly, their causes and, secondly, possible solutions to them. First, Matthews cites Odum and Moore (1938), who used a functionalist perspective to explore regional inequalities in American society. They concluded that regionalism per se was not a negative phenomenon, and that the strength of the centre depended on the interdependence of each regional sub-unit. For Odum and Moore, the regional division of labour was the guarantee of societal strength and functional integration.

Perroux (1970:94), using the *territorial-geographic approach* to analyze regional inequalities, argues that a consistent rate of economic growth cannot be expected to "appear everywhere at the same time; it becomes manifest at points or poles of growth, with variable intensity; it spreads through different channels, with variable terminal effects upon the whole of the economy." However, Perroux suggests that this differential economic growth pattern can be altered through government action, specifically, to create new growth poles in regions where they did not previously exist. This social activist approach to economic growth anticipates the transformation of economically backward regions, through the growth of large urban centres with core industries and an altered social, cultural, and economic structure.

According to Matthews (1983:43-44), however, this approach may be more idealistic than practical. First, it does not take into consideration the power of multinational and monopolistic corporations to affect market conditions in their own interests, and to prevent the success of independent ventures in the "hinterland." Second, most of the economically deprived regions of Canada are plagued with high unemployment, and require not core industries employing a small pool of highly skilled workers, but labour intensive industries that can provide employment for the surplus labour force. And third, while one can applaud the "growth pole theory" for its economic goals, it gives little consideration to social and cultural institutions which, as Matthews (ibid) states, do not necessarily benefit from improvements in economic status.

The seriousness of regional disparities in Canada is demonstrated in Table 9.1. Here, 1983 statistics on regional employment most dramatically show the unemployment rate for Newfoundland to be almost twice as high as Ontario's unemployment rate. A report by the Economic Council of Canada [ECC] (1977:32-59) found major differences among the regions in rates of population growth, migration, urbanization, family size, fertility rates, and youth and dependency rates. Taken in conjunction with per capita income, unemployment, and labour participation rates, these variables point to a major problem of regional inequities. In addition, the ECC study indicates that quality of housing, health, and education varies widely across the country, notwithstanding federal efforts to introduce national standards in these institutional services.

There are five basic approaches to the problem of regional disparities: the staples approach; the development approach; the neoclassical approach; the Keynesian approach; and the Marxist approach. The *staples approach*, according to the Economic Council of Canada, explains regional economic imbalances in terms of the presence or absence of natural resources. However, as Matthews (1983:45) notes, the wealth of Southern Ontario is not attributable to any strong resource base, while the Atlantic provinces, which have an abundance of resources, have been poor for most of this century. The *development approach*, which is more applicable to the problems of Third World countries than it is to Canada, attributes regional disparities to differences in social, economic, political, and cultural conditions in the various regions. The underlying presump-

Table 9.1
Labour Force Participation Rates and Unemployment Rates, Canada and Provinces,
1979–1983

| | Labour Force | | | | | | | | | |
| | Participation Rate | | | | | Unemployment Rate | | | | |
	1979	1980	1981	1982	1983	1979	1980	1981	1982	1983
Newfoundland	52.3	52.7	52.6	52.1	52.1	15.1	13.3	13.9	16.8	18.8
Prince Edward Island	59.0	59.2	58.7	57.8	60.2	11.2	10.6	11.2	12.9	12.2
Nova Scotia	56.6	57.4	57.3	57.0	57.4	10.1	9.7	10.2	13.2	13.2
New Brunswick	55.0	55.6	56.2	55.0	55.5	11.1	11.0	11.5	14.0	14.8
Quebec	60.2	61.2	61.5	60.0	60.9	9.6	9.8	10.3	13.8	13.9
Ontario	66.5	66.7	67.6	67.3	67.1	6.5	6.8	6.6	9.8	10.4
Manitoba	63.6	64.5	64.8	64.9	65.6	5.3	5.5	5.9	8.5	9.4
Saskatchewan	62.7	63.0	63.5	63.9	65.2	4.2	4.4	4.7	6.2	7.4
Alberta	69.7	70.9	72.3	71.4	71.6	3.9	3.7	3.8	7.7	10.8
British Columbia	63.2	64.1	65.1	64.3	64.1	7.6	6.8	6.7	12.1	13.8
Canada	63.4	64.1	64.8	64.1	64.4	7.4	7.5	7.5	11.0	11.9

Source: D. Forcese and S. Richer, eds., *Social Issues*, 2nd ed. (Scarborough: Prentice-Hall, 1988), p.74. Reprinted by permission.

tion here is that certain regions in Canada lack what McClelland (1971) calls "achievement motivation." Whether at the national or regional level, underdevelopment is related to the inability to create "need achievement" and an entrepreneurial ethic. The difficulty with this approach vis-à-vis regional disparities in Canada lies in the impossibility of definitively showing that entrepreneurship, on a qualitative level, is any greater in Ontario than it is in Nova Scotia. Ontario's economic success may be more related to its geographical proximity to Canadian and U.S. markets, than to any special personality traits in its people.

The *neoclassical approach* places its emphasis on the free market supply-and-demand principles of nongovernment interference in the economy. Accordingly, it opposes government subsidies and social welfare payments to deprived regions. Against this approach, Matthews (1983:66–67) argues that it is a fallacy to suggest that mass migration from poor to wealthy provinces on a theoretical supply-and-demand basis will solve the problem of regional disparities. This is because high unemployment in, for instance, Atlantic Canada is usually related to an economic slowdown in other regions—hence the limited opportunities for work in the more prosperous regions. In addition, the suspension of transfer payments by the federal government would spell disaster for Canada's economically deprived regions. The *Keynesian approach*, on the other hand, argues that it is the role of government to provide economic incentives to encourage business to locate in have-not regions. The paradox of this approach is that, while governments have accepted it as conventional wisdom since the Second World War, the economic disparities among regions remain as acute as ever.

More recently, regional differences in Canada have been analyzed on the basis of a modified *Marxist* interpretation of causation, which encompasses social as well as economic factors. Clement (1980) suggests that ruling elites in prosperous regions of Canada have been co-opted by multinational corporations. In order to maintain their positions of power, these elites assist in the economic exploitation of the underdeveloped regions. Further, Cuneo (1978) suggests that Canada's social class structure creates regional disparities in wealth. Depending on the type of production in which they are involved, wealthier regions have a disproportionate representation in skilled and industrial workers, while poorer regions are overrepresented in terms of primary and unskilled workers.

THE CASE OF QUEBEC

If the problems associated with regionalism are to be muted, then the historical view of Canada as "two nations—English and French—warring within one bosom" must be altered. As Hiller (1986:152–53) notes, language and ethnicity have been at the heart of the French–English conflict. According to Hiller, the British conquest had three major impacts on Quebec society: (1) it created resentments and antagonisms on the part of Quebec toward the British, which have never been obliterated; (2) it resulted in English control over Quebec's economic and political institutions; and (3) it impelled French Canadians to turn to the Church in order to insulate themselves from the institutions of the British, and at the same time preserve and maintain their own cultural and social institutions.

While the French-Canadian community succeeded in preserving its cohesiveness—mainly as a rural, agricultural entity—the British were content to allow cultural self-determination in exchange for political and economic control. By the 1940s, however, increasing urbanization, secularization, and industrialization brought the French-Canadian population into direct conflict with the British minority. As Gagnon (1988) observes, the election of the Lesage government in 1960 marked the true beginning of the Quiet Revolution. State economic intervention and the secularization of social services and education were viewed as instruments for the creation of a modern social movement that would realize the aspirations of all French Canadians. The emergence of an urban proleteriat and a new middle class of public sector employees set the stage for a determined advance on Anglophone dominance and control of Quebec society. However, because Anglophones controlled the ownership of capital and the decision-making process, the rising Francophone middle class was increasingly frustrated in its attempts at changing the dynamics of English–French relations, which saw the bulk of the Francophone community in subordinate socio-economic positions.

It was not until the 1970s that language came to be seen as a potential instrument of social and economic change in Quebec. French-Canadian nationalists saw language as pivotal to the preservation of their identity, and were convinced that the domination of English in the workplace was a major variable in the low status of Quebeckers. Increasingly, the Liberal government of Robert Bourassa was pressured to introduce laws that would change the working language of Anglophone businesses in Quebec and force immigrant children to be educated in French. Nationalist sentiment culminated in the 1976 election of the pro-separatist Parti Québécois under the leadership of René Lévesque.

The Parti Québécois proceeded to introduce a series of landmark nationalistic legislation, the most controversial being Bill 101, passed in 1977, which ensured that French would not only be the official language of Quebec, but that it would, with minor exceptions, be the language of schools and the workplace. In addition, the government proceeded toward its goal of separatism by introducing a White Paper on sovereignty-association, which advocated political independence and, at the same time, economic co-existence with the rest of Canada. A referendum on the issue was promised and the debate between the Quebec and federal governments ensued. Lévesque's basic position was that every people had the right to territorial integrity, to live and work in its own language, and to choose its own destiny. The federalist forces, led by Prime Minister Trudeau, argued that Quebec's special status was and would continue to be protected in a federalist state, and that Quebec had more to lose economically and politically by opting for independence. In a public referendum held on May 20, 1980, the sovereignty-association position of the Parti Québécois was rejected by a narrow margin. Ironically, it would appear that the success of the PQ in improving the self-esteem and socio-economic status of the Francophone majority had inadvertently lessened the appetite of Quebeckers for independence.

Despite the rejection of sovereignty-association, the Parti Québécois was re-elected to power in 1981. Increasingly, the Quebec government had become the centralizing force behind regional policies that challenged the federal government. This was most clearly seen in the refusal by the Lévesque government to sign the new federal Constitution in 1982, on the ground that the new document did not guarantee Quebec's special status within Confederation.

Let us consider now the forces that contributed to the phenomenal rise in Quebec nationalism in the 1970s. Kallen (1982:192) suggests that the separatist movement in Quebec served to revitalize those seeking politico-economic sovereignty and cultural transformation. In this sense, it was a revolutionary response to longstanding injustice and inequality.

Had the evolution of Quebec proceeded on the basis of equality there would have been no need for the radical shift in the political, economic, and cultural components of nationalism espoused by many Francophones in Quebec. As Lee (1979) observes, traditional nationalism, which saw its role as preserving French-Canadian culture, had given way to modern nationalism. The impact of industrialization, modernization, and urbanization had altered the utility of the status quo, and convinced many Francophones of the need to control their political and economic institutions. Throughout the 1970s Quebec nationalism championed political independence as the only means of attaining social, political, and economic equality. It was with this platform that the Parti Québécois swept to power in 1976. Another example of the transition from traditional to modern nationalism among the Québécois was the shift from the earlier goal of bilingualism and biculturalism for French Canadians throughout Canada, to one of unilingualism and uniculturalism for the Québécois in a Quebec state. As Kallen (1982:195) notes, the French-Canadian identity, as it grows stronger, increasingly involves a disassociation from Canada and a redefinition of the "state" of Quebec.

Hiller (1986:158) ascribes the growth of nationalism in Quebec in the period following the Quiet Revolution in the 1960s, firstly, to the continuation of the historical phenomenon of resistance to colonialism, which was aggravated by increased Francophone interaction with the Anglophone community during this period of rapid industrialization and urbanization, and, secondly, to the realization by the Francophone majority that economic nationalism needed to be combined with cultural nationalism if socio-economic status mobility was to be attained. The growing Francophone middle class, in particular, seeing their aspirations stymied by Anglophone corporations, pushed for greater regulation of the economy by government agencies and Crown corporations. Finally, the rapid social change that occurred in Quebec in the last thirty years destroyed the old order, leaving in its wake a vacuum in terms of values. For some, it was the opportune time to unite on a collective basis against the structural threat (in this case, the federal government and Anglophones). Under the rallying forces of the Parti Québécois, the new order sought to unite ethnicity and regionalism under the rubric of nationalism.

At the present time, Quebec's political and social relationship with English Canada and with its own English-speaking minorities has taken on a more conciliatory tone. That the Liberal Government of Bourassa has accepted the Meech Lake Constitutional Accord of 1987, which reaffirms the special status of Quebec in Confederation, augurs well for future federal–provincial relations. However, the thorny issue of Bill 101, which restricts the use of English in schools, business, and government remains, despite attempts by the Bourassa government to placate the fears of minority communities by allowing for the limited use of English in various jurisdictions. The very uniqueness of Canada—its bilingual framework—continues to be a major divisive force in majority–minority relations, not only in Quebec, but in other provinces as well.

Is it possible that a new model of French–English relations can be instituted? According to Schermerhorn (1970:22), subordinate groups in pluralistic societies often perceive conflict as the only way in which they can first identify, and then escape from, their inferior positions. In this sense, the power conflict approach utilized by Francophones in Canada was not unreasonable. As Schermerhorn (1970:67) notes, integration should be conceived as a continuing process, and conflict of goals among interest groups as not necessarily seriously disruptive. It has been suggested that the more firmly Quebec's language and culture is enshrined, the more tolerant the province will become of minority cultures and languages. To a large degree, social, structural, and legislative changes in the last decade have removed many of the cultural barriers to Francophone aspirations. Reducing economic inequalities by, for example, placing in Francophone hands many of the senior management positions in Quebec, and a proportion of those elsewhere in Canada, has removed another major source of irritation. In terms of political equality, the federal–provincial relationship can be adjusted to meet some of the pressing demands of Quebec, while stopping short of granting it political sovereignty. For example, power sharing in the areas of communication, immigration, trade, or legal structures would recognize the special interests of Quebec without compromising the authority of the federal government. Cultural sovereignty may be the hardest problem to resolve. The difficulty lies in allowing for the distinctiveness of Francophone culture—especially in the area of language rights—while at the same time maintaining the culturally pluralistic nature of the federal state. The present approach of the Quebec government, to reduce interaction with Anglophones, and to remove the rights of ethnic minorities in the language and cultural spheres, can only generate further conflict.

We can conclude by suggesting that, while historically co-operative federalism may have worked against Quebec's interests, current federalist initiatives, which grant Quebec almost total control of its social policies and which are working toward co-operative strategies on economic and political policies, cannot realistically be condemned out of hand. For a federalist state to operate efficiently, though, not only the interests of the minority but the interests of the nation as a whole must be protected. Undoubtedly, in this intricate balancing act not all of Quebec's aspirations will be fulfilled. Despite this, and despite continuing French–English conflict over language issues and regional inequality, Quebec's relationship with the rest of Canada appears to be headed in the direction of conciliation and co-operation.

WESTERN REGIONALISM

Separated from central Canada by the Canadian Shield, the West has no natural ties with the East (Hiller 1986:119). In the early settlement period, an attempt was made to integrate western Canada with the rest of Canada through an East–West transportation system, a tariff system, and a land settlement system. Western Canada, in other words, was to be an extension of central Canada. But instead the West has developed into a unique regional entity, with a distinct economy and distinct social values.

Predominant among Westerners is the perception of the West as a hinterland whose natural resources are being exploited for the economic benefit of central Canada. In the 1970s, the Prairie provinces—particularly Alberta—saw the rise in oil prices as a golden opportunity to shift the centre of economic development westward. With the transfer of billions of dollars to the Prairie provinces through energy sales, and a rapid diversification of their economies, the economic structure of the West took on a new shape. This development coincided with a downturn in the economies of Ontario and Quebec, which resulted in a large shift in population out of these provinces. The early years of the 1980s saw a gradual alteration of the traditional relationship between central Canada and the Western provinces. As the West increased its economic clout, regional issues which had been dormant prior to the 1970s took on a sudden urgency.

Gibbins (1980:167) suggests that Western regional conflict has its roots in the West's view that the economic elite in central Canada has conspired to keep the West backward and in a position of economic dependency. Over the years this attitude has developed into a regional ideology—a shared set of beliefs—based on animosity to the centre. Gibbins further cites the long history of discord between the federal and provincial governments and substantial regional differences in federal electoral support as evidence of regional distinctiveness. Further complicating the regional nature of our political culture are major disputes between the federal and provincial branches of the major political parties. For example, on the thorny issue of French language rights there are major policy differences between the federal Conservative Party and its provincial counterparts in Manitoba and Saskatchewan.

While it was not until the 1970s that western separatism became a major political issue, discontent in the region dates back to the early colonization and development of the West. At that time, western dependence on an economy based on the exportation of raw materials and natural resources to the industrial centre of Canada lent credence to western suspicions that the West was being held captive in a national plan that made it economically dependent on central Canada. However, the 1970s and 1980s have seen a dramatic change in the social and economic structure of the West, and, for that matter, the whole of Canada. In the economic sphere, an analysis of the distribution of income among provinces shows a marked narrowing of the gap among Western provinces. In 1981, for instance, the per capita incomes of Alberta and British Columbia were higher than that of the perennial leader, Ontario. Economic diversification has left the economies of the Western provinces no longer totally dependent on primary production. On the political front, the election of the federal Tories in 1984, accompanied by wide representation in the West, has brought Western regional interests to the forefront of national policy, as seen in the recent Meech Lake constitutional conference. In addition, the Western provincial governments have given unanimous support to Mulroney's initiative for a free trade agreement with the United States. Of course, it is not possible to undo the historical pattern of regional exploitation and the creation of regional dependency in a single decade. However, it seems just as clear that the national government is open to change and to the creation of policies that allow for national conciliation and the creation of regional equality.

EASTERN REGIONALISM

It is no coincidence that Atlantic Canada has become known as the Maritimes. The sea and its products have been the backbone of its distinct regional identity and heritage. Before Confederation, the provinces of Nova Scotia and New Brunswick were thriving centres of trade and industry, and major trading partners with Great Britain, the West Indies, and the United States. In the nineteenth century, central Canada was the disadvantaged region, cut off in the winter months from sea-going trade routes and lacking opportunities for expansion (Matthews 1983:99). It was only after federal promises of transportation routes and enhanced industrial growth that the Maritime provinces joined Confederation. However, the much-anticipated prosperity of post-Confederation never materialized in the Maritimes. Hiller (1986:125) suggests four factors for the economic decline of the Maritimes in the latter part of the nineteenth century: (1) the decline of the overseas trade in fish and lumber products; (2) the inability of the region to compete with the industries of central Canada, due in part to a change in the freight rate structure, which made it difficult for Maritime industries to ship goods to the West; (3) the lack of both capital and markets, which forced Maritime industries to sell out to competing central Canada interests, with the result that consolidation of industry and manufacturing became concentrated in that part of the country; and (4) the addition of the Western provinces to Confederation, which reduced considerably the political clout of Maritime politicians and began the gradual consolidation of political power in central Canada.

Forbes (1979:19) links the growth of Prairie and Maritime regionalism in the first few decades of the twentieth century to central Canada's burgeoning social and economic dominance of the country. As their economy waned, Maritimers began migrating to the new industrial heartland of Ontario, further strengthening that region. At the same time, economic policies of the central government ensured that the West would be primary producers of goods, and that manufacturing, with its higher profit base, would be concentrated in central Canada. Not surprisingly, the pro-central-Canada bias of the federal government stirred Eastern resentments. In the post-World War Two period, the Maritime provinces began to develop what Rawlyk (1979:102) calls "a paranoid style of regionalism," which was based on the conspiracy theory that central Canada had deliberately set out to make the Maritimes a region whose inhabitants were destined to be the "hewers of wood and drawers of water" for the economic elite of central Canada. In the interests of national unity, the federal government established in the 1960s a Fund for Rural Economic Development (FRED), a program which Matthews (1983:106) calls "the most comprehensive and systematic effort in regional planning and development ever undertaken in Canada." The goal was to develop the rural hinterland through farm consolidation, and to assist in the migration of surplus population from rural areas. While the program had the support of the provincial political leaders, and could have been successful, it was cancelled after the election of Pierre Elliott Trudeau in 1968.

Trudeau immediately introduced the Department of Regional Economic Expansion (DREE), which had four major goals: infrastructure assistance, industrial incentives, social adjustment, and urban growth. This program was implemented in various parts of the Atlantic provinces. Industries were to be attracted to these special areas through the dispensing of cash grants and interest-free loans to establish manufacturing plants. Matthews (1983:108) notes that while economic development became the priority of the department, little effort was made to examine the social structure and social problems of the areas where DREE programs were established. Plagued with criticisms of financial mismanagement and provincial antipathy, the program was modified in the late 1970s to allow for more provincial involvement in its administration. However, despite the expenditure of billions of dollars, the goal of reducing regional inequality in the Maritimes has not been achieved. As Daniels (1984) notes, the Maritimes, notwithstanding thirty years of regional planning, have been able to raise their relative incomes by only about 15 percent, which leaves them 20 percent below the national average, while the gap between the regions in terms of employment has not been narrowed at all, with the Maritime provinces showing an unemployment rate roughly twice that of Ontario for the last decade (see Table 9.1).

Given the failure of government programs, how might the problem of regional inequalities in the Maritimes be resolved? According to Matthews (1983:116–17), a successful policy for eliminating regional disparities may be impossible as long as the pattern of regional development policies continues to favour the central regions over the peripheral ones. He proposes instead that Canada first abandon the master industry approach to regional development, which in the past has served only the central and dominant interests, and second, that mass migration out of the deprived Maritimes region be discouraged through policies that attempt to eliminate the historic pattern of dependency of the peripheral regions. Economic self-sufficiency must be encouraged in the developing regions by supporting local resources and industries geared to meeting local needs. Every effort must be made to reduce unemployment by promoting labour-intensive over high-technology industries. The emphasis should be on regional economic viability, rather than on industrialization and urbanization. In short, a new perspective on social and economic change must be devised if regional inequality in the Maritimes is to be reduced.

FUTURE PROSPECTS

The problems associated with regionalism have been a recurring subject in Canadian history. Due to a combination of cultural and physical factors, Canada has developed more as a cluster of regional units than as a national entity. From the sociological point of view, ethnicity, occupational and industrial specialization, attitudes, identity, and values are all variables that have produced and sustained regionalism in Canada. As Schwutz (1974:5) notes, regionalism has a political dimension that involves both a collective identity and a defence of territorial interests.

In simple terms, we can differentiate among four clear regional cleavages: the West, Ontario, Quebec, and the Maritimes. According to Cairns (1977), the creation of a distinct Canadian society will depend on the extent to which regionalism, in the form of a collective consciousness, can be modified such that the population sees the national unit rather than the regional unit as its primary identity reference. Needless to say, this task is not made easier by the uneven distribution of population groups by ethnicity and other characteristics, and by regional disparities in income, power, and wealth distribution, which have produced numerous grounds for conflict within the societal unit (Hiller 1986:35). Pammett (1976) found that approximately 60 percent of Canadians think of themselves in terms of a regional identity, 30 percent in terms of a national identity, while 10 percent are ambivalent. Furthermore, reflecting the perception of regional inequality in the society, residents of both the Western and Atlantic provinces are more likely to have a regional identity than are Ontario residents. Regional distinctiveness and national unity are not, however, necessarily mutually exclusive goals. Ornstein

(1986) believes that a national Canadian ideology is slowly emerging, noting for example, that, in terms of political ideology, within English Canada there are few differences among the nine provinces, with the major differentiation noted between English and French Canada. Additionally, the issue of separatism in Quebec, while not buried, is dormant at the present time. It augurs well for the future of national unity that even in this province with the highest level of regional consciousness, the majority of Québécois view themselves as being "Canadian."

SUMMARY

1. Canadian regionalism refers to a myriad of factors, including cultural distinctiveness, identification with and loyalty to the region (as opposed to the nation), and resentment over regional disparities in economic and political power. A central aspect of Canadian regionalism is embodied in the view of Canada as "two nations—English and French—warring within one bosom."

2. Quebec, the West, the Atlantic provinces, and Ontario represent the four major regional cleavages in Canada. Each of these regions reflects fundamental differences in terms of population growth, urbanization, per capita income, employment, housing, health, and education.

3. There are six major sociological approaches to the problem of regional disparities. The *territorial-geographical approach* suggests that unequal rates of economic growth across regions can be altered through government action to revive economically deprived regions. The *staples approach* explains regional economic imbalances in terms of the presence or absence of natural resources. The *development approach* attributes regional disparities to the presence or absence of "achievement motivation." The *neoclassical approach* opposes government subsidies to deprived regions on the basis of free market supply-and-demand principles. The *Keynesian approach* emphasizes the role of government support to have-not regions. Modified *Marxist* approaches attribute regional disparities to Canada's social class structure.

4. The British conquest forced French Canada to cede political and economic control to the British. The growth of industrialization in the 1940s brought French Canadians into direct conflict with the British minority for the first time.

5. The election of the Lesage government in 1960 marked the beginnings of the Quiet Revolution. The 1970s saw the emergence of language as a pivotal issue in French–English relations. Quebec nationalism crystallized with the rise to power of the Parti Québécois in 1976.

6. Quebec's rejection of sovereignty-association in 1980 marked a victory for the federal government over the Parti Québécois. The more conciliatory relationship between Quebec and the federal government today is exemplified by Bourassa's acceptance of the Meech Lake Accord. The federal government must continue to promote the special interests of Quebec, while at the same time protecting the rights of minorities within that province.

7. Through a combination of historical, geographical, and political factors, the West has developed into a highly distinct regional entity, with a view of itself as an exploited hinterland whose natural resources are being used for the benefit of central Canada.

8. Rising oil prices in the 1970s vastly improved Western economic fortunes. At the same time, hitherto dormant regional issues—e.g., French language rights—rose to the surface and led to clashes between the federal government and its Western provincial counterparts. The Meech Lake Accord appears to have set a more positive agenda for federal–Western relations.

9. Before Confederation, the Atlantic provinces were thriving centres of industry and trade. However, the latter part of the nineteenth century saw their economic decline, which continued to be reinforced by central Canada's growing social and economic dominance.

10. Over the last thirty years, the federal government has introduced into the Atlantic provinces regional development programs designed to reduce economic inequality and to promote economic diversification. In the main, these programs have failed. Today, Eastern Canada reflects the highest poverty and unemployment levels in the country. Future regional development policies must emphasize the creation of a labour-intensive economic base and economic self-sufficiency.

11. Regional distinctiveness and national unity are not mutually exclusive goals. The creation of a distinct Canadian society will depend on the extent to which regions come to see the national unit, as opposed to the regional unit, as their primary identity reference.

10

Visible Minority Groups

INTRODUCTION

The issue of race relations is of major importance to sociologists. ("Race" we can define as an arbitrary classification of human populations, which uses *biological* criteria—e.g., actual or assumed physiological and genetic differences—to distinguish among the world's peoples.) While Canada espouses the values of egalitarianism, in practice we have fallen short of the ideal. According to Kallen (1982:22), Canada reflects a strong degree of racial inequality, with majority white groups (e.g., the British) controlling the power structure and visible minority groups assuming inferior roles. The result has been the institutionalization of inequality and discrimination in the society. This chapter will provide an analysis of the unequal role and status of visible minorities in Canadian society, with particular reference to the causes and consequences of the problem, and possible solutions to it.

PERSPECTIVES ON RACISM

Proponents of the *functionalist perspective* argue that the problems of minorities in Canada arise out of social disorganization, and that the low status of minority groups has created a dysfunctional situation not only for the groups themselves, but for society as a whole. The institutionalization of inequality has been most directly responsible for the growth of discrimination and prejudice against minorities. From the functionalist perspective, racism and its dysfunctional consequences can be alleviated by social structural changes, such as introducing a better balance into power sharing and eliminating institutional discrimination, in addition to reducing prejudicial attitudes, and promoting among the general population an acceptance of the culture and rights of minorities as equal to those of majority groups. From the functionalist perspective, prejudice and discrimination are seen as causative of social problems, mainly because of their disruptive affect upon the smooth and efficient operation of the social system.

While functionalists analyze the problem of racism in terms of its societal impact, *conflict theorists* see it in terms of how it affects minority groups in society. From this point of view, interracial conflict develops as a result of inequalities between groups in terms of power, prestige, and status. In the struggle for scarce resources, each group attempts to attain control of the resources by denying others access to them. In the Canadian context, their position of dominance in the early settlement period allowed the British to claim the positions of power and influence in society. All other groups later entering Canada were assigned particular entry-status positions based on this structure of inequality, which over time has become institutionalized. From the conflict perspective, then, racism stems not so much from conflict over physical or cultural differences, as it does from a struggle for power and social and economic rewards. The dominant group simply uses the assumed cultural and physical differences of other groups to justify its superior status.

RACIAL INEQUALITY AND IMMIGRATION

Racial inequality in Canada dates back to the original contact between the European colonizers and the native Indian and Inuit peoples. The Europeans, with their firearms and their economic and technological skills, soon held a position of military, cultural, and political dominance over the indigenous peoples. This early contact led, firstly, to the subjugation of the native peoples through the introduction of the reserve system, and secondly, to the perception of the colonizing white race as superior. Following the conquest, the British assumed a dominant status in Canadian society. While English and French Canadians were given equal status in theory, English Canadians assumed dominance at the institutional level, both inside and outside of Quebec. As the dominant national group, they exercised control of federal immigration policies, determining which groups would be allowed entry, where they would settle, what jobs they would hold, and how they would be ranked in the social stratification system (Hughes and Kallen 1974:112). To consolidate their majority status and cultural superiority, English Canadians offered a "preferred status" to immigrants from Britain and northern and western Europe who were culturally or socially similar, while the less preferred ethnic and racial groups (e.g., southern Europeans and Asians) received an entry status with low occupational and social roles (Porter 1965:63). Until 1962, in fact, the Canadian Immigration Act openly discriminated against nonwhite immigrants, strenuously limiting, and at times prohibiting, their entry into the country. In the post-1967 period, however, changes in the Immigration Act removed this type of discrimination, with the result that nonwhite immigration into Canada today surpasses immigration from the "preferred" countries.

With immigration in the pre-1967 period concentrated among those from Britain and northern and western Europe, the majority group broadened from being English Canadian to being Euro-Canadian in ethnic composition (Hughes and Kallen 1974:113). While changes in Canada's immigration laws in 1967 altered Canada's racial composition, resulting in a multiracial society, the domination of the Euro-Canadian majority in the stratification system has not significantly altered. Reitz (1980:153) notes that, despite a reduction in ethnic inequality in our time, immigrants from southern European continue to exhibit a lower socio-economic status than their northern-European counterparts. Finally, while other Euro-Canadian and French-Canadian groups have been able to achieve upward mobility into middle- and lower-upper-class social positions, the lower status position of many visible minority groups—particularly of our native peoples—has been virtually unchanged.

According to Kallen (1982:112), visibility was a major variable in the original ascribing of the *visible minorities* (that is, nonwhite minorities) to an inferior socio-economic status position in society. Visible minorities have been a part of the Canadian scene for over two hundred years, if only in small numbers at the outset. Blacks were brought in as slaves as early as the sixteenth century, and escaped slaves from the southern United States fled to Canada—particularly to Nova Scotia and Southern Ontario—after the abolition of slavery in Canada in 1834. Other visible minorities that trickled into Canada in the period prior to 1962 included blacks from the West Indies and the United States, and Chinese, Japanese, and East Indians from Asia. Despite the severe restrictions put on Asian immigration prior to 1962, by 1921 Canada's Asian population numbered over 60,000. The majority were Chinese and Japanese who originally came as labourers to build the railways. However, so successful were campaigns against the "yellow peril" that the census of 1941 listed only 74,000 residents of Asian origin.

Changes to the Immigration Act in 1962 opened the door to immigration on a nonracial basis, but since at this time the vast majority of immigration offices were located in Europe, there was no significant increase in nonwhite immigration to Canada. In 1967, precise non-discriminatory criteria were introduced. The "points system," whereby all immigrants who met basic health and educational requirements were allowed entry, resulted in an unprecedented rise in visible minority immigration to Canada. Between 1968 and 1978, the number of visible minority immigrants totalled 556,000, or approximately 34 percent of the total number of immigrants entering Canada (Immigration Statistics: 1968–1978, Dept. of Manpower and Immigration 1980). Taking into account nonwhite immigrants from earlier periods, Statistics Canada (1983) estimates the total visible minority immigrant population at one million. In 1976, the federal government, faced with public opposition to the rising number of immigrants (in addition to growing unemployment and economic recession), attempted to curb the free flow of immigrants to Canada by introducing, in the Immigration Act of 1976, a nondiscriminatory quota system which limited on a yearly basis the number of immigrants.

RACIAL DISCRIMINATION AND PREJUDICE

Kallen (1982:20) notes that Canadian concern for human rights is largely a post-World War II phenomenon. Awareness of institutionalized racism, stimulated both by reports from Human Rights Commissions and incidences of racial violence, has challenged notions of Canada as an egalitarian and just society. But the mere inclusion in our Charter of Rights of human rights guarantees for equality does not by itself qualify Canada as a tolerant and egalitarian society. The evidence suggests that racism, prejudice, and discrimination against our visible minorities constitutes a major problem.

In a national study, Berry et al. (1977:16) found among respondents a striking degree of social distance vis-à-vis their relations with visible minorities (the groups ranked lowest among all Canadian ethnic groups). Henry (1978), in a study of the demographic correlates of racism in Toronto, developed a racism scale, which showed that half of her sample expressed some degree of racism, with 16 percent classified as very racist. The variables most often associated with racism were age, education, social and economic status, and religion. While these studies suggest that racism in Canada is in the main covert, the evidence in the last few years of increased violence and discrimination against the visible minorities (Pitman 1977; Ramcharan 1982) suggests that overt racism is on the rise. Abella (1985:3–4), noting the evidence of discrimination against visible minorities by employers (see Table 10.1 for a comparison between perception and experience), recommends affirmative-action programs as the best means of removing barriers to equality.

Theoretical Perspectives

One of the assumptions underlying racism in Canada is the belief in the innate inferiority of visible minorities, through which allocation of inferior opportunities and social status is often rationalized. As Kallen (1982:25) notes, the fact that over time these groups become locked into inferior roles is used by the majority group to justify unfair treatment, thus perpetuating the cycle of discrimination.

From a theoretical perspective, racism involves the elements of ethnocentrism, prejudice, stereotypes, and discrimination. The interplay of these four components can create a structural situation whereby groups are assigned role and status positions on the basis of ascribed rather than achieved characteristics. *Ethnocentrism* involves the evaluation of all groups and cultures in terms of one's own cultural standards and values. As Kallen (1982:26) suggests, in this comparative process the culture and values of the "outgroup" are perceived as inferior to those of the "in

Table 10.1

Perception and Experience of Discrimination by Members of Minority Ethnic Groups and by Majority Canadians (%)

	German %	Italian %	Jewish %	Portu-guese %	Ukrainian %	Chinese %	West Indian %	Majority Canadian %	Other English %
A. Discrimination as far as jobs, pay, or working conditions are concerned									
As very and somewhat serious problem	31	3	19	16	31	9	60	5	8
Not too serious problem	46	17	41	45	26	32	22	18	15
Not a problem	20	77	39	36	36	55	13	76	76
Don't know	3	4	1	4	7	3	5	1	1
Number of interviews	(153)	(320)	(350)	(348)	(163)	(354)	(150)	(230)	(267)
B. Employers perceived as discriminating a lot or somewhat									
By the group itself	57	19	32	43	36	27	75	—	—
	(140)	(301)	(338)	(312)	(128)	(334)	(132)	—	—
By the majority group	51	19	40	43	56	20	79	—	—
	(212)	(209)	(223)	(212)	(201)	(184)	(218)	—	—
By others	45	23	37	34	48	23	70	—	—
	(1569)	(1353)	(1536)	(1440)	(1543)	(1086)	(1682)	—	—
C. Have experienced discrimination									
When trying to get a job	15	5	6	12	5	11	21	1	5
In other areas	15	20	20	31	6	14	17	5	12
Number of interviews	(153)	(321)	(351)	(348)	(164)	(354)	(150)	(230)	(267)

Source: R. Breton, "West Indian, Chinese and European Ethnic Groups in Toronto: Perceptions of Problems and Resources," in J. Elliott, ed., *Two Nations, Many Cultures* (Scarborough: Prentice-Hall, 1983), p.432. Reprinted by permission.

group." Unlike ethnocentrism, which focuses on the in-group, *prejudice* is often directed toward specific out-groups. Simpson and Yinger (1972:24), for example, define prejudice as an emotionally rigid attitude rooted in prejudgement of a particular group or category of people. One of the most dangerous characteristics of prejudice is that it is a learned behaviour in which people assume, without thought or question, the validity of unsubstantiated opinions.

Another of the components which operates in the sphere of inter-group relations is the *stereotype*. Glaser and Possony (1979:90) define stereotypes as overgeneralized and rigid cognitive maps or pictures in our heads, which are, in essence, unsubstantiated beliefs about members of a given group. While stereotypes about groups may not be totally errone-ous, they offer a distorted picture of the truth and reinforce existing prejudices in the society by exacerbating differences between peoples and cultures. To a large extent, stereotypes about minorities mirror the degree of acceptability society confers upon them. Table 10.2, for exam-ple, suggests an unwillingness on the part of majority Canadians in Toronto to form close relationships with visible and ethnic minority groups.

Racial or ethnic *discrimination*, which often results from the nega-tive attitudinal framework developed through ethnocentrism, stereotyp-ing, and prejudice, may be defined as the negative treatment meted out to people because of their membership in a minority group. Minorities in Canada have been subjected to three forms of discrimination: individual, institutional, and cultural. Of these forms, *individual discrimination*, which results from the conscious act of a prejudiced person, is the most blatant. *Institutional discrimination* occurs when the values of a preju-diced society drive the individual to discriminate. According to Kallen (1982:37), the most powerful and dangerous form of institutional dis-crimination in Canada is legislative or legal discrimination, which has in the past been exemplified by Canada's (until 1967) blatantly discrimina-tory immigration laws, and by the various Indian Acts passed by Parlia-ment, which imposed colonial rule on the native peoples and thereby entrenched their unequal and subordinate position. A further example of this form of discrimination was the institution of slavery, which flourished openly in Canada until 1833, with blacks treated as property to be bought and sold at the will of the master (Winks 1971:26). While such forms of legal discrimination have since been removed, negative behaviour and attitudes toward these groups are indicative of the legacy they left behind.

Finally, there exists a covert, subtle form of discrimination that Kallen (1982:38) calls *cultural discrimination*. While Canada promotes itself as a multicultural society, tolerant and accepting of the cultures of minority groups, in reality groups whose cultures are most alien to the dominant ones (visible minorities, for example) experience greater

Table 10.2
Perception of Social Acceptance by Majority Canadian Group and Attitudes of Majority Canadians and Others vis-à-vis Each Group (%)

	Chinese %	German %	Italian %	Jewish %	Portuguese %	Ukrainian %	West Indian %
A. 1 Perception of acceptance as neighbours							
Very easily	33 ⎫ 85	68 ⎫ 94	45 ⎫ 89	22 ⎫ 77	52 ⎫ 85	58 ⎫ 92	21 ⎫ 57
Somewhat easily	52 ⎭	26 ⎭	44 ⎭	55 ⎭	33 ⎭	34 ⎭	36 ⎭
Not easily	5	3	8	17	9	4	35
Don't know	10	3	2	6	6	4	8
Number of interviews	(152)	(321)	(351)	(348)	(161)	(353)	(150)
A. 2 Acceptance as neighbors by							
Majority group*	83	92	85	89	84	91	67
Others**	84	82	83	84	83	85	66
Number of interviews	(1861)	(1706)	(1696)	(1698)	(1844)	(1643)	(1862)

Table 10.2 (continued)

	Chinese %	German %	Italian %	Jewish %	Portuguese %	Ukrainian %	West Indian %
B. 1 Perception of acceptance as relatives							
Very easily	11 ⎤ 56	62 ⎤ 89	41 ⎤ 89	8 ⎤ 41	42 ⎤ 77	49 ⎤ 84	10 ⎤ 33
Somewhat easily	45 ⎦	27 ⎦	48 ⎦	33 ⎦	35 ⎦	35 ⎦	23 ⎦
Not easily	23	3	7	45	8	7	45
Don't know	21	8	5	14	15	9	21
Number of interviews	(152)	(320)	(350)	(347)	(162)	(353)	(150)
B. 2 Acceptance as relatives by							
Majority group*	65	87	84	77	68	87	49
Others**	50	64	65	66	62	69	38
Number of interviews	(1887)	(1727)	(1699)	(1699)	(1863)	(1664)	(1883)

*The number of interviews for the "Majority Group" ranges between 224 and 229.
**"Others" include all non-Majority Canadians except the respondents for the group concerned. Since this combined category changes with each group, the base of the percentage varies from column to column.
Source: R. Breton, "West Indian, Chinese and European Ethnic Groups in Toronto: Perceptions of Problems and Resources," in J. Elliott, ed., *Two Nations, Many Cultures* (Scarborough: Prentice-Hall, 1983), p.428. Reprinted by permission.

rejection by the majority than do those groups whose cultures are more similar to that of the majority group. Since minority groups, in order to fully participate in the wider societal institutions, must conform to the dominant value system, cultural discrimination can be said to be built into the institutional structure of society. From another perspective, D'Oyley (1978:138) argues that the education system, which moulds young Canadians into accepting the values of the dominant cultures that control it, is at the vanguard of the acculturation process. Wyatt (1982) notes that minority groups, particularly visible minorities, continue to encounter cultural and political roadblocks in their attempts to gain the respect and acceptance of the majority group for their cultural values and traditions.

Discriminatory behaviour in Canada may be analyzed from two other perspectives—the "colour-class" and the "stranger" theses. According to the *colour-class thesis*, the majority group in society identifies visible minorities with the lowest social class mainly because of the historical relationships between the two groups. The *stranger thesis*, on the other hand, suggests that the majority group reacts to visible minorities with distrust and antipathy because they differ both in appearance and behaviour.

CANADA'S NATIVE PEOPLES

Introduction

Canada's native peoples fall into five categories: registered treaty Indian, registered nontreaty Indian, nonregistered Indian, Métis, and Inuit. While these groups have differential status depending on their legal relationship with the Crown, they have all faced the prejudicial attitudes and discriminatory behaviour of the majority. For the purposes of this analysis, therefore, there will be no attempt to differentiate among the above categories. Nevertheless, while they share many of the same problems, it should be emphasized that the native peoples do not share a common identity or culture.

According to Frideres (1983:14–18), in the early period of settlement the French and English differed markedly in their approach to native peoples. While the French settlers attempted to integrate and devise methods for harmonious intergroup relations, under the English the native peoples were confined to reserves. The Indian Act of 1951 made official the role and status of Indians as nonpersons in Canada by designating native peoples as different from the rest of the Canadian population, with separate rights and privileges. The Act legitimated the physical and social isolation of reserves, which, however close they were to a town or city, would remain separate and unequal.

Demographics

Canada's Indian population numbers around 500,000, the Métis population around 200,000, and the Inuit approximately 30,000 (Statistics Canada 1988). The total group, then, comprises about 3 percent of the total population. As Nagler (1975:xiv) notes, their small numbers, combined with their geographical isolation, have made native peoples a relatively invisible minority in Canadian society. However, they are fast becoming more visible. The migration of native peoples to the cities has increased in recent years, with about 30 percent of the group now resident in urban areas (Frideres 1983:187). While the ramifications of this trend will be discussed later in the chapter, the fact that the reserve is still home to the majority of native peoples suggests that if their socio-economic status is to improve, changes will have to occur on rather than off the reserves (the latter was recommended in the 1969 White Paper on Indian Affairs).

While the native birth rate is twice the national average, it is the high infant mortality rate among natives—three times the national average—that best illustrates their position of deprivation and poverty. In terms of income, occupation, and education, native peoples represent the lowest level of any group in Canada. The per capita income of natives is one-fifth of that of Euro-Canadians, and, according to the Senate Committee's poverty lines for 1988, over 80 percent of Canada's native peoples live in poverty.

Employment

Native peoples are overrepresented in low-status occupations, and underrepresented in high-status occupations. A comparison of the census data for the period 1971–1981 shows that the occupational status of the group has improved only marginally, with less than 4 percent of native peoples holding occupations in the professional or managerial categories, compared with 10 percent for people of British origin and 38 percent for people of Jewish origin (Statistics Canada 1983). In addition, the average duration of employment for natives is five months, with less than 25 percent employed for more than nine months of the year—a statistic that supports the belief that most native peoples are gainfully employed only in seasonal and poorly paid occupations.

Education

Given the importance of education in achieving high occupational and social status, it is not surprising that native peoples have the lowest educational attainment levels of all the groups in Canada. As Nagler (1975:173) suggests, until recently the attempt by the federal government to impose a white, middle-class education system on reserve natives resulted in a high dropout rate among children, as well as in the fragmentation of families. According to Frideres (1983:174), the problem stemmed not from a lack of educational funding for native peoples, but from the fact that native peoples were never involved in the educational process, having no control over spending, the curriculum selection, and the teaching process itself. Furthermore, teachers brought in from the outside had little knowledge about the culture or way of life of natives and, as Nagler (1975:24) notes, "were often of second-rate calibre."

As a result of this form of institutionalized discrimination, less than 50 percent of Canada's native population completes elementary school (Frideres 1983:167). For high school, where overt discrimination from both teachers and white children is commonplace, the dropout rate is even higher. The number of natives between 15 and 19 who reach secondary school has been estimated to be 5 times lower than the national average (Frideres 1983:168–69). Of all the variables influencing equality of opportunity, education is the most tangible. While minorities may be faced with discrimination and prejudice in mainstream society, education enhances an individual's chances of obtaining a job commensurate with training and ability. Without the technological skills necessary in today's labour market, however, native peoples are doomed to a low socio-economic status. Finally, until native peoples are given control over their education system high dropout rates at all levels of the system will remain the norm.

Deviance

In view of their dependent status, it is not surprising that many natives resort to acts which are defined as deviant by the majority society. Poverty, health problems, substandard housing, negative stereotypes, discrimination and prejudice have all contributed to the anomie that has developed in the native communities. Social and cultural conflict, and an inability to adjust to the norms, values, and laws of mainstream society have led to an overrepresentation of natives in the criminal statistics of the nation, particularly in the areas of alcohol abuse, vagrancy, prostitution, petty theft, robbery, homicide, and auto theft. Reasons (1972) blames much of the deviant behaviour among native peoples on their lack of commitment to white society, and to the frustration that stems from their inability to attain their ends through legitimate means.

For many native people, disillusionment has taken two tragic forms— alcoholism and anomic suicide. Both alcoholism and suicide rates are higher for native peoples than for any other group in Canada. Nagler (1975:69) suggests that "native drinking is a social pastime which serves as a response to the frustrations and boredom encountered not only on the reserve, but in urban centres as well." It is significant that within the native community there is no stigma attached to alcoholism. Frideres (1983:182) notes that the suicide rate for native peoples is three times the national average, with suicide accounting for one out of every ten native deaths. Nagler (1975:73) ascribes the anomic nature of suicides among the native peoples to their existence in a social and cultural vacuum. Many, unable to adjust to the alternative normative standards of the society, become alienated, isolated, aggressive, and finally suicidal.

Future Prospects

In recent years, the growth of Pan-Indianism and the Red Power movement has led to a greater national unity among natives, a historically diverse people (Cardinal 1977:169). The common goal of these organizations is to develop the human and natural resources of native peoples on the reserves, making them comparable, in terms of role and status, with other groups in society. If native peoples are to control their destiny, it is essential that their leadership be involved in the economic development of the reserves. Further, as Frideres (1983:316) recommends, the administration of the federal Department of Indian Affairs should be "placed under the control of native peoples with little or no outside interference."

The recent growth of a common consciousness and solidarity among native peoples, based on their experiences of inequality, has made for a stronger coalition and sense of commitment to the achievement of shared goals. In addition, the various social control mechanisms used by the federal government to diffuse the conflict and maintain the status quo, while successful in the past, are no longer working (Frideres 1983: Chapter 11). However, years of co-option, insulation, sanctions, and persuasion have left their legacy, the most long-term and harmful example being the success of the majority in keeping natives out of power positions in the society by providing them with training programs geared toward semiskilled and blue-collar occupations, rather than toward the higher-status economic positions through which they would be able to challenge the status quo.

CHANGING RACE RELATIONS

In the past two decades, over half a million visible minority immigrants have entered Canada. During this period, race relations as a social problem can be said to have evolved from a latent to a manifest form, particularly in our large cities, where interracial conflict has become overt. While the problem is not as endemic as it is in South Africa, the United States, or Great Britain, racial discrimination and prejudice is an entrenched part of Canadian society. Racial inequality in Canada is a direct consequence of prejudice and discrimination. Perceived as outsiders and strangers, visible minorities have been relegated to inferior socioeconomic positions. While the dysfunctional nature of inequality is recognized by governments and concerned groups, there is at present little acknowledgement of the fact that only extensive changes to legal, economic, and education systems can put a dent in the attitudinal traits that allow inequality to persist. The widespread perception that groups of racially and culturally different people have invaded the majority's social and economic space has led both adults and children to form attitudes about these groups based mainly on stereotypes.

In terms of possible solutions to the problem, there is a clear need for multicultural and multiracial programs in teacher-education institutions aimed at raising the level of racial tolerance in schools. As Pitman (1977:184) suggests, the school "can provide not only language skills, but can orient the newly-arrived student to the customs and habits of the host community." In addition, both teachers and the curriculum should emphasize in a positive way the social and cultural values of minorities.

Also required for the improvement of interracial relations is an education in multicultural reality, extending to the whole community, which utilizes such institutions as the school system, libraries, churches, the news media, and ethnic associations. As Adair and Rosenstock (1977) note, negative racial attitudes are related to negative cultural attitudes, which can only be eradicated by parents, teachers, and school administrators working together. While fear of discussing racial issues in public may be understandable, the lack of communication amongst (and between) the majority group and minorities has merely served to perpetuate interracial conflicts.

Finally, we may consider the role multiculturalism has played in Canadian race relations. Baker (1978) suggests that the perception of Canadian society as one that encourages tolerance toward its minorities, allowing them to retain much of their cultural distinctiveness, is more an ideological model than a reality. He cites as evidence the ethnically and racially stratified nature of Canadian society, the persistence of racist attitudes, and the widespread discrimination and prejudice practised against minorities. In practical terms, our cultural mosaic is not operating functionally, and may in fact be generating interracial conflict as minorities experience wide disparities between their goals and what society offers.

Another problem posed by the policy of multiculturalism is that it can reinforce the differentiation among groups to the extent that we fall into the trap of identifying some groups—particularly visible minorities—as "separate but unequal." Racial affiliations should not be a criterion for the allocation of rights, privileges, and responsibilities between groups and individuals. Ideally, our goal should be a pluralistic society, but not a vertical mosaic based on race or ethnicity, which has been the institutional arrangement of the past. Racial or ethnic group identification may serve neither as an integrative force, nor as a method for the procurement of equality in the economic system. The problem, as Vallee (1969) points out, is that racial or ethnic groups cannot exhaust their limited resources on maintaining specific institutions and at the same time prepare their members for achievement in mainstream society. He suggests that by dispersion into the majority institutions, minorities can become part of the power structure, alter traditional roles, and increase the group's chances of success and upward mobility.

SUMMARY

1. From the functionalist perspective, racism has evolved out of the institutionalization of inequality in society. The best way to alleviate racism and its dysfunctional consequences is to introduce changes into the social structure.

2. For conflict theorists, racism stems less from conflict over physical or cultural differences, as it does from the tendency of the dominant group to control social and economic rewards by denying less powerful groups access to them.

3. After the conquest, the British ethnic group became the dominant group in Canadian society. To consolidate their power, English Canadians offered "preferred status" to white European immigrants. Despite the eventual removal of this type of discrimination from immigration policy, the Euro-Canadian majority continues to dominate the stratification system.

4. Visible minorities have been a part of the Canadian scene for over two hundred years. Estimates put Canada's total visible minority population today at over one million people.

5. Growing evidence of institutionalized racism challenges the view of Canada as an egalitarian and just society. Among the variables most frequently associated with racism are age, education, social and economic status, and religion. While racism in Canada is in the main covert, research points to a rise in violence against visible minorities in recent years.

6. Racism can be broken down into four components: ethnocentrism, prejudice, stereotypes, and discrimination. Discrimination can be individual, institutional, or cultural in its context. Discriminatory behaviour can be analyzed from either the "colour-class" perspective or the "stranger" perspective.

7. Canada's native peoples fall into the following categories: registered treaty Indian, registered nontreaty Indian, nonregistered Indian,

Métis, and Inuit. All groups are subjected to discrimination by the white majority.

8. Income, occupational, and educational levels are lower for native peoples than for any other group in Canada. It is estimated that over 80 percent of the native population lives in poverty.

9. While the urban native population has grown in recent years, the reserve is still home to the majority of native peoples. If native peoples are to ever control their own destiny, native leaders must play a major role in the economic development of the reserves.

10. The incidence of crime, alcoholism, and suicide among native peoples is disproportionately high. Sociologists see this as inevitably arising from the state of chronic social disorganization and anomie in which natives live.

11. The growth of a common consciousness and solidarity among native peoples has strengthened native commitment to shared goals and led to the creation of political activist movements (e.g., Pan-Indianism and Red Power).

12. Positive change in the area of race relations must involve a combination of structural and attitudinal changes, in addition to a reexamination of Canada's policy of multiculturalism in terms of how it affects interracial relations.

PART 4

DEVIANCE

11

Mental Disorders and Suicide

MENTAL ILLNESS AS A SOCIAL PROBLEM

Coleman and Cressey (1984:332) define a mental disorder as "a severe disturbance that makes coping with routine, everyday life difficult or impossible." The incidence of mental disorders in Canada is much higher than is commonly supposed. It is estimated that at any given time over one million Canadians may be in need of mental health care, while as much as 20 percent of the population suffers from emotional disorders, ranging from mild depression to stress-related breakdowns (Canadian Mental Health Association 1983). According to Statistics Canada (1980), one out of every eight Canadians can be expected to be hospitalized for a mental disorder at least once during his or her lifetime. In addition, of the more than 3,000 suicides that occur in Canada yearly, almost half are committed by people suffering from a severe mental disorder. The major causes of admission to psychiatric in-patient facilities include *neurosis, psychosis, schizophrenia,* and *alcoholism.*

PERSPECTIVES ON MENTAL DISORDERS

According to the *medical model,* a mental disorder is an incapacitating illness that results from an organic dysfunction. While this definition may explain many forms of mental disorders, there is a growing sense that nonorganic factors, including stress and alienation, demand consideration as well. According to Scheff (1984:18), mental disorders can be seen as a form of social deviance—that is, as a refusal on the part of the individual to conform to the institutional expectations of society. When people are nonconformist, it is easy to label them "mentally ill," a role and status that is reinforced by the mental health professions which treat them as such.

Let us consider the view of "mental disorders as a myth" expounded by Szasz (1961:22). While he does not dispute the reality of psychological and emotional breakdowns, Szasz believes that it is erroneous and dangerous to attempt to treat them as illnesses. Rather, he suggests that all nonorganic mental disorders should be viewed as unresolved "problems in living." In treating the problems which arise out of social relationships as psychological problems, the medical approach ignores the fact that conflict, stress, and tension are an integral part of the human interactive process. The implication of this for Szasz is that by labelling all of these variables as illnesses, we absolve individuals of their responsibilities to family and community, and suggest that causation is external and hence beyond the individual's control.

On an even more sinister note, Church (1978:11) argues that the label "mentally ill" can be seen in social and political terms—that is, as a means of controlling those who fail to conform to the established social order. Thus "misfits," such as alcoholics, homosexuals, and political dissidents, are frequently labelled as sick individuals in need of psychiatric treatment. The authority of the medical profession is such that few question this labelling process. And nonconformist patients who choose to rebel against their treatment simply reinforce the "mentally ill" image.

Finally, Coles (1970:54) notes that standards of mental normality are established by those who hold high social, economic, and political status, and for whom the most expedient way of preserving the status quo is to define nonconformist or deviant behaviour as an illness and treat it accordingly.

Functionalist theory attributes the rise in mental disorders to structural dysfunctions in society, which can impose on people debilitating emotional, psychological, and economic pressures. From this perspective, the stress, isolation, and alienation created by rapid technological change has its strongest impact on those individuals who have not developed successful coping mechanisms. Srole et al. (1978:38) have shown that a higher incidence of mental disorder exists among the urban poor. Society, according to functionalist theory, has failed to provide such groups sufficient means to alleviate the problem.

From the *conflict perspective*, mental disorders and other psychological problems are linked to the highly competitive economic systems that characterize industrialized societies. As Coleman and Cressey (1984:358) note, the insecurities that result from the constant struggle to compete and be successful lead to increased alienation and stress. Laing (1967:27), in fact, contends that mental disorders are a normal reaction to the tensions of modern life. Like their functionalist counterparts, conflict theorists express deep concern for the high rates of mental disorders found among deprived groups. However, they differ as to causation, arguing that this in large measure is a result of social, political, and economic exploitation, which can lead underprivileged groups to experience frustration, powerlessness, and alienation—feelings that can develop into serious mental disorders.

TREATING MENTAL DISORDERS

In past centuries, mental disorders were viewed as evil spirits to be exorcised by surgery. In medieval Europe, the church condemned the mentally disordered as heretics and witches, and subjected them to floggings, starvation, hangings, or burning at the stake. As late as the nineteenth century, in fact, both the church and state regarded the mentally disordered as moral degenerates, to be chained and imprisoned. More humane treatment of the mentally ill began in postrevolutionary France through the work of Philippe Pinel (1745–1826), who was chief physician at an asylum in Paris. By the late nineteenth century, many of Pinel's reforms had gained popularity throughout Europe, and there were dramatic improvements in care and living conditions for the mentally disturbed. However, treatment was minimal, and people committed to asylums generally spent the rest of their lives there.

In Canada, until the late nineteenth century there were, with the exception of Quebec, no special facilities for the mentally disordered. The majority of the mentally disturbed were confined to prisons or poor houses (Williams et al. 1972). It was not until the 1840s that concerted efforts were made to house the mentally disordered in special institutions. By 1920, large mental institutions were to be found across Canada. However, these institutions saw their role not as providing therapeutic care or treatment, but rather as ridding society of dangerous and troublesome elements. Indeed, almost all patients in these institutions were involuntarily admitted, and received custodial care rather than active treatment. Today, with a more sophisticated health care delivery system, patient care for the mentally disordered (both as in-patients and out-patients) is more geared to treatment and rehabilitation. The philosophy of the medical model of treatment is that, with proper diagnosis, medication, and therapy, the mentally ill can be rehabilitated and returned to normal living. We shall examine five major treatments: drugs, psychotherapy, behaviour therapy, community mental health, and institutionalization.

Drugs

When not used simply as a control mechanism, drug therapy can have positive effects on patients with neurotic and psychotic disorders. However, as Scheff (1984:165) notes, drug therapies do not cure mental disorders, but as of now simply alleviate symptoms. Until the link between mental disorders and chemical imbalance is more firmly established, drug therapy will remain a palliative and not a panacea.

Psychotherapy

Psychotherapy involves personal interaction between the therapist and patient. While there are many forms of psychotherapy, most are based on Freud's theory that mental disorders are defence mechanisms that people develop to avoid psychological and emotional problems. The therapist sets out to gain the confidence of the patient and thus achieve insights into his or her problems. The ultimate aim is to encourage patients to work toward an understanding of their problems from which they can alter their behaviour.

Behaviour Therapy

Behaviour therapy, also described as *behaviour modification*, takes as its starting point the assumption that mental illness is a learned behaviour. According to Rimm and Masters (1974:51), people develop maladaptive behavioural traits because they feel positively rewarded by the results of the negative behaviour. As such, the goal of behaviour modification is to alter the specific maladaptive behaviour by removing the rewards that it brings to the patient. While behaviour modification has become popular because of its simplicity, it is most effective in the treatment of maladaptive behaviours with specific symptoms (e.g., alcoholism and drug addiction) and may not be useful in cases involving emotional disturbances or depression.

Community Mental Health

The community mental health approach to the treatment of mental disorders may include various psychiatric therapies, but its emphasis is on the role of the community and society as a whole in contributing to the individual's problem. Central to community mental health treatment is the acknowledgement that stress, anxiety, or depression might be the result of external factors such as unemployment or family problems. Short-term counselling to encourage the individual to adjust to his or her situation may temporarily alleviate the disorder, but a more long-term solution would be to provide a broad spectrum of community services for individuals with psychological or social problems, treating the problem in the context in which it occurs, and reducing the need for psychiatric services in hospitals. Keeping patients out of institutions eliminates the stigma of hospitalization and allows for the maintainance of family and community responsibilities.

Advocates of the community mental health approach argue that not only is it the most successful approach to the rehabilitation of the mentally disordered, but that it is the only form of treatment that reaches those in society who otherwise would receive no psychiatric treatment at all. Its success, however, depends on the quality and degree of primary, comprehensive, and continuous care provided. As Williams et al. (1972) note, primary care should focus on preventive services. A comprehensive service should attempt to provide help for all problems of living. We have numerous programs to assist in the treatment of alcoholism, drug addiction, emotional disturbance, marital and family problems, as well as psychiatric disorders. While these programs incorporate much expertise from the helping professions, the services are usually unco-ordinated, disjointed, and fragmented. The goal of the health services should be the development of a rational system whereby the helping professions can be organized to resolve the social, financial, psychological, or emotional problems that may be at the root of the disorder. The community mental health approach to mental disorders would appear deserving of both governmental and public support, since it opens the door to wider public remedial services, reduces the need for hospitalization (and hence stigmatization), and involves the community and the family in the rehabilitation process. However, there is concern that, since the community may be partially responsible for the cause of the disorder, keeping those with severe mental disorders in the community may, in fact, be counterproductive, and, in some cases, dangerous. While this argument has some validity, the vast majority of patients with mental disorders pose no physical risk to the community, and the benefits of community integration in the long run far outweigh the serious negative effects of institutionalization.

Institutionalization

The institutionalization of the mentally ill, a longstanding method of treatment, has received immense criticism in the last two decades. A major argument is that prolonged hospitalization, a depressing and depersonalizing experience, can worsen rather than improve the conditions of patients. The validity of the institution as a means of treating mental disorders is being increasingly questioned. One of the major problems is that the institution forces patients to adapt to the needs of the system, creating what Goffman (1961) calls a "total institution," in which the patient loses touch with reality and becomes passive, dependent, and blindly accepting of authority. This situation, which is aggravated the longer the stay in an institution, makes it impossible for the majority of patients to readjust to the outside world once they are discharged. Critics of Canadian mental institutions both within and outside the medical community have pointed out the many instances in which patients' disorders are worsened by the dehumanizing influences of the institution. The majority of patients adopt the "sick role" as a coping mechanism, and since extended periods of hospitalization reduce the probability of successful rehabilitation, they can develop chronic mental illnesses. Health care officials in Canada have responded to the devastating criticisms of mental hospitals by attempting to reduce dependence on institutionalization as the primary treatment mechanism (mental hospitals have become instruments of last resort), and by working toward a goal of voluntary admission of all patients. Community health clinics

Table 11.1
Admissions and Separations in Psychiatric Hospitals, Canada, 1975–1980

Year	Number of Hospitals	Admissions	Separations
1975	59	49,696	51,469
1976	58	45,697	47,384
1977	55	42,814	44,578
1978	55	42,467	42,738
1979–80	46	39,276	38,267

Source: Statistics Canada, *Mental Health Statistics*. Vol 1. *Institutional Admissions and Separations*, Cat. no. 83-204, Ottawa. Reprinted by permission.

have become early-crisis-intervention, detection, and treatment centres. The result has been a drastic reduction in admission of patients to mental institutions. In the period between 1975 and 1980, there was a 20 percent reduction in patient admissions to institutions (see Table 11.1), and a drop from 3.2 to 1.5 per 1,000 population.

While at first glance, the deinstitutionalization of the mentally disordered can be seen as an important first stage in the introduction of community-based treatment programs, the release into the community of so many people, without the adequate provision of out-patient rehabilitative programs, has created severe problems (Stebbins 1988:204), particularly for many of the poor and deprived, as well as for those who lost their families during hospitalization. Isolated, uneducated, and unable or unwilling to cope with their new world, many ex-psychiatric patients form a new "psychiatric ghetto" in our inner cities. Hence the urgent need for increased funding to the community health centres, so that mental health and social services might be successfully integrated.

Conclusion

It should be clear from the above that, in the context of socially based disorders, the community mental health centre is perhaps the most effective in terms of (1) preventing mental disorders; (2) rehabilitating the individual through immediate community intervention; and (3) reducing the stigma attached to mental illness.

Of course, unless there is a significant change in current public attitudes toward mental disorders, the stigma will persist and discourage people from bringing early symptoms to the attention of the helping professions. Research studies (e.g., Talbot 1984:94) show that long-term rehabilitation is not only greatly facilitated by early intervention and treatment, but is also strongly influenced by public attitudes, which must alter if ex-mental patients are to be successfully integrated into the community. On a positive note, given that between 10 and 30 percent of the population experiences some form of mental disorder (Stebbins 1988:182), old prejudices should give way to an awareness of the nature of the problem, and to the realization that an individual from any social group can become affected by a mental disorder.

In conclusion, the complex interrelationship among physiological, emotional, and socio-cultural variables as they affect people suggests that solutions to the problem of mental disorders must involve the interdisciplinary co-operation of medicine, psychology, and sociology. From a sociological standpoint, the causes, consequences, and treatment of mental disorders can be effectively analyzed only if we understand the impact that labelling has on individuals, and, more generally, the critical role that society plays in creating mental disorders.

SUICIDE AS A SOCIAL PROBLEM

The prevalence of suicide in Canada represents a staggering cost in human resources. According to Statistics Canada (1983), between 1961 and 1981 suicide and suicide rates tripled. In 1981, 3,700 people were officially listed as having committed suicide, with another 29,000 having attempted the act. Since these acts are still stigmatized in society, incidences of both suicide and attempted suicide are usually covered up to protect individuals and their families. According to Allen (1977:15), a more reliable estimate would be to double the official rate. Of major concern is the alarming increase of both attempted suicide and suicide among the 16–29 age group.

The suicide rate is higher for males than females (see Figure 11.2). Although several studies report a higher female *attempted* suicide rate, males outnumber females in terms of successful conclusion of the act. While it has been suggested that the stressful nature of male occupations and the traditional role of the male breadwinner, as well as early gender-role socialization, has placed an intolerable burden on men, as women increasingly enter stressful occupations, a corresponding increase in the female suicide rate can be expected.

Other variables associated with suicide rates include marital status, occupation, race, education, and religion. According to Labovitz (1968), married people reflect a lower suicide rate than single, widowed, or divorced persons. The explanation most frequently offered for this phenomenon is that the absence of important social relationships among the single, and the dissolution of these ties among the widowed or divorced, leave them without social constraints.

While suicide rates for the under-age-15 population is minimal, for those between 15 and 29, and for the over-65 age category, the incidence of suicide is higher than normal. Peck (1977:165–170) attributes the

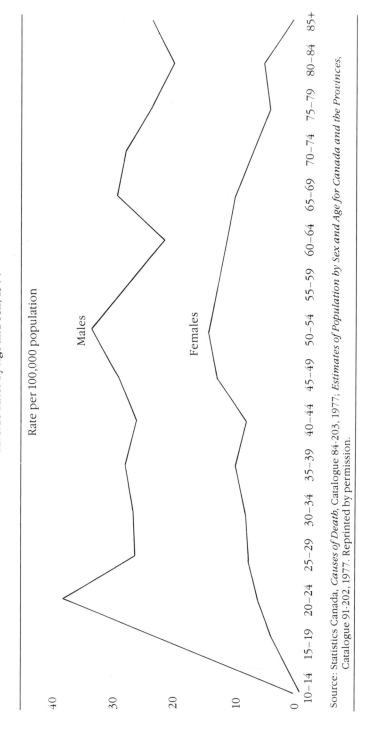

Figure 11.1
Suicide Rates by Age and Sex, 1977

Rate per 100,000 population

Males

Females

40

30

20

10

0

10–14 15–19 20–24 25–29 30–34 35–39 40–44 45–49 50–54 55–59 60–64 65–69 70–74 75–79 80–84 85+

Source: Statistics Canada, *Causes of Death*, Catalogue 84-203, 1977; *Estimates of Population by Sex and Age for Canada and the Provinces*, Catalogue 91-202, 1977. Reprinted by permission.

significant increase in teenage suicide to societal and parental pressures to succeed, which can lead to stress, unhappiness, and humiliation, as well as a lack of communication between teenagers and their parents, leading to isolation. Noting that suicide is the second most common cause of death among college students, Grollman (1971:127) suggests that the stress of developing new friendship and social networks, coupled with the pressure to succeed academically, can place immense emotional and psychological strain on the students, which can lead to depression, and, in extreme cases, suicide.

Of all ethnic and visible minority groups in Canada, native peoples have the highest incidence of suicides, particularly among males between the ages of 15 and 45. Nagler (1975:71–73) attributes the high rate in part to a lack of educational and economic opportunities, social disorganization, and a growing sense of anomie among native peoples, while the contributory variables for Disman (1972) include acute alcoholism, family instability, social and emotional deprivation, low self-esteem, and cultural conflicts.

PERSPECTIVES ON SUICIDE

Few types of human behaviour have received as much scholarly and scientific attention as suicide. To many people it is a puzzling and frightening phenomenon, and is regarded in most of the world's cultures as a deviant act. Negative public attitudes make suicide a manifest social problem, yet most of the studies on the subject seem to focus on the causes rather than the prevention of this act of self-destruction. The classic sociological explanation for suicide was provided by Emile Durkheim (1858–1917), who examined suicide statistics in France around the turn of the century. Durkheim (1951) categorized suicide into three types: egoistic, anomic, and altruistic.

Egoistic suicide, the most common form, usually occurs among individuals who are unable to integrate into social groups that are meaningful to them. The isolated or the elderly, who have either been unable to form close-knit ties or who have lost contact with family or church or friends, are examples of people who are prone to committing egoistic suicide. In contrast, individuals who participate in and are integrated into group structures may be constrained by their involvement from participating in an act that would bring grief and sadness to loved ones.

Anomic suicide occurs under conditions of rapid social or cultural changes, or when norms of behaviour are suddenly destabilized. For example, business persons who have lost a fortune or divorced couples who have had their dreams shattered are in anomic situations where norms of behaviour and social regulations no longer apply. On the other hand, *altruistic suicide* occurs, according to Durkheim, when group norms and group conformity take precedence over individuality. This would include the soldier who sacrifices his life for his country, or the religious fanatic who puts ideology above personal survival.

In contemporary Canadian society, suicide can be viewed as a moral-philosophical, psychological, and sociological problem. Gibbs (1968:2) notes that suicide traditionally has been viewed as a classical "moral" problem. Because it is legally proscribed, and yet condoned, there is a degree of ambivalence about its evaluation. The present debate in Canada over euthanasia as a means of ending terminal or painful illness, and the controversy over the right-to-die movement illustrate clearly the moral dilemma facing theologians, medical practitioners, and, in the final analysis, society itself.

As a *psychological* problem, suicide has been analyzed from three major perspectives. In very simplified terms: (1) Freudians see it as a conflict between love and the death wish, with the Oedipal conflict the source of the personality disorder through which the death wish becomes dominant; (2) Jungians see it as the individual's response to an inability to balance the needs of the self, in which the meaning of life is embodied, with the demands of the ego; and (3), according to Adlerians, suicide occurs when feelings of insecurity and self-hate begin to dominate the personality. All of these theories emphasize the individual personality at the expense of society and the role of its institutions in creating the conditions whereby an individual believes that self-destruction is the only solution.

From the *sociological* point of view, problems arising out of the social system are directly related to suicide. Porterfield (1968) notes that it is society which does or does not accord people satisfying roles, thereby linking the feasibility of suicide to one's social status. Accordingly, the problems in the society that create maladaptations in its people must be analyzed as a first step into solving the problem.

SUICIDE PREVENTION

Given the increase in suicide and suicide attempts in recent years, considerable effort has been made by various helping professions to diagnose and identify those in the population who may be suicide-prone. According to Schneidman (1968), the vast majority of individuals who are planning suicide still wish to have their deaths prevented. Most suicidal behaviour is provoked by the individual's sense of isolation and hopelessness, and the resultant suicide is an attempt to remove the intolerable conditions of life. Table 11.2 attempts to link symptoms with the degree of suicidal risk.

Potential suicides can exhibit four broad types of clues as to their problem. These can be either verbal, behavioural, situational, or syn-

Table 11.2
Assessing the Degree of Suicidal Risk

Behaviour or Symptom	Intensity of Risk		
	Low	Moderate	High
Anxiety	Mild	Moderate	High or panic state
Depression	Mild	Moderate	Severe
Isolation/ withdrawal	Vague feelings of depression no withdrawal	Some feelings of helplessness hopelessness and withdrawal	Hopeless, helpless, withdrawal and self-deprecating
Daily functioning	Fairly good in most activities	Moderately good in some activities	Not good in any activities
Resources	Several	Some	Few or none
Coping strategies/ devices being utilized	Generally constructive	Some that are constructive	Predominately destructive
Significant others	Several who are available	Few or only one available	Only one or none available
Psychiatric help in past	None or positive attitude toward	Yes, and moderately satisfied with	Negative view of help received
Lifestyle	Stable	Moderately stable or unstable	Unstable
Alcohol/drug use	Infrequently to excess	Frequently to excess	Continual abuse
Previous suicide attempts	None, or of low lethality	None to one or more of moderate lethality	None to multiple attempts of high lethality
Disorientation/ disorganization	None	Some	Marked
Hostility	Little or none	Some	Marked
Suicidal plan	Vague, fleeting thoughts but no plan	Frequent thoughts, occasional ideas about a plan	Frequent or constant thoughts with a specific plan

Source: Corrine Hatton, Sharon Valente, and Alice Rink, ed., *Suicide: Assessment and Intervention* (New York: Appleton-Century Crofts, 1977), p.56. Reprinted by permission.

dromatic. In many instances, individuals openly *state* that they are think-
ing of killing themselves, or make veiled threats as to their inability to
cope with life's problems. Too often these threats are not taken seriously
by family and friends, with tragic consequences. Others signal their
intentions in their *behaviour* by attempting the act as a kind of "dry run."
In addition, under *situations* of stress—e.g., medical, financial, or familial
crises—the patient can convey hints of emotional instability that should
be interpreted as warning signs. Finally, in terms of a *syndrome*, the
literature identifies four typologies: depressed, disoriented, defiant, and
dependent-dissatisfied. By far the majority of suicides follow the symptoms of depression.

It is the responsibility of family members, friends, and others close to
the individual to detect the above cues, assess the risk (see Table 11.2),
and attempt remedial action. Given the existence in most communities of
crisis or suicide prevention centres, the goal is to encourage potential
victims to seek aid. The rebuilding of social relationships and networks so
necessary to reducing feelings of isolation and alienation, however, is a
more difficult matter, often necessitating long-term counselling and the
support of other social agencies if the individual is to become integrated
into the society.

In a broader context, strategies for suicide prevention must recognize and attempt to change the social conditions that create an environment conducive to suicide. The early Durkheimian proposition that high
suicide rates characterize those groups that are not socially integrated and
lack "social regulation" still applies today. Teenagers faced with conflicting values, peer pressure, and a perception of not being understood, the
elderly, lonely and isolated and possibly living in poverty, and native
peoples, socially and culturally displaced and existing in a state of anomie
and hopelessness, are examples of groups with high suicide rates and
high indices of social maladjustment. This leaves little doubt as to the
correlation between suicide and social disorganization. Therefore, social
structural change, which places major emphasis on human resources and
solving the problems of socially, emotionally, and economically disadvantaged groups, can go a long way in integrating into society those individuals who feel that their lives are meaningless.

SUMMARY

1. While many forms of mental illness stem from organic or psychological factors, there is a growing sense that the individual's experience in
   society can trigger mental disorders. In this sense, mental disorders
   can be viewed as unresolved problems in living.
2. According to the functionalist perspective, mental disorders can be

attributed to structural dysfunctions in society which lead to stress, isolation, and alienation.

3. Conflict theorists link mental disorders to the tensions generated by the competitive economic systems found in modern industrial societies.

4. In past centuries, the mentally ill, who were seen variously as heretics, witches, and moral degenerates, were subjected to harsh and often brutal treatment. The work of Pinel (1745–1826) gave rise to more humane methods of treating mental disorders. Canada was slow to introduce special facilities for the mentally ill.

5. Modern treatment of mental disorders can involve drugs, psychotherapy, behaviour therapy, and institutionalization. The community mental health approach emphasizes the role of the community and society as a whole in the understanding and treatment of mental disorders. By contrast, institutionalization cuts patients off from the outside world, making it difficult for them to reassimilate into society upon release.

6. The stigma associated with mental illness discourages people from seeking treatment. Some sociologists view the label "mentally ill" as a means of controlling individuals who fail to conform to the established social order. Growing public awareness of the nature of mental disorders will probably lessen the stigma attached to them.

7. The incidence of suicide in Canada, particularly among teenagers, has risen dramatically over the last few decades. Common variables associated with suicide include marital status, occupation, race, education, and religion.

8. In his pioneering study on suicide, Emile Durkheim (1858–1917) categorized suicide into three types: egoistic, anomic, and altruistic.

9. The three major approaches to suicide are moral-philosophical, psychological, and sociological. Sociologists attribute suicide to problems arising out of the social system.

10. Most would-be suicides wish to have their deaths prevented. They may signal this by exhibiting verbal, behavioural, situational, or syndromatic clues as to their suicidal intentions.

11. Ideally, suicide-prevention strategies should recognize and attempt to change social conditions that create an environment conducive to suicide.

12

Crime and Delinquency

INTRODUCTION

According to Silverman and Teevan (1980:3), crimes involve "violations of norms, social rules which attempt to regulate behaviour and tell us what to do and what not to do in various situations." Violations of social rules range from minor violations of social conventions to the more serious violations of important ethical rules, known as society's mores. Most crimes represent violations of mores, and have been defined as harmful to society. Because social control in modern societies is obtained through formal laws enforced by the legal system, one can say that a *crime* is an act that is prohibited by criminal law. While sociologically we can define a crime as a socially harmful act to which penalties are attached, legally a crime is any act forbidden by the legal statutes and punishable under the Criminal Code. In addition, while some acts—e.g., murder—are classified as criminal in order to preserve social order, other acts are prohibited depending on the values of the particular society. Since laws define crime, and as society changes so does its laws, what may be classified as criminal behaviour also changes over time.

Statistics on crime rates across Canada suggest that between 1971 and 1981 crimes increased by 33 percent, with a marked increase in violent crime. It should be noted, too, that a large proportion of criminal activity is never reported to police authorities, and much of what is reported is not officially recorded. However, while criminal statistics do not represent the totality of criminal activity in Canada, from a comparative perspective—taking robbery and murder as indices—Canada demonstrates a considerably lower rate of violence than the United States and most other industrialized nations (Stebbins 1983:409).

THEORETICAL PERSPECTIVES

From the *functionalist perspective*, crime and deliquency are social problems because they produce social disorder and deviance, disrupting the consensus on values and the integration of the society. The common goals of Canadian society, together with the preservation of its social order and the protection of its people, is based on the laws and the legal principles of the Criminal Code. According to functionalists, inadequate socialization and structural deficiencies in society cause people to turn to crime and delinquency to attain their goals. Rather than follow the prescribed channels for goal achievement utilized by the majority, the

deviant, either because of inadequate opportunities or inadequate inter-
nalization of values, choses the non-normative route. According to
Durkheim (1951), modern societies offer the individual greater opportunities for violating social norms because they present less stringent social
controls on behaviour. Furthermore, in a heterogeneous mass society, the
rapid growth of urbanization and industrialization has created a climate in
which deviance can flourish.

According to the *conflict perspective*, by contrast, society is com-
prised of competing interest groups, and it is the ability of powerful
groups to impose their values and laws on the less powerful that defines
normative or non-normative behaviour. Conflict theorists argue that,
while there is consensus on the need for laws proscribing acts of a severe
criminal nature (e.g., murder, rape, or robbery), powerful groups in
society often label "criminal" those behaviours that conflict with their
own interests and values, such as marijuana use (Turk 1969:29). From this
perspective, crime and delinquency are products of a social order that
oppresses the powerless, creating social conditions of deprivation and
alienation. Discussing the political nature of crime, Quinney (1974:291)
suggests that criminal law is an instrument used by the state to maintain
and perpetuate the social and economic order.

No one theory, of course, can adequately explain what causes each
and every form of criminal behaviour. A man does not murder his wife for
the same reason a student uses marijuana, or a father commits incest, or a
woman resorts to prostitution and a man to bank robbery (Silverman and
Teevan 1980:121). The only common thread to these behaviours is that
they are all defined as criminal. Why do only some people who are in
environments that are conducive to crime actually resort to crime? For
example, why do not all slum dwellers become delinquent, if slum-living
is conducive to delinquency? We shall now examine some of the more
important contributions in the literature on this difficult question of
causation.

Since crime is generally perceived to be one of the most socially
harmful forms of deviance, theories of deviance have served as the major
focus in the search for causation. Early deviance theory tried to discover
physical characteristics that would differentiate the criminal from the
noncriminal (see, for example, Lombroso's [1911] study of criminals in
prisons). Research has since shown, however, that there is no common
physical typology of criminals, and further that biological determinism
has no bearing in the study of this socially and culturally related problem
(Sutherland and Cressey 1981).

Crime as a learned behaviour is the dominant focus in the theory of
differential association expounded by Sutherland (ibid). His position is
that one learns criminality in the same way one learns any other
behaviour. If the socialization process provides exposure to deviant

activities and at the same time encourages scorn toward the legal codes, then the seeds will be sown for a career in crime. Using other variables in his theory (including the frequency, degree, and intensity of contact with known criminals, as well as the age at which contact occurs), Sutherland hypothesizes that a person becomes delinquent because of conditions favourable to violation of the law, and that criminal behaviour is a learning process like any other. Despite its clear insights into the criminal subculture, and into the learning process of criminality, Sutherland's theory has become less prominent today, mainly because it offers no clear explanation as to why some persons learn criminal behaviour (while others interacting with the same people do not), and because its concepts are difficult to test in research studies.

A variation of the differential association theory is the *culture conflict* theory of Sellin (1938), which links crime to the norm and role conflict that occurred in the United States during the post-World War II period of high immigration. The thesis has not been particularly useful in its application to Canada, for two reasons. Firstly, immigrants' norms are generally similar to those of Canadian society, and, secondly, crime rates are no higher among immigrants than they are among native-born Canadians. As Silverman and Teevan (1980:138) note, culture conflict cannot be used as a major explanation of criminal activity in Canada.

Merton's (1968) theory of *anomie* attempts to link deviant behaviour to the presence of social disorganization in the society. It suggests that the social structure, by exerting pressure on individuals to become successful, can cause those unable to succeed legitimately to turn to illegal means to attain their goals. The discrepancy between the goals of society and access to the legitimate means to obtain them is classified as anomie. And the greater the degree of anomie in the society, the greater the likelihood of crime occurring, since this state of anomie or normlessness places the individual in a situation where the norms of the society are rejected and behaviour becomes unregulated. Merton, in relating deviance to the norms and values of society, argues that North American society invites deviance and crime by valuing, for example, material possessions but denying people equal access to them. (In general, Merton's theory has been able to explain lower-class crime, rather than white-collar crime.)

In terms of Canadian society, Silverman and Teevan (1980:139) suggest that while there may be less discrepancy between goals and means here than in the United States, in general both Merton's and Sutherland's theories are flexible enough for most of their concepts to be applicable to the Canadian context. It should be noted, however, that these two theories offer only partial explanations of crime causation, and also that, while both societies are culturally similar, there are sufficient differences between them to caution against generalizations.

Subcultural theories of crime causation, put forward by criminologists such as Cohen (1955), Cloward and Ohlin (1981), and Miller and Reissman (1968), start with the basic argument that the cultural values and norms of certain subcultural groups (e.g., delinquent or motorcycle gangs) are in conflict with those of mainstream society. The skid row member, for instance, is likely to violate existing norms and laws, through common activities of the subculture, for example, theft or panhandling. Similarly, as Cohen (1955:66) notes, working-class male adolescents who are frustrated in their attempts to attain middle-class goals often band together, developing new norms and values, and deriving status and self-esteem from within the subculture of the group. Generally speaking, subcultural and delinquent gang theories, while appropriate for analyzing nonconformity among working-class delinquents, do little to explain middle-class deliquency. Furthermore, as Hagan (1984:86) observes, subcultural theories simply explain what we already know, without providing explanations as to the conditions that create the climate for delinquent behaviour. In addition, from a Canadian perspective, gang subcultures are not nearly as predominant in our cities as they are in American cities. The real value of subcultural theories is that they allow us to study groups of people whose values and norms differ from those of the majority.

Because cultural and subcultural theories of criminality focus on social structural problems, many Canadian criminologists have turned to socio-psychological theories, which attempt to focus on individual adaptations to society. Two of these which have gained support in recent years are the social control and labelling theories. *Social control* theory sees crime as the result of inadequate social control over individual behaviour. If the socialization process, which trains us to conform, is ineffective, and the threat of punishment minimal, then people have little pressure to conform and can consequently turn to deviant behaviour. Hirschi (1969) suggests that attachment, commitment, and involvement, as ingredients in the socialization process, are essential if the bond between the individual and society is to be strong enough to constrain the individual from deviating from normative values. Social control theorists argue, therefore, that we could reduce our crime rate not through conventional punishment, but rather through strengthening the socialization process.

The *labelling theory* of criminality, as developed by Becker (1981), suggests that deviance is a social process and that the deviant is simply a person who has been labelled as such by society. Thus, people who engage in certain illegal activities may not regard themselves as "criminals" until the label is attached to them. For example, it is not until teachers, the police, and the courts become aware of petty delinquent behaviour by a teenager that he or she becomes labelled as a delinquent. This imposed label becomes a self-fulfilling prophecy once the individual accepts this definition and begins to act out the behaviour in order to conform to the image, thus establishing the pattern of deviance. Criminologists who have adopted the labelling perspective are concerned with how laws are made, and with distinctions as to why, when, to whom, and under what circumstances the deviant or criminal label is applied.

While labelling theory has become an important source of analysis of criminal behaviour, it has also been widely criticized as having only limited applicability. According to Sagarin (1975:47), the concept of special interest groups enforcing their moral values by labelling certain behaviour as criminal, cannot, for example, be generalized to include violent crime, which is defined on the basis of societal consensus. In addition, the hypothesis that a causal relationship exists between labelled criminal and further criminal behaviour has not been empirically validated. Notwithstanding, labelling theory provides valuable insight into society's role in making rules and labelling rule breakers. Together with the other theories discussed in this section, it has widened our knowledge of crime causation, and hence laid the groundwork for productive approaches to crime prevention.

PATTERNS OF CRIMINAL BEHAVIOUR

Because the term "crime" is an extremely broad one, there is wide diversity in types of crime and criminal behaviour. As we mentioned at the beginning of this chapter, often the only common denominator is that they constitute a violation of criminal law. In this section, the discussion will focus on the following categories of crime: common crime, organized or syndicated crime, white-collar crime, and juvenile delinquency.

Common Crime

Common crimes, which range in severity from petty theft to rape and murder, are committed by a wide variety of people, including occasional, habitual, and violent criminals (Clinard and Meier 1979: Chapter 7). The *occasional criminal* has not made crime a way of life and most often commits theft in the form of shoplifting, vandalism, or larceny. Occasional criminals do not, generally speaking, consider themselves criminal, although if caught and convicted they will undoubtedly be so labelled. *Habitual criminals*, including professional or semi-professional criminals, engage in robberies, burglaries, and larcenies for monetary gain and are confirmed in their way of life. Most of them spend a large portion of their adult lives in prison. *Recidivism*, which means repeating the offence, is high among this group of hard-core criminals who commonly perceive themselves as victims of an unjust society. The *violent criminal* commits crimes such as murder or rape. The majority of homicides occur in the home, are unplanned, and, in over half the cases, involve drinking by both murderer and victim (Jayewardene 1980). With regard to sexual assault, Koenig (1987) notes that the victim and the perpetrator were previously known to one another in more than half of all rape cases. As with homicide, premeditation in rape appears to be minimal, which suggests that crimes of violence may be more situational than deliberate. As Table 12.1 suggests, in recent years there has been a steady increase in most categories of common crime.

Organized Crime

There is little consensus in the literature as to definitions of organized crime. For Stamler (1987: 272–73), organized crime consists of "self-perpetuating, structured, and disciplined associations of individuals, or groups, combined together for the purpose of obtaining monetary or commercial gains or profits, wholly or in part of illegal means, while protecting their activities through a pattern of graft and corruption." Today, according to Stamler (1987:273), there are at least seven major crime groups operating in Canada. The Italian-based Mafia, the oldest and most efficient organization, has been joined by the Chinese Triads, the Colombian Mafia, motorcycle gangs, and other Canadian ethnic-based drug-trafficking groups.

Stamler (ibid) notes that by the 1930s the Italian *Cosa Nostra* crime syndicate was firmly based in Montreal, Toronto, and Vancouver. The Quebec Police Commission Inquiry on Organized Crime (1977) found that the Italian Mafia organization in Montreal was a significant factor in organized crime, with involvement in illegal drugs, prostitution, loan-sharking, and extortion. This organized-crime family syndicate operates somewhat like a corporation, with the godfather or family boss occupying the role of the chief executive officer, the underbosses or lieutenants acting as vice-presidents, heading various branches engaged in criminal activities, and the foot soldiers or lower-level workers engaged in the actual criminal street-level activities.

The *Chinese Triad* organization, which followed the immigration of Chinese to North America, adheres to the basic Triad principles of the parent Chinese organization (Stamler 1987:276–77). These organized crime groups are to be found in the large urban centres of Vancouver, Toronto, and Montreal, and operate in cells, with each cell controlling a particular criminal activity. They operate almost totally within the Chinese community and are involved in drug trafficking, black market activities, gambling, and extortion. As the East Asian population of Canada increases, it is to be expected that Chinese Triad crime syndicates will expand their activities.

The *Colombian Mafia*, which operates in Canada, specifically in drug

Table 12.1
Rates of Adults Charged by Sex Per 100,000 Population for Criminal Code and Federal Statute Offences, 1974, 1978, 1982, 1983, Canada

	1974 Adults Charged		1978 Adults Charged		1982 Adults Charged		1983 Adults Charged	
	Male	Female	Male	Female	Male	Female	Male	Female
Homicide	5.5	0.9	6.2	0.9	5.6	0.7	5.5	0.9
Attempted murder	4.7	0.5	6.2	0.7	7.8	0.9	6.8	0.8
Sexual offences	49.4	0.3	47.5	0.3	48.4	1.3	(1)	(1)
Assaults	389.0	34.6	392.3	40.9	399.7	47.6	(1)	(1)
Robbery	61.3	3.9	69.5	4.9	77.1	5.6	70.4	5.1
Crimes of violence—Total	509.8	40.3	521.6	47.8	538.6	56.1	634.0	66.5
Breaking and entering	340.9	11.8	431.6	17.7	535.9	20.8	538.2	20.8
Theft—Motor vehicle	145.5	4.7	136.2	6.2	119.1	6.6	112.1	6.2
Theft over $200	85.9	10.4	108.0	15.5	178.0	29.7	184.3	29.9
Theft $200 and under	454.8	196.0	517.3	256.5	650.1	291.1	652.9	292.4
Have stolen goods	106.9	11.9	126.3	16.8	145.4	18.4	144.9	19.3
Frauds	192.1	48.9	248.8	73.8	295.0	89.7	289.0	89.4
Property crimes—Total	1,326.1	283.8	1,568.3	386.6	1,923.4	456.3	1,921.4	458.1
Other crimes—Total	1,011.8	126.0	1,234.8	135.6	1,158.2	124.7	1,170.3	133.6
Criminal Code—Total	2,847.7	450.1	3,324.7	569.9	3,620.2	637.1	3,725.6	658.3
Drugs—Total	561.9	61.7	524.9	59.3	426.4	48.1	393.2	46.9
Other Federal Statutes—Total	251.6	19.6	344.6	35.1	150.3	22.8	141.6	22.8
Total	7,152.8	777.1	7,553.6	930.4	7,779.0	1,061.5	7,574.4	1,069.9

(1) Breakdown for these offences is not available due to the proclamation of Bill C-127 in 1983. However, this data has been included in the total crimes of violence category.

Source: *Canadian Crime Statistics*, 1983. Mnister of Supply and Services. Statistics Canada, Catalogue 85-205. Reprinted by permission.

trafficking in cocaine and marijuana, shares with the Italian Mafia a hierarchical and differentiated structure, with each part operating independently but reporting to a central controlling authority (Stamler 1987:278). It is estimated that 75 percent of the cocaine consumed in Canada is provided by this crime syndicate, and that its annual profits run into the hundreds of millions of dollars.

In the last two decades, outlaw *motorcycle gangs* have become a major crime grouping in Canada, with chapters of the major gangs found in the United States now established in most large Canadian cities. The Quebec Police Commission (1977) estimated that the province of Quebec has at least thirty different groups in existence. All of these groups are characterized by a rigid, hierarchical organization that facilitates the group's control over specific territorial jurisdictions. Most groups are involved in the major traditional organized crime activities, including extortion, prostitution, and drug trafficking.

It has been suggested that legalizing the products and services that organized groups provide would be an effective way of reducing organized crime operations. Both the enforcement and detection of organized crime-related activities have proved difficult, often because the crimes involve different territorial jurisdictions, or because the public is unwilling to co-operate with law enforcement agencies, or, most importantly, because in cases involving "victimless" crimes there is no social consensus that these activities should be illegal. Given this state of affairs, it is not surprising that crime syndicates are profiting immensely, and that the authorities seem impotent in their attempts to control or reduce their criminal activities.

White-Collar Crime

White-collar crime involves offences committed by middle- and upper-class members in the course of their business and professional occupations. Although common, such crimes are rarely prosecuted in the courts, and, except for those of a political nature, are seldom publicized. Yet their social and economic costs are enormous, for while in most instances companies, fearing the negative publicity that could arise simply write off the loss on their books, this type of crime can have a corrupting influence on the total organization, and eventually the capitalistic system as a whole.

While embezzlements and stock manipulations receive the lion's share of media attention, the most common form of white-collar crime is *consumer fraud*. Examples of consumer fraud include false advertising, repair fraud, violations of food and drug laws, and violations of the Combines Act by monopolistic corporations. Such frauds are so common that consumers feel helpless against them, and, moreover, public vulnerability to consumer fraud is to a large extent caused by widespread ignorance about our technological society; in other words, we are forced to trust others to satisfy our needs.

While there are in existence many government protection agencies designed to act on behalf of the consumer in cases of illegality, the minimal fines imposed on corporations for breaches of legislation do little to force compliance. According to Snider et al. (1980), in 1975, of the one hundred charges laid under the Food and Drug Act for consumer fraud, the average fine was less than $1,000; there were no imprisonments. Similarly, enforcement of the Combines Investigation Act, which forbids monopolistic practises, shows that in 1974 charges were laid in less than 3 percent of the 4,000 cases under investigation, and that of that 3 percent only two cases were prosecuted. Clearly, there is an obvious and vital need for public pressure on government agencies and the courts to eliminate loopholes in the laws pertaining to white-collar and corporate crime. As Snider et al. (1980) observe, regulating agencies often become controlled by those they are supposed to regulate, and view their function as mainly that of educating corporations to stay within the limits of the law. Rather than prosecuting offenders as criminals, the approach has been to levy minor fines and admonishments.

Juvenile Delinquency

Juvenile delinquency constitutes a major social problem for both the public and criminologists. Young offenders account for over 30 percent of all arrests for property crimes (see Figure 12.1). Over 66 percent of juvenile arrests occur among youths 15 to 18 years of age, with 11 and 12 year olds accounting for 10 percent of the total. The majority of arrests are for property offences, including larceny, auto theft, burglary, and vandalism. In addition, boys outnumber girls five to one in police records. Juvenile delinquency is still mainly an urban problem, with the highest rates in large cities, and the lowest in rural areas.

While the under-age-18 exemption of young offenders from adult criminal prosecution has doubtless improved their chances at rehabilitation by diverting them from the criminal justice system, the system as a whole still discriminates against certain groups of young offenders. According to Hagan et al. (1980), socio-economic status and residential density influence police conceptions of delinquent behaviour; for example, police tend to perceive working-class areas of the city as being more prone to crime and delinquency.

Most research studies have adopted Merton's (1968) theory of anomie to explain juvenile delinquency. This theory sees delinquency as arising from the discrepancy between socially approved goals and opportunities for achieving them. Cloward and Ohlin (1981), in studying the

Figure 12.1
Ratio of Persons Reported Charged by Offence Group, Canada, 1982

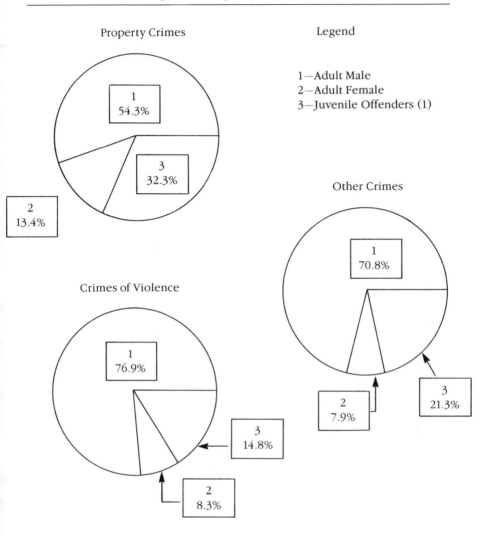

Source: Crime and Traffic Enforcement Statistics, 1982. Statistics Canada, Catalogue
No. 85-205. Reprinted by permission.

growth of the delinquent subculture and the working-class delinquent gang, found that boys who become members of gangs explicitly attribute their failures to the social order, rather than to personal inadequacies. In opposition to these theories, Matza (1964: 15–40), arguing that society has exaggerated the differences between delinquent and nondelinquent behaviour, suggests that most juveniles behave normatively most of the time, and only sporadically drift into deviant behaviour.

Finally, Scott and Vaz (1969) raise the important point that society has emphasized working-class and gang delinquency to the virtual exclusion of delinquency among middle-class youth. Structural changes in society over the last half-century, Scott and Vaz argue, have created opportunities among middle-class youth for extensive adolescent peer group participation, and the emergence of a mass youth culture. It is within the framework of this youth culture that both delinquent and nondelinquent behavioural patterns emerge. Because it occurs in the course of normal adolescent group behaviour, and within the limits of group norms, delinquent behaviour does not lead to the emergence of a separate delinquent subculture for this group. Scott and Vaz (1969) further stress the importance of the peer group in the adolescent socialization process, and the consequent decrease in the importance of parental influence and values. The increase in social status that is derived from conformity to peer group expectations makes conformity the keynote within the middle-class youth culture. Delinquent activities , such as drug use, drinking, gambling, stealing cars, or vandalism, are not perceived as deviant because they stem from legitimate behaviour (e.g., dating, dancing, or having "fun"), and are employed by youth to gain status and prestige among their peers. As such, middle-class juvenile delinquency does not seem to be related to the rejection of cultural goals, or to the inability to achieve desired goals legitimately, to the same extent as working-class juvenile delinquency.

THE CRIMINAL JUSTICE SYSTEM

Introduction

In modern Canadian society, crime is dealt with through an elaborate bureaucracy called the criminal justice system whose basic purpose is to preserve public order and the safety of the citizens. We begin our discussion of the criminal justice system with an examination of the focus and functions of the *criminal laws* upon which it is based.

There are two competing perspectives relating to the functions of law, namely, the "value consensus" (functionalist) and the "interest group" (conflict) theories (Hills 1974:3). The *value consensus*, or functionalist, position holds that criminal laws reflect the social values of the majority and the social consciousness of society as a whole. Underlying this proposition is the belief that society is well-integrated, exhibiting a consensus on basic values by all groups. The legal process, according to Hills (1974:8), simply regulates, harmonizes, and reconciles conflicts between people, always with the goal of enhancing the welfare of the social order. In opposition to this view, proponents of the *interest group* (conflict) theory argue that criminal law in Canada represents the interests of specific groups. Given our heterogeneity and our wide diversity of values and interests, there is minimal consensus in Canadian society on basic values. According to Quinney (1974:29–30), most societies are based upon power, coercion, and constraint, rather than consensus, and therefore laws are formulated and administered by those groups powerful enough to incorporate their interests into public policy.

While both of these theories have some merit, in accordance with interest group theory it can be suggested that Canadian criminal law is, in fact, beginning to reflect the diversified interests of our heterogeneous society. At the same time, value consensus theory is supported by the fact that there is broad public consensus that serious deviation from basic social norms should be punishable by law. It is on the subject of "victimless" crime (e.g., soft drug use) that the interest group perspective gains credence, for in this area there is widespread disagreement among groups, conflicting values, and intense lobbying on the part of powerful interest groups to affect legislation and the administration of justice.

Related to the fundamental purpose of criminal justice in Canada—to protect society and its members from harmful and dangerous conduct—is the idea that no conduct should be defined as criminal if it can be treated in a noncriminal (e.g., social or legal) context. Thus our system tempers the quick use of punishment with concern for human rights. The present dilemma is that, while criminal law emphasizes crime control, the legal rules for the administration of justice emphasize the rights of the accused. The crime control approach to justice is being modified by an increasing emphasis on rehabilitation, as opposed to retribution, as the main goal of the justice system. Let us turn now to the three main branches of this system: the police, the courts, and the corrections system.

The Police

Police officers represent the citizen's first link with the legal system. As the first on the scene after a crime occurs, they can have tremendous impact on the degree to which citizens will or will not feel confidence in the justice system. Only a small percentage of police work directly involves crime. The majority of the police officer's time is spent assisting people, in "peace keeping" functions, and in intervention in domestic disputes.

When involved in crime control, police must walk a fine line between maintaining law and order, and meeting the legal requirements of their authority. That this authority is being exceeded is a question that has been raised in recent years, particularly by minority communities in Canada. In Toronto, complaints by visible minorities about police brutality, harassment, and discrimination have become commonplace (Pitman 1977:38–41). In conclusion, it should be emphasized that, while the police have immense discretionary powers to arrest, these should be discriminately applied in order to avoid placing an intolerable burden on other criminal justice agencies.

The Courts

In Canada's adversarial system of justice, it is through the court system that lawbreakers are prosecuted, convicted, and sentenced. The role of the courts, therefore, is to protect citizens from government control and to uphold the concept of due process. More than 90 percent of Canadian criminal cases are tried in the provincial criminal justice system, and the clearest illustration of how our court system works can be obtained by following an arrested person through the system.

The Canadian Criminal Code requires that an arrested person be brought before a justice of the peace within twenty-four hours of the arrest, or soon thereafter, so as to avoid having the innocent spend time in detention. In an examination of the system in Canada, the Canadian Civil Liberties Association found that, of the accused who underwent a period of pre-trial incarceration, over 66 percent were able to post the required bail, and were set free until their trial. In the sense that posting bail is not an option equally available to all groups in society, it can be said that the system allows for discrimination by socio-economic status. Visible minorities argue that judicial discretion in determining the amount of bail often discriminates against them, as it does for economically disadvantaged groups.

According to Grossman (1974), the majority of criminal convictions are based on the acceptance by the court of a plea of guilty entered by the accused. In most cases, this plea is the result of pre-trial negotiations between defence and prosecuting attorneys. It is estimated that more than half of all guilty pleas are the result of *plea-bargaining* and the reduction of charges, which defendants, lawyers, prosecutors, and judges are pressured to encourage in the interests of efficiency. However, to encourage guilty pleas on lesser charges is to punish the innocent and to reward the guilty. Furthermore, when plea-bargaining results in reduced sentences for serious criminal offences, the deterrence factor operating in our criminal justice system is eroded. In addition, it has been suggested that the procedure discriminates against the poor, who, particularly if held in jail in lieu of bail, are in no position to resist the pressure to bargain. Often the presence of a legal aid lawyer, overburdened and underpaid, makes irresistible the temptation to settle for the best deal, regardless of the innocence or guilt of the accused.

In the Canadian court system, once the accused has been found guilty the magistrate or judge has wide discretion in the sentencing process. While mandatory sentences are applied in cases of first- or second-degree murder, in the vast majority of other cases there are wide variations in fines and jail sentences. For serious offences, variables such as educational and occupational background, length of criminal record, race, pre-sentencing report by officers of the court, character references, and age of the accused can enter into the picture.

The Corrections System

In Canada, the corrections system was formerly looked upon as a form of deterrence. Today, the term refers to the various means that society has adopted in order to manage its criminals. These include imprisonment, probation, and parole. As a theoretical goal, rehabilitation has replaced deterrence as the major goal of the corrections system. However, Cousineau and Veevers (1972:139–140) suggest that the present high rate of recidivism among prison populations shows that rehabilitation is at best minimal and at worst nonexistent.

Excepting certain categories of violent offenders, probation and parole may serve both the offender and society better than incarceration. Under *probation* the offender, subject to specific conditions and the supervision of a probation officer, is released into the community. Properly enforced, breach of the judicial provisions should result in the reimprisonment of the individual. Of all the options available to the courts, probation, a growing phenomenon in Canada, provides the most effective means of rehabilitating the offender within the community. According to the Canadian Committee on Corrections (1974), over 80 percent of all probationers successfully completed probation. Given this high rate of success, and the fact that it costs taxpayers an estimated $40,000 per year to keep an offender in prison, the system should be provided with adequate funding so that it might expand.

The final alternative in the corrections system is to release an inmate into the community prior to the expiration of the legally set prison term. Under *parole* released offenders must meet certain stringent regulations and report to a parole officer in exchange for their freedom. In Canada, all offenders are eligible for parole. For capital offences, the length of imprisonment before parole is clearly stated, while in most other cases it can be granted after one-third of a sentence is served. The National Parole Board is responsible for each candidate as to his or her suitability for parole. Before a parole is granted, the offender must sign an agreement to report to a parole officer and the police department on a regular basis, to accept supervision and maintain steady employment, to obey the law and avoid the company of criminals. Should these conditions be breached, the offender is liable to be returned to prison. It has been estimated that over 80 percent of inmates released on parole do not breach the terms of their release (Cousineau and Veevers 1972:139). However, both native people's groups and the Canadian Civil Liberties Association argue that the conditions for the granting of parole have resulted in visible minorities and the poor having the lowest success rate, first, in obtaining parole, and second, in avoiding violations of their release. (Frequently these groups are disadvantaged when it comes to finding and sustaining employment, are more socially isolated, and are more likely to drift back into the old friendship networks and lifestyles that led to their convictions in the first place. To facilitate parole, more halfway houses are required to alleviate the social adjustment problems of released inmates. Also needed are changes in public attitude, particularly where landlords and employers are concerned, so that the ex-convict can obtain housing and employment, two key variables in long-term rehabilitation.

With regard to the handling of juvenile delinquents, a popular movement in recent years has been to "divert" them from imprisonment in training schools and detention centres. A large part of the incentive to divert young people from the formal court process has stemmed from discontent over the failure of the traditional juvenile court process to rehabilitate youthful offenders. Moyer (1980:76) defines *diversion* as the routine suspension of criminal justice processing that occurs when an accused juvenile is referred to a community program and fulfils the obligations specified by the program. The basic premise is that the young offender, by avoiding the label and stigma of delinquent, may be encouraged to conform to social and legal norms and thereby escape the treadmill of crime.

While there are many variations of diversion programs operating in Canada, the aim of most is to keep youths out of the courtroom, and to channel them into nonjudicial helping institutions in the community. According to Moyer (1980), the underlying goals of diversion are (1) to remove discrimination associated with official processing, (2) to reserve entry into the criminal justice system for only the most serious offenders, (3) to give the victim a role in the justice process, and (4) to return to the community some of the responsibility for dealing with juvenile offenders. In view of the evidence that the label of delinquent can lead young people to adopt the adult criminal role, diversion can be seen as a success. According to Moyer (1980), both court-based and police-sponsored legal diversion programs have operated effectively in the Canadian jurisdictions where they have been tried. With clear and precise goals and objectives, adequate funding and public support, diversion will in all probability continue to be a positive force in handling less severe forms of deviant behaviour among young offenders.

SUMMARY

1. According to the functionalist perspective, inadequate socialization and structural deficiencies are directly responsible for crime and delinquency.
2. Conflict theorists argue that powerful groups in society often label as criminal behaviours that conflict with their own interests and values. In this sense, criminal law is a means by which the social and economic order is maintained and perpetuated.
3. There are five major theories of crime causation. Sutherland's theory of *differential association* views crime as a learned behaviour. Sellin's *culture conflict* theory links crime to the norm and role conflict that occurred in the United States during a period of high immigration. Merton's theory of *anomie* attributes crime to social disorganization. According to *social control* theory, crime results from failures in the socialization process. Finally, *labelling* theorists suggest that individuals are provoked into criminal activity once the label of "criminal" has been attached to them.
4. Common crimes range in severity from petty theft to murder. People who commit these crimes may be ranked as occasional, habitual, or violent criminals.
5. Among the major organized crime groups operating in Canada are the Italian and Columbian Mafias, the Chinese Triads, and outlaw motorcycle gangs. Extortion, prostitution, and drug trafficking are among their main criminal activities.
6. White-collar crime, the most common form of which is consumer fraud, while widespread is rarely prosecuted in the courts. Government agencies generally have been lax in their regulation of corporations.
7. One of Canada's major social problems is juvenile delinquency. Research suggests that both the courts and the police discriminate against young offenders of low socio-economic status. Juvenile delinquency among middle-class youth has not been regarded as a social problem to the same extent as working-class juvenile delinquency.
8. From the value consensus (functionalist) perspective, criminal laws reflect the social values of the majority. Against this position, interest group (conflict) theory holds that criminal laws represent only the interests of specific groups.

9. The three main branches of the criminal justice system are the police, the courts, and the corrections system. The system as a whole must balance the need for crime control with the need to uphold the rights of the accused.
10. The police must walk a fine line between maintaining law and order and staying within the legal limits of their authority. Charges of discrimination, brutality, and harassment are frequently levelled against the police regarding their dealings with visible minority and economically disadvantaged groups.
11. The central role of the courts is to uphold the concept of due process. Plea-bargaining and sentencing in the Canadian judicial system have been found to discriminate against the poor.
12. The corrections system has replaced deterrence with rehabilitation as its major theoretical goal. Research suggests that probation and parole may serve both society and the offender more effectively than incarceration. Canadian courts have lent their support to diversion programs aimed at keeping young offenders out of the courtroom.

13

Drug and Alcohol Abuse

INTRODUCTION

Drugs are an integral part of Canadian society today. According to the Addiction Research Foundation (ARF) (1982), 90 percent of Canadian adults have used alcohol (about 60 percent are regular users), more than one-third of the population smokes tobacco, and over 10 percent have smoked marijuana. Of particular concern has been the use of alcohol and various forms of depressants and "high" inducing drugs among our teenage population (see Table 13.1).

A *drug* can be defined as a chemical that is capable of altering a person's behaviour through its ability to affect moods, thoughts, feelings, or consciousness. The addictive or dependence factor associated with the use of some drugs is widely regarded as the most socially injurious aspect of drug use. Goode (1972:22) makes an important distinction between psychological dependence and *physical addiction*. Addicting drugs like heroin or barbiturates, taken in sufficient doses over a period of time, result in physical addiction, such that if use is discontinued physical symptoms of *withdrawal* occur. By contrast, withdrawal from a nonaddictive drug such as marijuana elicits no physical symptoms. From the sociological perspective, then, the two components in the addiction–dependence problem are not necessarily inseparable.

Table 13.1
Alcohol and Other Drug Use Among Students in Ontario:
Grades 7 to 13, 1977–1983

Drug	% Using Drug at Least Once in Prior 12 Months			
	1977	1979	1981	1983
Tobacco	30.4	34.7	30.3	29.1
Alcohol	76.3	76.9	75.3	71.1
Glue and other Solvents	10.5	10.1	5.5	7.3
Barbiturates	20.2	19.6	20.6	17.0
Heroin	2.0	2.3	1.5	1.6
Stimulants	13.8	16.3	18.2	20.6
Tranquillizers	13.5	12.3	12.6	11.5
LSD and other Hallucinogens	10.4	13.9	14.9	14.6
Cocaine	3.8	5.1	4.8	4.1

Source: Addiction Research Foundation, *Report of Alcohol and Other Drug Use Among Ontario Students in 1983, and Trends since 1977.* Toronto, 1984. Reprinted by permission.

In the Canadian context, *drug abuse* refers to the use of drugs which society, through social norms and the law, has deemed unacceptable and illegitimate. The physical, psychological, or social harm that can result from both legal and illegal drug use suggests that drug abuse as a social problem extends to socially acceptable drugs like alcohol, which, when abused, cause more social and individual problems than the majority of illegal drugs.

THEORETICAL PERSPECTIVES

From the *functionalist perspective*, the use of drugs, particularly in its medical application, is necessary for the maintenance of society, and, as such, is supported by social norms. However, when drug use turns to abuse and interrupts the smooth functioning of the society, it becomes dysfunctional. In other words, drugs become a social problem when they prevent individuals who use them from fulfilling their tasks and goals effectively, thereby promoting imbalance in society's institutions.

The *conflict approach* sees the problem as one of differential values and interests held by heterogeneous groups in the society. In our drug-oriented society, groups attach different values to different drugs. Illegal drugs tend to be labelled as deviant, and their users, when caught and convicted, often have a criminal label attached to them. However, both alcohol and tobacco, which may have more damaging sociological and physiological consequences, are regarded as normal and socially approved drugs. In this conflict of values, the dominant societal reaction is based not so much on the potential for harm in the use of the drug, as on the underlying perception of the group participating in the drug use. For example, when drugs such as heroin or marijuana were largely restricted to poor or marginal groups, they were never considered in terms of a social problem. It was only after their use spread to more influential groups in the society that they came to be seen as such, and accommodations were made; for example, when marijuana use became prevalent in the middle- and upper-classes of society, the laws were modified to limit the harmful effects of the criminalization process for convicted offenders.

From the *deviance perspective*, drugs constitute a social problem when there is a violation of the society's norms regulating their use. The drug abuser is an individual who either has not internalized, or else has rejected, the norms pertaining to drug use. Of interest to the deviance school are the social conditions that give rise to drug abuse. According to Robertson (1980:437), drug abuse can occur through differential association, that is, when people internalize the drug use norms of their subcultural group. As Lolli et al. (1958:15) note, while Italians are socialized into an alcohol-use subculture from childhood, with regular consumption of wine at mealtimes, in the Italian community there is a low incidence of alcohol abuse and alcoholism. On the other hand, in the Irish community, where there is less family-related alcohol consumption, the norms allow instead for periodic heavy drinking as a means of releasing tension and stress. Similarly, alcohol abuse among native peoples may in part derive from the absence in their culture of norms restricting the consumption of this drug, which in a sense has come to be regarded as a panacea for their disillusionment with society.

COMMONLY ABUSED DRUGS

Marijuana

According to Stebbins (1988:152), "after alcohol and prescription drugs, marijuana is the third most widely consumed psychoactive drug in Canada." The Le Dain Commission into the Non-Medical Use of Drugs (1972) reports increasing marijuana use among all social, educational, sexual, and ethnic groups. The use of this drug is considerably higher among high-school and college students, with 25 percent of college students reporting regular use while at school. The reports of the Addiction Research Foundation (1984) and the Le Dain Commission (1972) both indicate that marijuana use is more a legal than a social problem. While research concerning the physiological and psychological effects of marijuana is nonconclusive, the medical evidence suggests that the drug is not addictive. Whether or not to legalize marijuana, therefore, has become the controversial issue. In Canada, opponents of legalization contend that to add marijuana to the already serious problems of alcohol and tobacco abuse would set a dangerous precedent. While the drug may not be harmful in itself, when abused, loss of lives and accidents on the roads due to the effects of the drug can be horrendous. Proponents of legalization, on the other hand, argue that the drug is nonaddictive, has no harmful medical or social effects, is used by over two million Canadians, and has acquired a negative stereotype simply because interest groups have been able to affect public opinion, as well as the laws.

In 1972, the Le Dain Commission recommended that simple possession—but not distribution and trafficking—of marijuana be decriminalized, their main argument being that the label attached to an individual on conviction for simple possession was not justified. (It is estimated that over a quarter of a million Canadians have been visited with a criminal record because of this offence.) However, even though the Commission's recommendations met with widespread support in the legal and academic communities, and in some segments of the public, the law concerning simple possession has not been changed (though, overwhelmingly, fines rather than prison terms are levied, and charges are infrequently laid). Supporters of legalization contend that decriminalization for simple possession would not only remove the criminal label from basically nondeviant people, but it would also allow for the heterogeneity in values among different groups to be accepted. While at the present time public opinion is divided on the legalization issue, making simple possession of marijuana illegal has had no effect on users (except to alienate those who regard the law as hypocritical and discriminatory). At the same time, it has diverted the attention of the criminal justice system away from the serious problems engendered by the abuse of hard drugs such as heroin, cocaine, and a host of narcotics and addictive substances.

Narcotics

Of all the drugs being used by Canadians, narcotics evoke the most concern and fear in the public imagination. A *narcotic* can be defined as an addictive drug that provides relief from pain, reduces psychological distress, and provides a sense of tranquillity and euphoria in its users. Some of the common narcotics include opium and its derivatives, heroin, morphine, cocaine, and artificially created drugs such as methadone and demerol. Of these, the most problematic, in terms of widespread usage and damage to both the individual and society, are heroin and cocaine.

There are usually two paths to addiction. The first one is through the prescription of opiate derivative drugs. The second, and more common, method is through association with heroin and cocaine users, where drugs are initially used for social interaction and recreational purposes. According to Hicks (1975), only one in ten heroin or cocaine users becomes addicted. In 1972, the Le Dain Commission estimated that there were approximately 4,000 heroin addicts in Canada, while, in the same year, the Addiction Research Foundation estimated Canada's addict population at less than 6,000, with 1 percent of the adult population having tried the drug. Heroin addiction is mainly an urban phenomenon that effects males under age 40. In terms of numbers, then, the heroin-addicted population is much smaller than is our alcohol- or barbiturate-addicted population. What makes heroin (and cocaine) addiction such a serious problem is its link with criminal activities, which arises out of the exorbitant costs associated with it. Kasindorf (1975) suggests that the typical working-class heroin addict is under 30, lives in an urban area, has serious health problems, and a shortened life expectancy. Besides hepatitis, AIDS, and other infections related to intravenous injections, the addict often suffers from malnutrition. Addicts, particularly those from a working-class background, commonly resort to crime to support habits that can cost well over $100 a day.

In large Canadian urban centres, a widespread drug subculture has emerged within which users find sources of supply, socialization and interaction, and knowledge of new drugs and techniques. Hartjen (1978:94) perceives elements characteristic of other deviant groups beginning to appear in the growing drug subculture. Addicts are starting to develop a sense of solidarity, an elaborate ideology justifying addiction, status rankings, and the rejection of social norms. Furthermore, as with other groups, the subculture actively recruits new members. Normally, the drug user is forced into a pattern of criminal activity to support his or her habit. If caught and put through the criminal justice system, the individual acquires a negative label that makes reintegration into mainstream society almost impossible. Clearly, our drug laws and policies need reexamination. The assumption that punitive laws and rigorous enforcement will eradicate the use of both soft drugs such as marijuana, and hard drugs such as heroin, has proven erroneous. In fact, drug policies in Canada, which cost millions of dollars to enforce, have inadvertently increased the crime rate, and have contributed to the coffers of organized crime, which controls the importation of narcotics into the country and their distribution. Greater success may be obtained if we address, through rehabilitation programs, the underlying social and psychological problems that drive individuals to drug abuse in the first place.

Alcohol

The Le Dain Commission (1972) estimates that 6 percent of the Canadian population is alcohol-dependent. Between 1968 and 1978, deaths due to alcoholism increased by 75 percent for males, and 100 percent for females (in 1978, there were 1,200 alcohol-related deaths in Canada, including alcohol poisoning and cirrhosis of the liver). And between 1965 and 1980 the estimated number of alcoholics more than doubled, from 283,400 (2,500 per 100,000 population) to 682,000 (4,600 per 100,000 population) [Addiction Research Foundation 1984]. The World Health Organization estimates that, in Canada, alcohol addiction is 100 times greater than narcotic addiction. Hence, the general consensus that alcohol is the most individually and socially harmful drug in our society.

It is important, at this stage, to distinguish the alcohol dependent (or alcoholic) from the problem drinker. The *alcoholic* has an uncontrollable need to consume alcohol in a compulsive and excessive manner, and will, if frustrated in this attempt to achieve a peak of intoxication, develop painful withdrawal symptoms similar to those of narcotics withdrawal, including delirium tremens, nausea, and an increased heart rate (Strauss 1971). By contrast, the *problem drinker* may drink to the point of intoxication without becoming addicted to the drug; health and work problems are common, however, among heavy drinkers.

A variety of physiological, psychological, and sociological factors can trigger alcoholism. For instance, people who are unable to deal with frustration or depression in a constructive manner turn to alcohol as a panacea. As well, many cultures lack prescribed ways of handling alcohol consumption. One of the major problems concerning alcohol use in our society is that despite its potential dangers, it is, as a social facilitator and a pleasurable legal drug, generally accepted in our culture. Significantly, when it stops being a social utility and instead becomes a social and individual menace, the individual, rather than society, is blamed for the problem.

The negative social effects of excessive alcohol consumption are immense. Stebbins (1988:108) estimates that about one-third of all arrests in Canada are related to alcohol abuse, as, more tragically, are roughly one-half of all traffic fatalities and homicides and one-third of all suicides. Of further importance, while historically men were more prone to alcohol use and abuse, the present trend reported by the Addiction Research Foundation (1984) indicates a sharp rise in the female alcoholic population, an important causative factor being the stress that accompanies the high-status positions occupied by increasing numbers of women.

No area of interpersonal life is affected by alcohol abuse as much as the family. The alcoholism of one member can have devastating economic, emotional, and psychological effects on other family members. Marriage to an alcoholic often ends in divorce or desertion instigated by the nonalcoholic partner, who is unable to cope with the alcoholic's inability to perform normal roles. Even if the marriage survives, many alcoholics lose their jobs, with the result that the family drifts into poverty. Julian and Kornblum (1986:134) note that order can return to the household only when one spouse takes over the other's role, becoming the family's major source of financial, emotional, and psychological support. Discussing the lasting emotional maladjustment suffered by children of alcoholics, Cork (1972:275) suggests that the child of the alcoholic is often withdrawn, fearful, and ashamed, has few friends or social networks, and experiences problems in school. These characteristics are particularly common among adolescent children. The presence of an alcoholic parent in the home frequently means that the emotional bond so necessary in a child's life is absent. Finally, Cork suggests that these children often face life with more insecurity and less confidence and self-esteem than the average child. With no one to turn to for emotional support, they can become social isolates involved in anti-social behaviour.

Regarding the link between alcoholism and crime, Thio (1983:368) notes that up to 80 percent of homicides and assaults are committed by people under the influence of alcohol. In addition, especially among the poor, alcohol-dependent persons often turn to crime to support their drinking, and soon find their values and self-concept eroded by the criminal subculture. The criminal justice system, however, with its emphasis on arrests for drunkenness, puts undue strain on law enforcement agencies and clogs up our courts. Alternatives to the "revolving door syndrome," in which the public drunk is repeatedly arrested, sentenced, and released, are explored in the following section.

ALCOHOL AND DRUG REHABILITATION

Canada's major drug problem, both in terms of the social and economic costs and the size of the addict population, is alcohol abuse. Given that alcoholism cannot be legislated away, and that the norms for the use of alcohol have failed to influence the millions of Canadians who abuse it, efforts at prevention and rehabilitation must be increased. However, as noted by the Le Dain Commission (1972) Canada has no organized means of reaching those who are unwilling to seek help, for the social stigma attached to alcoholism remains despite growing recognition that it is a disease. Significantly, even after the problem is acknowledged, the type of treatment available often depends on the person's socio-economic status. In some Canadian provinces, for example, the public drunk is commonly thrown into a "drunk tank" without benefit of medical treatment. The skid row bum experiences an unending cycle of arrests and jail sentences. Only recently has the futility of incarcerating chronic alcoholics begun to seep into our judicial system, with the result that public detoxication centres, where humane treatment is provided the individual, have been instituted in most of our larger cities.

For the general public, while an effective medical method for the treatment of alcoholism has yet to be found, groups such as Alcoholics Anonymous offer moral support and group therapy in which the alcoholic is forced, first of all, to accept the nature of his or her condition, and then to develop a strategy for withdrawal from the drug. This community-based organization has introduced additional programs such as Al-Anon for partners and children of alcoholics. In terms of hospitalization, institutions should develop comprehensive programs, including follow-up care. The Donwood Institute in Toronto, with a rehabilitation success rate of 50 percent, is an example of such a facility. Drugs such as antabuse, which produce violent nausea when used in conjunction with alcohol, can, when combined with other therapy, lead to successful rehabilitation, provided the alcoholic is motivated enough to take the drug regularly. Finally, there is a growing recognition on the part of the public and private sectors that alcoholism is a disease, with increasing referrals of alcoholics by employers to treatment centres. Interestingly, employer-referred alcoholics appear to be more highly motivated than those referred by the courts, perhaps because this group is under immense pressure to succeed given the underlying threat of dismissal.

There are three main approaches to heroin and cocaine addiction: (1) to leave the situation to continue as is, with addicts having to commit criminal acts to support their habit; (2) to provide addicts with the drug, or with a suitable synthetic substitute; or (3) to recognize that the addict can be rehabilitated and offer a form of therapy and treatment. Since doing nothing reduces neither drug-related crime, nor the considerable waste of human potential, the Canadian approach has been, firstly, treatment aimed at total abstinence from narcotics, and, secondly, treatment aimed at less than total abstinence. The evidence suggests that techniques utilizing total abstinence from narcotics are a dismal failure. Le Dain (1972) notes that forced withdrawal, either in a prison, hospital, or therapeutic environment, has a less than 5-percent success rate. According to Vaillant (1970), the conventional model for the treatment of narcotic addiction has been ineffective, particularly in our correctional institutions, where few or no attempts are made to alter the perceptions of inmates toward their drug addiction.

Treatment aimed at less than total abstinence involves the dispensing of the opiate in dependence-maintaining amounts, or else substituting the opiate with another less physiologically harmful drug such as methadone. Once the addict has been weaned from dependence, through reduction of the dosage in conjunction with therapy and support, the rehabilitation process can begin. In Canada, the methadone substitution program has been introduced experimentally in many of our large cities as a way of controlling the heroin addict population. Great Britain has gone further than either Canada or the United States in establishing a register whereby drug addicts can obtain regular doses of their addictive drug from a licensed doctor; in some instances, a heroin substitute such as methadone is also prescribed. Legally registered, the majority of addicts can be controlled and assisted in achieving better social and occupational adjustment. Most importantly, the link between common crime and drug addiction is removed, as addicts are no longer forced to resort to criminal activities to support their habit. While there is evidence that under the British system the number of registered addicts have grown markedly, at the same time, the number of deaths attributed to drug overdoses or other drug-related illnesses have been reduced significantly. Underlying the British practice is an important ideological premise that widely departs from the North American one: the British consider addiction a medical problem, whereas we perceive it as a law-enforcement issue.

Let us turn now to the various self-help and therapy programs that provide housing, counselling, and employment for the addict. Many of these programs follow the model established by Synanon, an organization of ex-addicts founded in the 1960s, which operates in a manner similar to Alcoholics Anonymous in that the "self-help" and "group help" aspects are paramount for successful rehabilitation. On entering the treatment program, addicts must sever all former networks, including family ties before undergoing withdrawal "cold turkey," with the emotional and social support of the group, which plays an important part in probing the factors underlying the drug addiction. The structure of the community is hierarchical and authoritarian, with conformity to the rules enforced by group pressure. While the methods of the program may appear harsh, the goal of altering the personality traits and psychological needs of the hard-core addict is by itself a most difficult task. As Volkman and Cressey (1963) note, however, the success rate for rehabilitation in this form of group-therapy treatment, while less than 20 percent, is higher than for any other method. Unfortunately, the exposure of addicts to programs such as Synanon remains minimal, with less than 5 percent ever entering a treatment program. Given the motivation, the social and psychological predisposition, and the proper environment, the evidence suggests that rehabilitation for the heroin addict, while extremely difficult, is not in all cases impossible.

FUTURE PROSPECTS

The punitive, law-enforcement approach to solving the drug abuse problem has several negative consequences. Instead of recognizing that behind every abuse of a drug—legal or illegal—lies a troubled individual, we brand the users as deviant and process them through the criminal justice system. While the treatment of the alcoholic under the medical model has gained prominence in the last decade, other drug addicts are treated as criminals and implicitly encouraged to turn to crime to support their expensive habits. At the same time, organized crime thrives under the outdated drug policies of the government. Both the Addiction Research Foundation of Ontario (1984) and the Le Dain Commission (1972) have suggested that, since ours is a drug-oriented society, what is considered an abusive drug by the state may not be perceived as such by the groups that use them. Social psychologists and other researchers into the problem have shown that, given appropriate social, psychological, and emotional pressures, anyone can become a drug addict; for example, it is estimated by the Addiction Research Foundation that 5 percent of the medical profession uses drugs excessively.

Without question, the drug problem in Canada is directly related to our culture and social structure. As Rinehart (1987:131) notes, there is a basic discontent in society, with many people seeking to alleviate the stress or frustration in their lives through drugs, whether legal or not. According to Fort and Cory (1975:21), basic social institutions no longer seem to satisfy, family disorganization is growing, bureaucracies make us feel useless and alienated, job dissatisfaction in the industrial world is on the rise, and more and more people from all walks of life are becoming disillusioned and unhappy. It is not surprising, then, that for many in our society drugs have come to represent a form of help and comfort. Until the public shows more support for the medical approach to rehabilitation of the addict, and understands that rapid social and cultural changes have made more people prone to drug use, drug abuse will remain a problem.

Turning now to the inconsistency in labelling some drugs legal and others not, it is clear that whatever activity becomes defined as a social problem is dependent on how significant others interpret the activity, and, further, that this interpretation varies over time; for example, drug abuse as a social problem is dictated by our present drug laws, and is related to the traditional beliefs of influential groups in the society. Ironically, the most strictly controlled drugs are not the most dangerous to society (e.g., marijuana and heroin, while illegal, pose fewer health hazards than barbiturates, alcohol, or nicotine, which are legally obtained and which used indiscriminately can have devastating social consequences). A greater degree of rationality, therefore, is essential to our approach to drugs if positive solutions to the problem are ever to emerge.

In conclusion, Canadian drug policies clearly are bankrupt both in terms of enforcement and finding long-term solutions to the problem. While we may not agree with Szasz's (1974) position that *all* drugs should be legalized regardless of their potential ill-effects, we should at least examine the role of government in regulating what drugs we use. Certainly, if the use of a drug, be it alcohol or heroin, harms others then state involvement and punishment for drug abuse is entirely justified. However, since legislation and strict enforcement have proven ineffective in terms of reducing the numbers of drug users, it may be a more useful option for society to concentrate on the socially abusive aspects of *all* drugs. The artificial distinction between legal and illegal drugs, through which arbitrary moral values are imposed on groups, is not feasible in a heterogeneous society like ours.

SUMMARY

1. According to the functionalist perspective, drug use becomes a social problem when it prevents individuals from fulfilling their roles, thereby creating imbalances in the social structure.
2. Conflict theorists argue that the distinction between legal and illegal drugs is related not so much to the harmful effects of drugs in either category, as it is to powerful interest groups imposing their values and moral codes on others.
3. Reports on marijuana use suggest that it is more a legal problem than a social problem. In Canada, debate centres on whether or not to legalize the drug. The Le Dain Commission's (1972) recommenda-

tion that simple possession of marijuana be decriminalized has yet to be passed into law.

4. Of the narcotics, heroin and cocaine represent the greatest threat to both the user and society as a whole. Users commonly turn to crime to support their addiction. A community of addicts, or drug subculture, has become an integral part of Canada's large cities.

5. Stringent drug laws have failed to eradicate either soft or hard drug use. Greater success may lie in putting more of our resources into self-help and therapy programs aimed at addressing the social and psychological problems that drive people into drug addiction.

6. Between 1965 and 1980, the estimated number of alcoholics in Canada more than doubled. While alcohol abuse constitutes Canada's major drug problem in terms of social and economic costs, alcohol enjoys a high degree of social acceptability.

7. Alcohol abuse can have a psychologically and economically devastating impact on the family. Research suggests that the children of alcoholics suffer lasting emotional maladjustment.

8. Strong links have been established between alcohol and crime. However, the economically disadvantaged alcoholic—the "public drunk"—is needlessly shuffled and reshuffled through the criminal justice system in what is known as the "revolving door syndrome."

9. While there is no effective medical treatment for alcoholism, group therapy (e.g., Alcoholics Anonymous) and drug therapy can lead to rehabilitation. Socio-economic status has been found to be a major factor in determining the method of treatment available to the alcoholic.

10. With regard to the treatment of the hard drug addict population, Canada has three basic options:

- to preserve the status quo, thereby perpetuating addict involvement in crime;
- to adopt the British model whereby addicts are registered and provided with drugs under a doctor's supervision;
- to concentrate resources in rehabilitation programs and public education campaigns.

14

Deviant Sexual Behaviour

INTRODUCTION

Given the heterogeneity of values in Canadian society, it is not surprising that definitions as to what constitutes acceptable sexual behaviour continue to be debated. In analyzing this problem, it is important to remember that there is no biologically normal or abnormal type of sexual behaviour in human beings (Davis 1971). Any distinction, therefore, between normal and deviant sexual patterns is cultural and societal in its basis. The human being is capable of sexual satisfaction through a wide range of activities, including homosexuality, fetishism, pedophilia, masturbation, oral, anal or genital intercourse, bestiality, heterosexuality, exhibitionism, masochism or sadism (Buckner: 1971:7). Canada accepts some of these activities while prohibiting others, in both legal and social terms. Today, formerly illegal activities such as homosexuality have gained legal, if not social, acceptance.

Why do certain sexual acts provoke public hostility and condemnation? Goode (1978: 297) notes that what makes a sexual act deviant is its inappropriateness along one or another of the following dimensions: "(1) the degree of consent, (2) nature of the sexual partner, (3) nature of the sex act, and (4) setting in which the sex act occurs." Thus our laws prohibit rape, which involves an absence of consent and violence. In addition, our norms of sexual behaviour proscribe certain sex partners, including those of the same gender, close relatives, minors, and animals. Other aspects of our sexual behaviour that are classified as deviant include the selling of sexual favours (prostitution), the selling, acting in, making, and, in some instances, purchasing of pornographic materials, and the public display of sexual acts (exhibitionism).

THEORETICAL PERSPECTIVES

The *functionalist approach* gives us some insight as to why some forms of sexual behaviour—in particular, homosexuality, prostitution, and pornography—are labelled deviant and stigmatized. Stebbins (1988:68) suggests that in earlier times the maintenance of the society depended on a stable family system with high birth rates. Heterosexual intercourse, therefore, was regarded as the functional way to sustain population growth and economic stability, while homosexuality, particularly if condoned and popularized, was seen as a potential instigator of immense social disorganization in the society. Similarly, prostitution contributed nothing to the reproduction rate, as well as undermining the stability of the family institution. Finally, prostitution, pornography, and homosexuality, being highly visible forms of sexual experience, further threatened marriage and the family by exposing to the public non-normative forms of sexual behaviour. Today, we have modified our position on many forms of sexual behaviour. The relationship between sex and reproduction is minimal, while small families are perceived as functional. Other traditional attitudes and values, however, have not adapted as quickly to our heterogeneous society, and the majority of Canadians still believe that certain sexual activities are abnormal and should be rejected.

From the *conflict perspective*, given the diverse interests, lifestyles, and values of our heterogeneous population, divergencies from sexual norms within the society are inevitable. At issue is a clash between the values of those groups who feel that sexual variation should be tolerated, and the values of those groups who believe that the state has a moral and legal responsibility to regulate the sexual behaviour of its citizens. The debate, which centres on the legal and civil rights of homosexuals, spills over into such issues as the legalization of prostitution, the effects of pornography on children, the sexual inequality of women in pornographic materials, and the rights of the state to censor.

HOMOSEXUALITY

Of the many forms of sexual variance practiced in Canada, homosexuality is one of the most stigmatized, despite the fact that its legal status as a deviant form of behaviour has been removed for acts committed in private. *Homosexuality* can be defined as the limitation of sexual interests to members of the same sex. As Goode (1978:361) notes, in the face of widespread hostility, fear, and denunciation, most homosexuals still keep their sexual preferences hidden from heterosexuals, thus involving themselves in deception, play-acting, and an elaborate presentation of self to the outside world. The homosexual community faces myriad forms of discrimination, in employment, housing and social services, as well as from the police, and from gangs who fear no reprisals for their acts of violence against a stigmatized minority (Adam 1978:24). It is not surprising, therefore, that the homosexual community in Canada identifies in many ways with our discriminated-against visible minority groups.

While it is difficult to assess the size of the homosexual community in Canada, Salamon (1988) estimates that 4 percent of the population is exclusively homosexual, while another 4 percent is bisexual, that is, engaging in or sexually stimulated by both homosexual and heterosexual acts. The problem with estimating incidence is that, while the public neatly categorizes people into two sexual categories, people fall in a continuum between the two (see Figure 14.1). Hunt (1974:310) suggests that 10 percent of American males and 5 percent of females have had extensive homosexual experience. It has been estimated that the homosexual *lifestyle*, which involves active participation in the subculture and the adoption of a homosexual self-concept, has been taken up by no more than 20 percent of the homosexual community. Despite widespread public disapproval, homosexuality and the homosexual lifestyle continue to attract many. Social and natural scientists, in attempting to provide explanations as to the processes by which people become involved in this form of sexual behaviour, have proposed theories involving such variables as biological determinism, early childhood experiences, family environment, social learning, and self-definition.

The *biological* explanation of homosexuality suggests that genetic or chromosomal factors predispose an individual toward either homosexuality or heterosexuality. In other words, people are "born that way." This theory, which does not explain the wide variations in rates and patterns of homosexuality among cultures (or among groups within the society), becomes more plausible when coupled with social and environmental factors.

The *psychological* school has analyzed in depth early childhood socialization and the family environment as determinants of homosexuality. Bieber (1962) found that a significant number of male homosexuals have domineering, possessive mothers and ineffectual or hostile fathers, while female homosexuality is strongly correlated with broken homes, in which the child strongly prefers one parent over the other. This theory, however, fails to account for the fact that many heterosexual people also come from broken or conflict-ridden family environments. Furthermore, as Bell et al. (1981) note, in most instances there are no personality differences between homosexuals and heterosexuals. Therefore, psychological factors, while they may play a role in the decision of an individual to become homosexual, do not offer a complete explanation in terms of causation. In this sense, the Canadian Psychiatric Association's position that homosexuality is not a mental illness supports those homosexuals who do not consider their sexual behaviour or their lifestyle abnormal.

Sociological explanations have stressed the conditions under which the behaviour is learned, as well as the processes whereby individuals come to identify and define themselves as homosexual. The basic contention is that social or situational factors play an important role in the decision to engage in homosexual acts or to participate in the homosexual lifestyle and subculture. Because our society frowns on heterosexual relationships at the very early stages of sexual development, it is not surprising that the first sexual activity for many young people is a homosexual one. Homosexuality is also widespread in institutions such as prisons or the armed services where heterosexual contacts have tradition-

Figure 14.1
The Kinsey Heterosexual–Homosexual Continuum

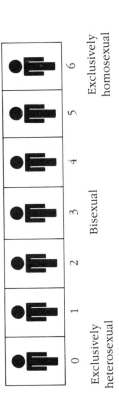

Exclusively   Bisexual   Exclusively
heterosexual   homosexual

0. Exclusively heterosexual
1. Predominantly heterosexual, only incidentally homosexual
2. Predominantly heterosexual, but more than incidentally homosexual
3. Equally heterosexual and homosexual
4. Predominantly homosexual, but more than incidentally heterosexual
5. Predominantly homosexual, but incidentally heterosexual
6. Exclusively homosexual

Source: Adapted from Alfred C. Kinsey, Wardell B. Pomeroy, and Clyde E. Martin. *Sexual Behavior in the Human Male* (Philadelphia: W. B. Saunders, 1948), p. 638. Reprinted by permission.

ally been barred. In most instances, participants engage in these activities either as a form of sexual gratification, or out of fear of violence, motivations that do not make them homosexual in terms of identity or lifestyle. It is when individuals perceive themselves as homosexual and take on the lifestyle and behavioural patterns expected of them, that their self-definition is completed. Finally, in terms of labelling theory, it has been suggested that a person labelled as a homosexual by his or her significant others—e.g., friends or family—may be more likely than otherwise to accept the definition and act out the expected role.

What all of the above conceptualizations suggest is that only a multifaceted approach, involving both predisposing and situational factors, can provide us with insights into causation. At the present time, however, there remain many unanswered questions as to why, in the face of powerful social norms proscribing the behaviour, so many individuals become exclusively homosexual.

While much has been written about male homosexuality, in terms of both lifestyle and subculture, little has been reported about the female homosexual or lesbian. This may be due to the fact that lesbians have not been seen as societally threatening by powerful interest groups, nor have they formed subcultures or publicized their lifestyle to the same extent as male homosexuals. Goode (1978:387) suggests that the most striking difference between male and female homosexuals "has to do with the nature of their sexual—and emotional—relationships." Gagnon and Simon (1973:139) note that male homosexual acts tend to be relatively anonymous and impersonal, with 60 percent reporting at least two hundred partners. Further, the vast majority reported that their homosexual affairs lasted less than one year, and that more than half of their partners in casual relationships were strangers. (However, given the present AIDS epidemic in the homosexual community, there has been a decrease in promiscuity among members of the group, and an accompanying rise in stable monogamous relationships.) Lesbians, in contrast, tend to have fewer and longer-lasting sexual relationships, with romantic and emotional involvement figuring more prominently than for male homosexuals. In this respect, they more closely resemble their heterosexual sisters. Kinsey et al. (1953:336), for example, found that the number of sexual partners for homosexual and heterosexual women was virtually identical, with the majority having sex with one partner, and less than 10 percent with six or more partners (Saghir and Robins [1973:59] note a similar pattern). The implication here is that, for women, whether heterosexual or homosexual, romance and commitment, and the total person are more important to the relationship than sex. Goode (1978:196) observes that, while male homosexuals have a more intense genital fixation, lesbians see their orientation as mainly a romantic issue, and their lifestyle as a way of being.

Saghir and Robins (1973:236) note further differences between male and female homosexual lifestyle in terms of "cruising" and place of sexual activity. While more than one-half of urban male homosexuals engaged in sex both in public and private locales, none of the female homosexuals in their sample had ever engaged in sexual activity in a public place. Finally, less than half of the male homosexuals in the Saghir/Robins sample had had previous sexual relations with a woman, while 80 percent of lesbians reported sexual intercourse with men at least once. In addition, the majority of lesbians in the sample had received marriage proposals, a fact that belies the notion that lesbians are sexually undesirable to men. According to Stebbins (1988:75), the evidence suggests that most lesbians seem to have lost emotional or sexual interest in men after negative experiences in their relationships with them.

In the last decade there has evolved in Canada—particularly in our large cities—an active homosexual community, which, first of all, provides an escape from the pressures of being a minority in an unfriendly environment, and, secondly, acts as a base for the socialization of new members into the norms and values of the homosexual subculture. Bruner (1981), while noting the diversity to be found among Toronto's gay population, suggests that it is bound together as a community by a common identity, and by common goals and interests. In short, it is a well-organized group with a well-defined system of interaction and communication, and growing economic and political strength. Bruner estimates the Toronto homosexual community to number around 200,000, making it the largest in Canada. Community centres, restaurants, and bookstores have been established in Toronto to cater to this growing market. In addition, the downtown gay scene includes dozens of gay bars and other entertainment centres for male and female homosexuals.

The issue of homosexual acts in public places has created an immense furor in our large cities—particularly Toronto—in the last few years. The locales that best represent impersonal sex in Toronto include steam baths, public washrooms, and public parks. Bruner (1981) suggests that members of the gay community in Toronto first engage in public sex during the secretive or fearful stage of their "coming out," at which time they are facing up to their homosexuality. Regardless of the rationale for their utility, police raids on bath houses and other public places frequented by homosexuals have generated much of the conflict and hostility between this minority and the police, who represent the guardians of public morality. In the absence of understanding and co-operation between these two groups, the present climate of suspicion and animosity can be expected to continue. Notwithstanding, liaison committees comprising both members of the police and the homosexual community, as established in Vancouver, can be seen as an example of a positive approach in the application of the Criminal Code to sexually related matters.

PROSTITUTION

While prostitutes can be male or female, and can sell their sexual favours to same- or opposite-sex clients, in Canada the vast majority of prostitutes are female. As with homosexuality, the condemnation of prostitution is linked with moral and religious values, although Bell (1971:227) notes that, historically, "in some Eastern religions prostitution was a basic part of the religion itself and sometimes involved sacred prostitutes." By contrast, Western religions became obsessed with "sins of the flesh," with the result that restrictions on all types of sexual expression were over a period of time built into the culture. In Canada today, however, while soliciting for the purposes of prostitution is illegal (prostitution per se is not), most Canadians neither condemn nor condone the behaviour. We only become concerned when prostitution becomes associated with other social problems (e.g., child prostitution, drug addiction, and the spread of venereal diseases or AIDS).

Why do men turn to prostitutes? According to Bell (1971:231), for those men who are unable to compete for women, either because of emotional insecurity or physical or mental handicaps, the prostitute provides a sexual outlet without risk of rejection. Some men may, as well, wish to avoid emotional involvement with women, and by paying for sexual favours feel no obligation or responsibility. Still others may have unusually high sexual needs, or may find that they can only have their fantasies fulfilled in a formal prostitute–client relationship. To a large extent, prostitution reflects the values and institutions of society as a whole. In a male-dominated society, prostitution serves to devalue and oppress women, and to cater to the whims, desires, and pleasures of men. Goode (1978:331) argues that prostitution is a reflection not of a permissive society, but a repressive one. That is, as long as sexual freedom is restrained by institutions such as marriage, and by cultural repressions, the needs of the populace will only be fulfilled through the formal mechanism of prostitution. Most clients of prostitutes are sexually deprived men who for various reasons have become prisoners of the restricting verbal, emotional, and behavioural games of masculinity, and for whom the prostitute serves in a confessional as well as sexual role.

Explanations as to why women become prostitutes have been as varied as the number of books written on the subject. Greenwald (1970:406) records early family experiences of parental conflict, neglect, and rejection as common variables in the prostitutes he studied; many, too, had financially rewarding sexual experiences with older men and came to look upon sex as a commodity that could be used for monetary gain. As Benjamin and Masters (1964:93) observe, prostitution brings far greater economic rewards than most other occupations given the level of education and skill it requires. This may be the major predisposing factor, with the anticipation of "glamour" and "adventure" a subsidiary reason. Interestingly, Lemert (1972:105) notes that prostitutes rarely have any moral guilt about their role, and are usually quite secure in their lifestyle. As a society, however, we refuse to accept that prostitution could be a rational occupational choice taken by some women. To a large degree, the label of deviant we attach to the prostitute (or the homosexual) is a rationalization by the majority to compensate for the fact that some in society have rejected total conformity to mainstream values.

Similar to other groups that exhibit deviant lifestyles, many prostitutes function within a subculture. In fact, the largest proportion of sexual events defined as prostitution take place in this subcultural setting, a social network of pimps, police, customers, and other prostitutes (Gagnon and Simon 1967:10). Regarding the link between prostitution and drug use, a widespread subcultural activity, Lemert's (1972:105) sample found a higher incidence of drug use leading to prostitution than vice versa. As in the homosexual community, it is within the subculture that the roles and norms related to the practice of prostitution are learned. Given the negative image of prostitution, the introduction of the apprentice into the life is an important and significant stage. Generally, both the street prostitute and the higher-status call girl drift into the profession without much conscious planning. The specific skills and values are learned through imitation and through tutoring by an experienced practitioner. While competition is keen among prostitutes, because theirs is a deviant and hence isolated occupation, a degree of interdependency usually develops among them; in times of sickness or arrest, the commonality of interests works to their collective advantage. As a business person, the prostitute's major goal is to please the customer and obtain repeat business. In her code of behaviour, the customer can depend on confidentiality and anonymity.

We conclude our discussion of the subculture in which the prostitute operates with a brief examination of the role of the pimp. While call girls frequently work on their own, the majority of streetwalkers are dependent on pimps for a number of things. Perceived by society as the lowest form of social parasite, the pimp takes the bulk of his prostitute's earnings and at the same time functions as her lover, bodyguard, business manager, and, in some instances, her drug source (Bell 1971:243). According to Bryan (1965), the pimp's main function is psychosexual in nature, with the sexual relationship forming the strongest bond between himself and the prostitute. Hirschi (1969:202) discerns a similarity between the pimp–prostitute relationship and the husband–wife relationship, with the economic roles reversed. Whereas mainstream society views the relationship with contempt, and from a middle-class perspective, Hirschi feels that the occupational roles are symbiotic and, from a working-class perspective, reasonably functional.

While the continued existence of prostitution in Canada appears more or less secure, at the same time it is unlikely that the activity will ever be totally decriminalized. In fact, because of public furor in various parts of Canada—particularly Vancouver, Toronto, and Halifax—over the increased visibility of prostitutes in residential areas, the laws against soliciting are being toughened. As our values relating to sexual expression change, however, more women may begin to view their sex lives in a more positive light and be less tempted by the economic lure of prostitution, while men may feel less compelled to seek out prostitutes for recreational sex. Of course, there will always be people, unable to obtain sexual partners in the normative way, for whom prostitutes will remain the sole source of sexual outlet. In addition, the world of the high-price call girl and the escort agency, which caters to the pleasures of big business, seems unlikely to wane in popularity. In short, although sexual freedom among women in and out of marriage may decrease the need for paid sex, the role of the prostitute will always be functional to certain groups in society.

What are Canada's options with regard to prostitution? The two basic ones are (a) to continue to view it as a deviant activity punishable under the Criminal Code, or (b) to introduce measures to legalize and regulate the activity—a position adopted by such groups as the Canadian Organization for the Rights of Prostitutes (CORP). Given the ambivalent attitude of a male-dominant society toward this form of sexual behaviour, it seems that the trend will be to condone the activity as long as it remains invisible—a trend reflected, for example, in the thriving operation of "hidden" massage parlours in our cities. Similarly, if street walkers can avoid becoming public nuisances, they also may find their activities increasingly tolerated. In the case of juvenile prostitution, the Fraser Report on Prostitution and Pornography (1985) recommends a thorough investigation into its causes, the establishment of more halfway houses for teenage runaways and prostitutes, and the instituting of measures for their social rehabilitation.

PORNOGRAPHY

Pornography can be defined as written or visual sexually explicit material designed to produce sexual excitement and stimulation. At the present time, there is widespread disagreement over the social effects of pornography. Part of the difficulty in resolving the problem lies in the subjectivity with which it is viewed. For some individuals and groups, *Playboy* and *Penthouse* magazines are pornographic, while for others only live sex shows and adult movie houses fall into that category. While the legal definitions have been modified over time, the Criminal Code of Canada defines as pornographic material lacking in social value, which portrays sexual conduct in an offensive way. Significantly, community standards play an important role in the interpretation by the courts of what material can be deemed "offensive" and "without social value." What this means, essentially, is that what may be viewed as pornographic in a small community like Belleville, Ontario, may not be classified as such in a heterogeneous city like Montreal, with its more liberal values and multifaceted interest groups. The Criminal Code also gives provincial governments the right to restrict the access of minors to pornographic material. In some provinces, this is accomplished through censorship boards and the licensing of adult movie houses and bookstores. Finally, as agents of the government, the police have the right to seize material they deem pornographic and to arrest the distributors of these materials.

Central to the pornography debate are questions concerning the potentially negative social and psychological effects of visual or written pornography. Does exposure to pornography contribute to the number of sexual assaults in society, and to the general debasement of women? Research is split among two models: the catharsis model and the imitation model. The *catharsis model* suggests that pornography acts as a safety-valve mechanism, permitting individuals to act out their fantasies harmlessly. Polsky (1972) draws an analogy between pornography and prostitution as "functional alternatives." Both provide, he suggests, "for the discharge of what society labels antisocial sex, i.e., impersonal, nonmarital sex: prostitution provides this via real intercourse with a real sex object, while pornography provides it via masturbatory, imagined intercourse with a fantasy object."

On the other hand, proponents of the *imitation model* argue that pornography stimulates aggressive tendencies in males, and that in most forms of hard-core pornography women are treated as sexual objects to be debased and exploited, an attitude which men exposed to pornography carry over into their own lives, thereby contributing to sexual violence against females in general. Indeed, over the last decade the content of pornographic materials available in the mass media has become more sexually explicit, violent, and debasing to women. Researchers have suggested that, compared to soft-core pornography with its emphasis on the simply "erotic," hard-core material, which is based on the exploitation of women, is unequivocally negative in terms of its societal impact. Donnerstein (1980), for example, found that pornography which portrays sex in conjunction with violence against women can lead to increased aggression and feelings of domination in men. Thus the imitation model, which links pornography and sexual violence, cannot be dismissed lightly.

In terms of societal attitudes toward pornography, a 1982 Gallup poll indicated that 75 percent of Canadians believe that pornography encourages people to commit sex crimes. Feminist groups in Canada have adopted the position that crimes of violence against women (including wife abuse, incest, and sexual assaults) are encouraged by pornography. On the issue of child pornography, civil libertarian groups, which denounce censorship of all forms on the grounds that our Charter of Human Rights guarantees a free press, find themselves in a highly unpopular position, for, while public opinion is divided on the societal effects of adult pornography, there is enormous public demand that the government protect children from being exploited as the subjects of sexually explicit written and visual material. On the consumer level, while industry self- regulation and other informal controls may be useful in monitoring pornography for adults, there is strong public support for tough policies that will reduce the availability of pornography to minors, in addition to successfully prosecuting the producers and distributors of child pornography.

In conclusion, despite what critics have condemned as their socially harmful effects, pornographic materials will in all likelihood continue to be widely available, in large part because of the considerable public demand. As a solution to the problem, censorship simply drives the product underground, making it even more difficult to control, and allowing organized crime syndicates to reap immense profits. The most utilitarian approach may be to enforce the recommendations of the Special Committee on Pornography and Prostitution (Fraser 1985) to restrict the availability of pornography to those people who wish to be exposed to it, and to introduce legal measures to protect our youth from exploitation.

LABELLING AND SEXUAL DEVIANCE

What are the effects of labelling on individuals and groups? A summary of the literature reveals that rule breakers labelled "deviant" by others can become entrenched in deviant roles and thus excluded from resuming normal social roles in the community (Gibbons and Jones 1975:148). Douglas (1970:367) argues that the official people-processing organizations are primarily responsible for creating career deviance (e.g., prostitution); that official stigmatization, in other words, does more than anything else to alter an individual's social self and self-image, thereby provoking a commitment to a deviant lifestyle. According to the labelling school, then, society's imposition of negative labels on people, far from being a means of dissuasion, may actually compel them into adopting a permanent nonconformist behaviour. Labelling homosexuals or prostitutes "deviant" does not lead to their readjustment into normative society.

All it does is to create homosexual or prostitute subcultures whose members act out the deviant roles expected of them, attempting to obtain emotional or psychic gratification apart from the majority group that spurned them. When homosexuals campaign for the protection of their human rights, they are in large part attempting to alter community norms and remove the stigmatizing label they have been assigned.

Along with the labelling of all forms of nonconformist behaviour, we must reappraise efforts to legislate morality, which have so far had little success. Prostitution and homosexuality, for example, are still here despite societal condemnation and punitive laws, and public demand for pornography has not diminished. The fact is, Canada is a heterogeneous society, diverse and multifaceted in its values and normative standards. We must, therefore, begin to approach the issues discussed in this chapter with an understanding and acceptance that interests and lifestyles among groups inevitably vary, and that nonconformity to the majority's moral codes does not necessarily translate into deviance.

SUMMARY

1. Distinctions between sexual deviance and social normality are based upon socio-cultural rather than biological factors.
2. In the past, according to the functionalist perspective, sexual acts were considered deviant if they did not contribute to high birth rates and the overall stability of the family system. While the emphasis today on small families has altered perceptions of sex as exclusively a reproductive function, certain sexual activities continue to be stigmatized by the vast majority of Canadians.
3. Conflict theorists suggest that divergencies from sexual norms are inevitable in any heterogeneous society. Sexual deviance is a social problem only because powerful interest groups insist on imposing their sexual values on others.
4. Despite its legal status, homosexuality is one of society's most stigmatized forms of sexual behaviour. As do visible minorities, homosexuals face widespread discrimination in such areas as employment, housing, and social services.
5. There are three major theories of causation with regard to homosexuality. Proponents of the *biological* explanation suggest that genetic factors predispose an individual toward either homosexuality or heterosexuality. In the *psychological* explanation, early childhood socialization and the family environment are regarded as the major determinants of homosexuality. Finally, from the *sociological* perspective, homosexuality is a learned behaviour (i.e., caused by a variety of social and situational factors).
6. For various reasons, female homosexuality has received significantly

less attention than male homosexuality. Lesbianism is generally considered the less socially threatening of these two forms of sexual deviance.

7. The past decade has seen the evolution of a homosexual subculture and the emergence of homosexual rights groups in our large cities. The subculture serves a primary socialization and interaction role for homosexuals. A climate of suspicion and hostility has developed between the police and the homosexual community.

8. While men turn to prostitutes for a variety of reasons, women generally become prostitutes for monetary reasons. Prostitution can be said to reflect the values of a male-dominated society in which women are devalued.

9. Most prostitutes operate within a subculture, or social network, consisting of pimps, police, clients, and other prostitutes. Within this subculture, the aspiring prostitute is socialized into accepting the norms and rules associated with the life.

10. While it is unlikely that prostitution will ever be totally decriminalized in Canada, it will probably continue to be tolerated, so long as it remains invisible. Even with positive changes to social values relating to sexual expression, prostitution will probably always serve a functional role for certain groups in society.

11. There is little consensus as to the potentially harmful effects of pornography on society. Community standards play an important role in interpreting pornography as it is defined in the Criminal Code.

12. According to the *catharsis model*, pornography acts as a safety-valve mechanism, permitting people to act out their fantasies harmlessly. By contrast, advocates of the *imitation model* argue that pornography stimulates male aggression, thereby contributing to violence against women.

13. While public opinion reflects ambivalence on the issue of adult pornography, there is widespread support for tough policies designed to eliminate child pornography and to protect minors from exposure to adult pornography.

14. According to labelling theory, the labels that society imposes on individuals may inadvertently provoke them into adopting nonconformist behaviours. Attempts to legislate morality have similarly failed to eliminate sexual deviance. Approaches to nonconformist behaviour, therefore, must take into account the heterogeneous nature of Canadian society.

Epilogue

Our objective throughout this text has been to analyze the causes and consequences of social problems from a Canadian perspective, and to suggest options for reducing them. We enter the post-industrial world with the knowledge that rapid social, economic, and cultural change over the last three decades has precipitated many of the social problems that now confront us—problems that will only become exacerbated if our organizations and institutions fail to accommodate the new and complex values, attitudes, lifestyles, and groups arising out of change.

To examine the relationship between rapid change and social problems more closely, as Horton and Leslie (1978:701) note, social problems normally occur as a result of the breakdown of traditional social systems, brought on by social change. In Canada, the price we have paid for modernization and increased individuality has been an intensification of many of our social problems. In contrast to more traditional systems, where consensus on values was easily obtained, in today's world the erosion of established ways of asserting control and authority has served to heighten social and group conflict. And since the pace of social and cultural change is not uniform in our institutional structure, some parts of that structure have adapted to change more rapidly than other parts. For instance, while many groups have changed to reflect the impact of technological and communication advances, our legal system plods on with archaic codes of law and methods of social control. However, the interdependence of all the components of our social system inevitably requires that change in one institution be followed by readjustment in another.

Canada today is in the midst of this search for a renewed equilibrium. The task is a formidable one, for institutional breakdown is occurring at an alarming rate. Our post-industrial economy has not eradicated—and in some cases has worsened—problems of worker alienation, bureaucratization, and unemployment. In addition, severe strains have been placed on the nuclear family as groups labelled deviant attempt to displace traditional values by directly challenging the legal system and established codes of behaviour. Such challenges are timely, for, generally speaking, our social and cultural institutions have not kept pace with the advances of science and technology that have been the hallmark of Canada's development in the last four decades. Yet as Toffler (1980) comments, the post-industrial era, with its increased information flows and complexity of social interaction, demands that old ideologies and old ways of problem solving give way to new approaches.

Critical to any new approach will be a holistic rather than fragmentary examination of social problems. It is senseless, for example, to suggest Alcoholics Anonymous as a long-term solution to the high alcoholism rate among native peoples. Any lasting solution to the problem will be the end result of long analysis of the role and status of native peoples, and specifically the anomie and social disorganization that characterize their lives. Similarly, in our approach to ageism we must take into account the ethnic and socio-economic heterogeneity of the aged population and be prepared to adopt a wide diversity of solutions to deal with the multifaceted problems facing seniors today. Finally, in terms of our youth subculture, we must abandon the common (but misguided) belief that deviation from conventional behaviour is by itself abnormal.

On the positive side, we have become more aware of problems in our midst. We are taking steps to improve the social and ecological environment. In terms of urban decay and crime rates, Canadian cities are models for other countries to replicate. The issue of worker alienation is beginning to be addressed by all partners involved—workers, management, and government. Public pressure to improve conditions for seniors has brought unprecedented attention to their problems. However, although we have taken positive steps to remedy these and other acute conflictual problems, our approach has remained one of segmentalization. Almost always, problems are seen as isolated issues, which is why policy recommendations are so often piecemeal and fragmentary. Our inability to develop comprehensive and co-ordinated solutions to our pressing social problems is due in large part to our failure to confront these issues as interconnected and overlapping.

Another crucial factor in the development and implementation of solutions to our social problems is public opinion. Traditional values and attitudes must give way to new ways of acting and behaving. Efforts to improve the economic status of the poor or the aged will undoubtedly involve some degree of financial sacrifice on the part of more privileged groups. Similarly, the technological innovations needed to solve our environmental problems will place a heavy financial burden on both government and big business, and will invariably necessitate that moral, ethical, and economic choices be made. Unfortunately, at the present time it would appear that Canadian public opinion has not been aroused to the extent that an ethic of activism for solving our social problems can be said to be imminent. On a more positive note, growing public awareness and concern over problems that were once latent in the public consciousness is an important first stage in the long road to reform.

How will we cope with social problems in the twenty-first century? According to Bell (1973:53), Western technological society shows signs of a radical disjunction that will spell its eventual decline. He suggests that our emphasis on rational bureaucracy, impersonality, and the values of the Protestant work ethic appears to be on a collision course with social and cultural change, and predicts increasing group and class conflict. By contrast, Kahn (1976) foresees a bright technocratic future, with continued growth and prosperity for western industrialized societies. In all likelihood, we will neither collapse as a society nor produce the kind of social engineering that would effectively eliminate all of our social problems. In typical Canadian fashion, we will probably continue to respond swiftly to nation-threatening problems, as we did when Quebec sought sovereignty-association, and to introduce changes to mitigate our most serious social problems. On the majority of issues, however, we can anticipate that the societal consensus necessary for the implementation of structural changes in the social and economic system will be less easily achieved.

SUMMARY

1. Modernization and a greater emphasis on individuality have led to an intensification of many Canadian social problems. The erosion of traditional systems has heightened social and group conflict, while, at the same time, the failure of the institutional structure to keep pace with social and cultural change has resulted in the breakdown of many institutions.
2. In the post-industrial era, old ideologies and methods of problem solving must give way to new approaches to social problems. The examination of social problems must be holistic rather than fragmentary if we are to develop comprehensive, co-ordinated, and long-term solutions.
3. Public opinion is a crucial factor in determining our response to social problems. While public opinion has not been aroused to the extent of promoting an ethic of activism with regard to social problems, growing public awareness of formerly latent problems is a positive sign.
4. Sociologists vary in their predictions as to how western industrialized societies will deal with social problems in the twenty-first century. Some anticipate eventual decline, others a bright technocratic future. Canada will probably continue to react swiftly only to those problems on which there is a high degree of societal consensus.

Glossary

Absolute deprivation. The absence of basic necessities.

Addiction. Physical dependence on a habit-forming drug, the discontinuation of which produces physical withdrawal symptoms.

Ageism. Discrimination against the elderly, which is reinforced by stereotypes and misconceptions about the aged.

Alcoholics anonymous. Alcohol rehabilitation program emphasizing group therapy.

Alienation. Workers' feelings of powerlessness, meaninglessness, and isolation over their lack of control over the organization and conditions of the workplace.

Altruistic suicide. Durkheim's classification of a suicide that occurs in situations where group identity and loyalty take precedence over individuality.

Anomic suicide. Durkheim's classification of a suicide that occurs in situations where norms of behaviour and social regulations no longer apply.

Anomie. A term used by Merton to describe the deviance that results when individuals are unable to attain goals through legitimate means.

Automation. A system in which the functions of the workplace are performed, controlled, and regulated by automatic means.

Behaviour modification. Management strategy for improving worker productivity and satisfaction through the manipulation of intrinsic motivations.

Behaviour therapy. Treatment of mental disorders in which therapist's goal is to replace negative behaviour patterns with positive ones.

Bureaucracy. An organizational structure characterized by a hierarchical arrangement of officials who have specific tasks, and who work under formal rules.

Case study. Research method employed by sociologists to examine a phenomenon in considerable depth.

Catharsis model. Theory that pornography acts as a safety-valve mechanism, permitting people to act out their fantasies harmlessly.

Chinese triad organization. Organized crime groups which operate in large urban Chinese communities, and which adhere to the Triad principles of the parent Chinese organization.

Citizens' groups. Special interest groups of concerned citizens whose aim is to decentralize the power structure and increase public input into the decision-making process.

Cohabitation. See *Common-law relationship*.

Colour-class thesis. Perspective that attributes discrimination to the historical relationship between white society and visible minorities.

Columbian mafia. Organized crime syndicate primarily involved in drug trafficking.

Common crime. Crimes ranging in severity from petty theft to murder, and committed by a wide variety of people.

Common-law relationship. Cohabitation outside of legal marriage.

Communal marriage. See *Group marriage.*

Community. Primary group ties among people who share common goals, interests, and experiences over time.

Community mental health. Form of medical treatment stressing the role of the community and society as a whole in the causation of mental illness.

Compulsory retirement. See *Mandatory retirement.*

Conflict perspective. A sociological view emphasizing the conflict between competing groups in society.

Conglomerate. A large holding company that controls various companies in different areas of production and manufacture.

Consensus perspective. See *Functionalist perspective.*

Consumer fraud. Common form of white-collar crime. Includes false advertising, repair fraud, and violations of food and drug laws.

Corporate crime. See *White-collar crime.*

Corporate state. An interchangeable structure of power created by the alliance of government and big business.

Cosa nostra. In Canada, crime syndicate based in Montreal, Toronto, and Vancouver.

Crime. An act that violates criminal law.

Criminal subculture. Environment that socializes new members into adopting criminal roles and values.

Cultural discrimination. See *Discrimination.*

Culture of poverty. Theory attributing the cycle of poverty to the inability of the poor to transcend debilitating cultural characteristics.

Cycle of poverty. The continuation of poverty through generations.

Decriminalization. Removal of a specific act from the Criminal Code.

Delinquent subculture. Response of working-class youth to their failure to attain middle-class goals. Also perspective on deviance developed by Cohen.

Demography. Scientific study of the size, composition, and distribution of human populations.

Depersonalization. The loss of self, power, and personal autonomy, brought on by the constraints of institutional life.

Deviance. Variation from a social norm.

Differential association. Process by which deviant behaviour is learned through maximum exposure to deviance and minimal exposure to normative values.

Discrimination. The practice by which a majority group denies a minority group equal access to opportunities, resources, and social rewards. There are three types of discrimination:

a) **Individual discrimination**. A blatant form of discrimination resulting from the conscious act of a prejudiced person.

b) **Institutional discrimination**. Discrimination arising out of the values of a prejudiced society.

c) **Cultural discrimination**. A subtle form of discrimination by the majority culture against minority cultures.

Diversion. Routine suspension of criminal justice procedures against an accused juvenile, followed by referral to a community program.

Division of labour. Specialization in the production of goods and services whereby work roles are fragmented and the worker is separated from the end product.

Drug abuse. Violation of social rules concerning the regulation, acceptability, and legitimate use of drugs.

Drug subculture. Environment within which individuals are socialized into patterns of drug use.

Due process. Procedural safeguards in the legal system designed to protect the public from arbitrary government power. The Criminal Code guarantees all accused persons the right to speedy trial, bail, legal counsel, and the assumption of innocence until proven guilty in a court of law.

Ecology. Science of the mutual relationship between organisms and their environment. Human ecology studies the relationship between human groups and their environment.

Egoistic suicide. Durkheim's classification of a suicide that occurs in situations where people lack the ties of strong group interaction that would normally constrain them from acting out suicidal feelings and attitudes.

Environment. Conditions and circumstances surrounding and affecting the development of an organism or group of organisms.

Equality of opportunity. Equal access of all groups in society to social rewards.

Ethnic group. Individuals who share distinctive cultural traits, beliefs, values, attitudes, and customs.

Ethnicity. Characteristics shared by an ethnic group.

Ethnocentrism. Tendency to evaluate all groups and cultures in terms of one's own cultural standards and values.

Experiment. A basic component of sociological research.

Extended family. A family unit comprising a nuclear family plus other relatives.

Extrinsic motivation. Workers' concern with pay and job security.

Fertility. The number of births to women of childbearing age, measured as the crude birth rate.

Functionalist perspective. A sociological view emphasizing the relationship between parts of the system and the system as a whole.

Gender role. Expectations, responsibilities, and personality traits based upon gender.

Geriatrics. Medical specialization dealing with old age and its diseases.

Gerontology. Scientific study of aging and the problems of the aged.

Group marriage. Two or more couples living together as one marriage unit.

Group therapy. Psychotherapy practised in a small group setting, in which members learn to change negative behaviour on the basis of insights gained from group interaction.

Guaranteed national income. Proposal that would guarantee the working poor an income above the poverty line.

Habitual criminal. Professional or semi-professional offender for whom crime is a confirmed way of life.

Homosexual subculture. Community in which new members learn the values, norms, and lifestyle patterns of homosexuality.

Homosexuality. Sexual feelings, fantasies, and acts directed toward members of the same sex.

Imitation model. Theory that pornography stimulates male aggression, thereby contributing to violence against women.

Individual discrimination. See *Discrimination.*

Industrialization. Organization of work in a factory environment where labour and management are separated in the production of goods and services.

Inner city. An urban environment characterized by physical deterioration, overcrowding, poverty, unemployment, racial and ethnic segregation, and a disproportionately high crime rate.

Institutional discrimination. See *Discrimination.*

Institutionalization. The placing of the elderly and mentally ill in institutions where all aspects of their lives are controlled.

Interpersonal relations model. Theory that examines marriage on the basis of internal and external sources of gratification, and constraining factors.

Intrinsic motivation. Workers' concern with autonomy, creativity, shared decision making, and innovation on the job.

Job dissatisfaction. See *Alienation.*

Juvenile delinquency. Crimes committed by offenders under the age of 18. Also refers to noncriminal acts (e.g., truancy, loitering, or incorrigibility) that contravene norms for adolescent behaviour.

Labelling. The imposition of labels on people, such that they are forced to relinquish normative roles and behaviours. Labelling theory contends that deviance would be vastly reduced with the elimination of negative labels.

Latent problem. A condition whose existence society must be aware of and perceive as threatening before it is labelled a social problem and targeted for remedial action.

Leisure. Activities outside the workplace, which nevertheless are affected by work activities.

Mafia. See *Cosa nostra*.

Mandatory retirement. Forced retirement of workers at age 65.

Manifest problem. A latent problem made manifest by public awareness of its existence.

Migration. Movement of individuals or groups from one place of residence to another, either within a country or from one country to another.

Multiculturalism. Federal government policy legitimizing the rights of ethnic and visible minority communities to maintain their cultural distinctiveness.

Multinational corporation. A large business company with subsidiaries—known as branch plants—in other countries.

Narcotic. Addictive drugs that produce feelings of euphoria in users.

Nationalism. Advocacy of national unity or independence. Nationalism may be cultural, economic, or political in its emphasis.

Native peoples. In Canada, term used to refer to the following categories: registered treaty Indian, registered nontreaty Indian, nonregistered Indian, Métis, and Inuit.

Neurosis. A functional disorder that stems from irrational anxiety commonly attributed to familial, employment, or group pressures.

Norms. The shared rules and expectations that dictate appropriate and acceptable behaviour in society.

Nuclear family. Family unit of a married couple and their dependent children.

Occasional criminal. Criminal who has not made crime a way of life.

Open marriage. Marital relationship in which both parties are free to seek emotional and sexual gratification outside the unit.

Organized crime. Large-scale and co-ordinated operation of criminal groups primarily involved in gambling, drug trafficking, prostitution, and pornography.

Parole. Release of an inmate from prison, under a parole officer's supervision, prior to the expiration of his or her sentence.

Plea-bargaining. Commonly practised procedure in which the accused enters a plea of guilty in exchange for a reduction of charges.

Pluralism. The recognition of social and cultural differences among various racial and ethnic groups. *— and accomodation* *— by la. the ~ system. gay.*

Pornography. Written or visually explicit material intended to cause sexual stimulation and excitement.

Poverty line. Amount of income needed to meet basic survival needs.

Power elite. Group that occupies the strategic command posts in the corporate structure.

Preferred status. Immigration policy provision discriminating against ethnic and visible minority groups.

Prejudice. A set of emotionally rigid attitudes based on faulty generalizations, which causes, supports, or justifies discrimination.

Probation. Court disposition whereby offenders are released into the community under the supervision of a probation officer.

Prostitution. Exchange of sexual favours for monetary rewards.

Protestant work ethic. A cluster of values, attitudes, and beliefs, which promotes hard work, frugality, asceticism, and success.

Psychosis. A grave mental disorder that can take the form of schizophrenia, or affective disorders such as depression.

Psychotherapy. Treatment of mental disorders in which a trained therapist attempts, through verbal interaction with the patient, to delve into the cause of the disorder, and then to resolve the conflicts associated with it.

Quality of working life (QWL). Programs designed to make the workplace a more humane and fulfilling environment.

Race. Arbitrary classification of human populations according to biological criteria.

Racism. The belief in the genetically based inferiority and superiority of different racial groups. Racism comprises *ethnocentrism, prejudice, stereotypes,* and *discrimination*.

Rationalization. A process whereby rules, regulations, orders, and hierarchies of positions are formally established in large organizations.

Recidivism. Tendency to fall back into criminal activity upon release from jail.

Reciprocal exchange model. Theory that the family unit should be based upon a sexual division of labour.

Regionalism. A sense of common identity and attachment to one's region, often accompanied by a separate ideology and value system.

Relative deprivation. The inability of individuals to achieve the higher standard of living enjoyed by others.

Residential concentration. The presence of significant numbers of people of similar racial or ethnic background in a particular urban geographical area. Also known as *residential segregation*.

Sample survey. Social research method which provides information on social characteristics and attitudinal changes over time.

Schizophrenia. A common type of psychosis characterized by disorganization in personality, thought patterns, and speech, withdrawal from reality, delusions, and hallucinations.

Single-parent family. A family form comprising a single parent and dependent children.

Social disorganization. Breakdowns in norms and institutions, often precipitated by rapid social and cultural change, which can result in normlessness and cultural conflict.

Social mobility. Upward or downward movement from one social class or status group to another in the social stratification system.

Social pathology. A model based on organic theory which suggests that social problems are caused by "sick" people who are incapable of operating within the normative structure.

Social problem. A condition affecting a significant number of people, which is perceived as a threat to social norms and values.

Social role. Behaviour which an individual has learned to enact in response to the expectations of others.

Social stratification. Hierarchical arrangement of roles and positions in society.

Socialization. Complex learning process through which individuals acquire the knowledge, skills, and motivation required for participation in society.

Sociogenic aging. Aging based on psychological/emotional factors rather than physical factors.

Stereotype. Exaggerated mental picture based on the presumed characteristics of a given social group.

Stranger thesis. Perspective that attributes discriminatory behaviour to the antipathy of the majority group toward the appearance and behaviour of minority groups.

Structural-functionalist perspective. See *Functionalist perspective*.

Structured inequality. Inequality in the social structure that prevents equality of opportunity for all groups in society.

Subculture. Group that differs from the dominant group in terms of its norms and values.

Subsistence conception of poverty. Refers to the above-average expenditure of income on food, clothing, and shelter.

Synanon organization. Drug rehabilitation program emphasizing self-help and group therapy.

Total institution. Term coined by Goffman to describe institutions— e.g., mental hospitals—where the individual is totally controlled by outside forces, and where the uniformity of social experience results in alienation and dehumanization.

Urban blight. Parts of the urban landscape considered undesirable by the majority of urban residents.

Urban renewal. Programs designed to improve housing conditions and living standards for inner-city residents. In Canada, the stabilization of neighbourhoods is a primary goal.

Urbanization. The demographic, economic, and socio-cultural changes that affect cities as a result of population increases.

Value conflict. Clashes between the values and interests of competing groups in society, which can create social problems.

Values. Socially based measures of what is desirable and worthwhile, and upon which the goals of a society are based.

Vertical expansion. Obtaining control or ownership of firms that produce at different stages in the manufacture of a product.

Visible minority. A term used to refer to native peoples, blacks, Asians, and others of non-European descent.

White-collar crime. Crime committed by a person of high socio-economic status in the course of his or her occupation. Such crimes include bribery, fraud, and embezzlement.

Withdrawal. Physical and psychological symptoms experienced by addicts upon the discontinuation of the addictive drug.

Zero population growth. Stationary population that results from an equalization of the birth and death rates.

References

Abella, R. 1985. *Equality in Employment*. Ottawa: Supply and Services Canada.

Adair, D. and J. Rosenstock. 1977. "Explaining Racial Attitudes Among Adolescents." *Multiculturalism* 1: 5–9.

Adam, B. 1978. *The Survival of Domination: Inferiorization and Everyday Life*. New York: Elsevier.

Adams, I. et al. 1971. *The Real Poverty Report*. Edmonton: Hurtig.

Addiction Research Foundation. 1982. *Statistics on Alcohol and Drug Use in Canada and Other Countries*. Toronto: Addiction Research Foundation.

Addiction Research Foundation. 1984. *Annual Report: 1983*. Toronto: Addiction Research Foundation.

Adler, H. and D. Brusegard, eds. 1980. *Perspectives Canada III*. Ottawa: Statistics Canada.

Allen, N. 1977. "History and Background of Suicidology." In C. Hatton et al., eds., *Suicide: Assessment and Intervention*. New York: Appleton-Century Crofts, 1977.

Baker, P. 1978. "Theory and Practice: Problems with the Mosaic Concept in Black Policy Formation." In V. D'Oyley, ed., *The Black Presence in Multi-Ethnic Canada*. Vancouver: Faculty of Education, University of British Columbia.

Balakrishnan, T. R. et al. 1985. "Contraceptive Use in Canada, 1984." *Family Planning Perspectives* 17(5): 209–15.

Becker, H. 1981. "Outsiders." In E. Rubington and M. Weinberg, eds., *The Study of Social Problems*. 3rd ed. New York: Oxford University Press.

Bell, A. and S. Weinberg. 1978. *Homosexualities: A Study of Diversity Among Men and Women*. New York: Simon and Schuster.

Bell, A. et al. 1981. *Sexual 'Preference': Its Development in Men and Women*. Bloomington: Indiana University Press.

Bell, D. 1973. *The Coming of Post-Industrial Society: A Venture in Social Forecasting*. New York: Basic Books.

Bell, D. 1987. "Regionalism." In M. Rosenberg et al., eds., *An Introduction to Sociology*. 2nd ed. Toronto: Methuen.

Bell, R. 1971. *Social Deviance: A Substantive Analysis*. Homewood, Ill.: The Dorsey Press.

Benjamin H. and R. Masters. 1964. *Prostitution and Morality*. New York: Lubian.

Berkowitz, S., ed. 1984. *Models and Myths in Canadian Sociology*. Toronto: Butterworths.

Berry, J. et al. 1977. *Multiculturalism and Ethnic Attitudes in Canada.* Ottawa: Supply and Services Canada.

Bieber, L. et al. 1962. *Homosexuality.* New York: Basic Books.

Blau, Z. 1973. *Old Age in a Changing Society.* New York: New Viewpoints.

Boyd, M. and Kenneth Mozersky. 1975. "Cities: The Issue of Urbanization." In D. Forcese and S. Richer, eds., *Issues in Canadian Society.* Scarborough: Prentice-Hall.

Breton, R. 1983. "West Indian, Chinese and European Ethnic Groups in Toronto: Perceptions of Problems and Resources." In J. Elliott, ed., *Two Nations, Many Cultures.* 2nd ed. Scarborough: Prentice-Hall.

Brody, E. 1973. "The Aging of the Family." *Annals of the American Academy of Political and Social Science*, pp. 423–33.

Bronson, H. 1979. "Multi-National Corporations and Canadian Food Policy." In J. A. Fry, ed., *Economy, Class and Social Reality.* Toronto: Butterworths.

Bruner, P. 1981. "The Homosexual Community in Canada." In the *Body Politic.* Toronto.

Bryan, J. 1965. "Apprenticeships in Prostitution." *Social Problems* (Winter): 287.

Buckner, H. 1971. *Deviance, Reality and Change.* New York: Random House.

Cadwallader, M. 1966. "Marriage as a Wretched Institution." *Atlantic Monthly* (218).

Cairns, A. 1977. "The Government and Societies of Canadian Federalism." *Canadian Journal of Political Science* (10): 695–709.

Campbell, A. et al. 1976. *The Quality of American Life: Perceptions, Evaluations and Satisfactions.* New York: Russell Sage Foundation.

Canadian Committee on Corrections. 1974. *Report of the Canadian Committee on Corrections.* Ottawa: Information Canada.

Canadian Mental Health Association. 1983. *Report on the Mental Health of the Nation.* Ottawa: Canadian Mental Health Association.

Canadian Teachers' Federation 1970. *Brief to the Senate Committee on Poverty.* Ottawa.

Cardinal, H. 1977. *The Rebirth of Canada's Indians.* Edmonton: Hurtig.

Carisse, C. 1976. "Life Plans of Innovative Women: A Strategy for Living the Feminine Role." In L. Larson, ed., *The Canadian Family in Comparative Perspective.* Scarborough: Prentice-Hall.

Caskie, D. M. 1979. *Canadian Fact Book on Poverty.* Ottawa: Canadian Council on Social Development.

Chafetz, J. S., 1974. *Masculine, Feminine or Human?: An Overview of the Sociology of Sex Roles.* Itasca, Ill.: Peacock Press.

Chambliss, W. 1973. "The Saints and the Roughnecks." *Society* 2: 24–31.

Chan, K. 1983. "Coping with Aging and Managing Self-Identity: The

Social World of the Elderly Chinese Woman." *Canadian Ethnic Studies* 15(3): 36–50.

Church, J. 1978. "Two Fly Over the Cuckoo's Nest." *New York Times Book Review*, March 26, 11.

Clement, W. 1975. *The Canadian Corporate Elite: An Analysis of Economic Power.* Toronto: McClelland and Stewart.

Clement, W. 1980. "A Political Economy of Regionalism in Canada." In J. Harp and J. Hofley, eds., *Structured Inequality in Canada.* Scarborough: Prentice-Hall.

Clinard, M. and R. F. Meier. 1979. *Sociology of Deviant Behaviour.* 5th ed. New York: Holt, Rinehart and Winston.

Cloward, R. and L. Ohlin. 1981. "Illegitimate Opportunities and Deviant Behaviour." In E. Rubington and M. Weinberg, eds., *The Study of Social Problems.* 3rd ed. New York: Oxford University Press

Cohen, A. 1955. *Delinquent Boys: The Culture of the Gang.* New York: Free Press.

Coleman, J. and D. Cressey. 1984. *Social Problems.* Cambridge, Mass.: Harper and Row.

Coles, R. 1970. "A Fashionable Kind of Slander." *Atlantic Monthly* (226): 54.

Commoner, B. 1971. *The Closing Circle.* New York: Knopf.

Connidis, I. 1987. "Life in Older Age: The View from the Top." In V. Marshall, ed., *Aging in Canada.* 2nd ed. Toronto: Fitzhenry and Whiteside.

Conservation Council of Ontario. 1981. *The State of Our Environment.* Toronto: Conservation Council of Ontario.

Cork, M. 1972. *The Forgotten Children.* Toronto: Paperjacks.

Cousineau, D. and J. Veevers. 1972. "Incarceration as a Response to Crime: The Utilization of Canadian Prisons." In C. Boydell et al., eds., *Deviant Behaviour and Societal Reaction.* Toronto: Holt, Rinehart and Winston.

Coward, B. et al. 1974. "The Culture of Poverty Debate: Some Additional Data." *Social Problems* 21: 621–34.

Cuneo, C. 1978. "A Class Perspective on Regionalism." In D. Glenday et al., eds., *Modernization and the Canadian State.* Toronto: Macmillan.

Cuneo, C. and J. Curtis. 1975. "Social Ascription in the Educational and Occupational Status Attainment of Urban Canadians." *Canadian Review of Sociology and Anthropology* 12: 6–24.

Daniels, M. 1984. "The Birth and Shaping of Regional Policies." *Policy Options* 2: 55–61.

Darroch, G. 1980. "Another Look at Ethnicity, Stratification and Social Mobility in Canada." In J. Goldstein and R. Bienvenue, eds., *Ethnicity and Ethnic Relations in Canada: A Book of Readings.* Toronto: Butterworths.

Darroch, G and W. Marston. 1971. "The Social Class Basis of Ethnic Residential Segregation: The Canadian Case." *American Journal of Sociology* 77: 491–510.

Davies, C. et al. 1975. *The Politics of Pollution.* 2nd ed. Indianapolis: Bobbs Merrill.

Davis, K. 1971. "Sexual Behaviour." In R. Merton and R. Nisbet, eds., *Contemporary Social Problems.* 3rd ed. New York: Harcourt Brace Jovanovich.

Davis, K. and W. Moore. 1945. "Some Principles of Stratification." *American Sociological Review* 10: 242–45.

de Beauvoir, S. 1973. *The Coming of Age.* New York: Warner Paperbacks.

Department of Manpower and Immigration. 1986. *Immigration Statistics 1968–1983.* Ottawa.

Disman, L. 1972. "Suicides among the Cheyenne Indians." In H. Bahr et al., eds., *Native Americans Today: Sociological Perspectives.* New York: Harper and Row.

Donnerstein, E. 1980. "Pornography and Violence Against Women: Experimental Studies." *Annals of the New York Academy of Sciences* 347: 277–88.

Dotson, F. 1974. "Marx and Engels on the Family." *American Sociologist* 9: 181–86.

Douglas, J., ed. 1970. *Deviance and Respectability.* New York: Basic Books.

D'Oyley, V., ed. 1978. *The Black Presence in Multi-Ethnic Canada.* Vancouver: Faculty of Education, University of British Columbia.

Dreidger, Leo. 1978. "Ethnic Boundaries: A Comparison of Two Neighbourhoods." *Sociology and Social Research* 62: 2.

Durkheim, E. 1951. *Suicide.* Trans. by J. A. Spaulding and G. Simpson. Glencoe, Ill.: Free Press.

Economic Council of Canada. 1977. *Living Together: A Study of Regional Disparities.* Ottawa: Supply and Services Canada.

Fisher, T. 1972. "The Many-Faceted Food Problem." In S. Reid and D. Lyon, eds., *Population Crisis.* Glensview, Ill: Scott Foresman and Co.

Feldberg, Rand and J. Kohen. 1976. "Family Life in an Anti-Family Setting: A Critique of Marriage and the Family." *The Family Coordinator* 25: 151–59.

Ferguson, B. 1988. "Studying the Family in Canada." In D. Forcese and S. Richer, eds., *Social Issues.* 2nd ed. Scarborough: Prentice-Hall.

Forbes, E. 1979. *The Maritimes Rights Movement 1919–1927: A Study in Canadian Regionalism.* Montreal: McGill-Queen's University Press.

Forcese, D. and Richer, S., eds. 1975. *Issues in Canadian Society: An Introduction to Sociology.* Scarborough: Prentice-Hall.

Fort, J. and C. Cory. 1975. *American Drug Store.* Boston: Little Brown.

200 / References

Fraser, P. 1985. Special Committee on Pornography and Prostitution. *Pornography and Prostitution in Canada*. Ottawa: Supply and Services Canada.

Frideres, J. 1983. *Native People in Canada: Contemporary Conflicts*. 2nd ed. Scarborough: Prentice-Hall, 1983.

Fuller, Richard and Richard Myers. 1981. "The Stages of a Social Problem." In E. Rubington and M. Weinberg, eds., *The Study of Social Problems*. 3rd ed. New York: Oxford University Press.

Gagnon, A. 1988. "Intercommunal Relations and Language Policy in Quebec: 1960–1986." In D. Forcese and S. Richer, eds., *Social Issues*. 2nd ed. Scarborough: Prentice-Hall.

Gagnon, J. and W. Simon, eds. 1967. *Sexual Deviance*. New York: Harper and Row.

Gagnon, J. and W. Simon, eds. 1973. *Sexual Conduct: The Social Sources of Human Sexuality*. Chicago: Aldine.

Gallup, G. 1982. *Public Opinion Sample Survey on Attitudes to Pornography*. Toronto.

Gallup, G. 1984. *Public Opinion Sample Survey on Efficiency in Government and its Employees*. Toronto.

Gans, H. 1972. "The Positive Functions of Poverty." *American Journal of Sociology* 78: 275–88

Gee, E. and M. Kimball. 1987. *Women and Aging*. Toronto: Butterworths.

Gelles, R. 1974. *The Violent Home: A Study of Physical Aggression between Husbands and Wives*. Beverly Hills: Sage.

Gibbins, R. 1980. *Prairie Politics and Society: Regionalism in Decline*. Toronto: Butterworths.

Gibbons, D. and J. Jones. 1975. *The Study of Deviance: Perspectives and Problems*. Englewood Cliffs, N.J.: Prentice-Hall.

Gibbs, J., ed. 1968. *Suicide*. New York: Harper and Row.

Gilbert, S. 1980. "Poverty, Policy and Politics: The Evolution of the Guaranteed National Income Experiment in Canada." In J. Harp and J. Hofley, eds., *Structured Inequality in Canada*. Scarborough: Prentice-Hall.

Gillespie, G. 1980. "On the Redistribution of Income in Canada." In J. Harp and J. Hofley, eds., *Structured Inequality in Canada*. Scarborough: Prentice-Hall.

Glaser, K. and S. Possony. 1979. *Victims of Politics: The State of Human Rights*. New York: Columbia University Press.

Goffman, Erving. 1961. *Asylums: Essays on the Social Situation of Mental Patients and Other Inmates*. New York: Anchor Books.

Goode, E. 1972. *Drugs in American Society*. New York: Knopf.

Goode, E. 1978. *Deviant Behaviour*. Englewood Cliffs, N.J.: Prentice-Hall.

Greenwald, H. 1970. *The Elegant Prostitute: A Social and Psychological Study.* New York: Ballantine.

Grollman, E. 1971. *Suicide: Prevention, Intervention, Postvention.* Boston: Beacon Press.

Grossman, B. 1974. "Discretion and Pre-Trial Practices." In C. Boydell et al., eds., *The Administration of Criminal Justice in Canada.* Toronto: Holt, Rinehart and Winston.

Hagan, J. et al. 1980. "The Differential Sentencing of White-Collar Offenders in Ten Federal District Courts." *American Sociological Review* 45: 101–20.

Hagan, J. 1984. *The Disreputable Pleasures: Crime and Deviance in Canada.* 2nd ed. Toronto: McGraw-Hill Ryerson.

Harp, J. 1980. "Social Inequalities and the Transmission of Knowledge." In J. Harp and J. Hofley, eds. *Structured Inequality in Canada.* Scarborough: Prentice-Hall.

Harp, J. and J. Hofley, eds. 1980. *Structured Inequality in Canada.* Scarborough: Prentice-Hall.

Hartjen, C. 1978. *Crime and Criminalization.* 2nd ed. New York: Praeger.

Henry, F. 1978. "The Demographic Correlates of Racism in Toronto." V. D'Oyley, ed., in *The Black Presence in Multi-Ethnic Canada.* Vancouver: Faculty of Education, University of British Columbia.

Henshel, A. and R. Henshel. 1983. *Perspectives on Social Problems.* 2nd ed. Don Mills: Academic Press.

Hicks, N. 1975. "Drug use called up among youths." *New York Times,* October 2nd, 1975, 22.

Hiller, H. 1986. *Canadian Society: A Macro-Analysis.* Scarborough: Prentice-Hall.

Hills, S. 1974. *Crime, Power and Morality: The Criminal Law Process in the United States.* Scranton: Chandler.

Hirschi, T. 1969. *Causes of Delinquency.* Berkeley: University of California Press.

Hobart, C. 1975. "Reactions to Premarital Intercourse." In S. Parvez Wakil, ed., *Marriage, Family and Society.* Toronto: Butterworths.

Horner, K. 1980. "On the Interpretation of Changes in Inequality." In J. Harp and J. Hofley, eds., *Structured Inequality in Canada.* Scarborough: Prentice-Hall.

Horton, P. and G. Leslie. 1978. *The Sociology of Social Problems.* 6th ed. Englewood Cliffs, N.J.: Prentice-Hall.

Hughes, D. and Kallen, E. 1974. *The Anatomy of Racism.* Montreal: Harvest House.

Hunt, M. 1974. *Sexual Behaviour in the 1970's.* New York: Dell.

Ishwaran, K. 1986. "Socialization." In K. Ishwaran, ed., *Sociology.* Don Mills: Addison-Wesley.

202 / References

Jayewardene, C. 1980. "The Nature of Homicide: Canada 1961–71." In R. Silverman and J. Teevan, eds. *Crime in Canadian Society*. 2nd ed. Toronto: Butterworths.

Johnson, L. 1979. "Income Disparity and the Structure of Earnings in Canada: 1946–74." In J. Curtis and W. Scott, eds., *Social Stratification in Canada*. 2nd ed. Scarborough: Prentice-Hall.

Julian, J. and W. Kornblum, 1986. *Social Problems*. 5th ed. Englewood Cliffs, N.J.: Prentice-Hall.

Kahn, H. 1976. *The Next 200 Years: A Scenario for America and the World*. New York: William Morrow.

Kalbach, W. E. and W. W. McVey. 1979. *The Demographic Bases of Canadian Society*. 2nd ed. Toronto: McGraw-Hill Ryerson.

Kallen, E. 1982. *Ethnicity and Human Rights in Canada*. Toronto: Gage.

Kammeyer, K., ed. 1969. *Population Studies: Selected Essays and Research*. Chicago: Rand McNally.

Kasindorf, M. "By the time it gets to Phoenix." *New York Times Magazine*, October 26, 1975, 92–105.

Kavolis, V. 1981. "A Universal Criterion of Pathology." In E. Rubington and M. Weinberg, eds., *The Study of Social Problems*. 3rd. ed. New York: Oxford University Press.

Kellough. G. 1980. "From Colonialism to Imperialism: The Experience of the Canadian Indians." In J. Harp and J. Hofley, eds., *Structured Inequality in Canada*. Scarborough: Prentice-Hall.

Kennedy, L. 1983. *The Urban Kaleidoscope: Canadian Perspectives*. Toronto: McGraw-Hill Ryerson.

Kinsey, A. et al. 1953. *Sexual Behaviour in the Human Female*. Philadelphia: W. B. Saunders.

Knapp, J. 1976. "An Exploratory Study of Seventeen Sexually Open Marriages." *Journal of Sex Research* 12:206–19.

Knight, S. 1979. "Work Orientation and Mobility Ideology in the Working Class." *Canadian Journal Of Sociology* 4:27–41.

Koenig, D. 1987. "Conventional Crime." In R. Linden, ed., *Criminology: A Canadian Perspective*. Toronto: Holt, Rinehart and Winston.

Komisar, L. 1971. "The Image of Women in Advertising." In V. Gornick and B. Moran, eds., *Women in a Sexist Society*. New York: Basic Books.

Labovitz, S. 1968. "Variations in Suicide Rates." In J. Gibbs, ed., *Suicide*. New York: Harper and Row.

Laing, R. 1967. *The Politics of Experience*. New York: Pantheon.

Langdon, S. 1980. "The Emergence of the Canadian Working Class Movement." In J. Paul Grayson, eds., *Class, State Ideology and Change*. Toronto: Holt, Rinehart and Winston.

Larson, L., ed. 1976. *The Canadian Family in Comparative Perspective*. Scarborough: Prentice-Hall.

Le Dain, G. et al. 1972. *Report of the Commission of Inquiry into the Non-Medical Use of Drugs*. vols. I and II. Ottawa: Information Canada.

Lee, D. 1979. "The Evolution of Nationalism in Quebec." In J. L. Elliott, ed., *Two Nations, Many Cultures*. Scarborough: Prentice-Hall.

Lemert, E. 1972. *Human Deviance, Social Problems and Social Control*. 2nd ed. Englewood Cliffs, N.J.: Prentice-Hall.

Lewis, D. 1972. *A Brief on Wife Battering with Proposals for Federal Action*. Ottawa: Canadian Advisory Council on the Status of Women.

Lewis, O. 1980. "The Culture of Poverty." In J. Harp and J. Hofley, eds., *Structured Inequality in Canada*. Scarborough: Prentice-Hall.

Locke, E.A. 1973. "Satisfiers and Dissatisfiers among White-Collar and Blue-Collar Employees." *Journal of Applied Psychology* 58: 67–76.

Lolli, G. et al. 1958. *Alcohol in Italian Culture*. New York: Free Press.

Lombroso, C. 1911. *Crime: Its Causes and Remedies*. Boston: Little Brown.

Lupri, E. 1986. *Reflections on Marriage and the Family in Canada*. Toronto: Holt, Rinehart and Winston.

Mackie, M. 1979. "Gender Socialization in Childhood and Adolescence." In K. Ishwaran, ed., *Childhood and Adolescence in Canada*. Toronto: McGraw-Hill Ryerson.

Maclean, M. and R. Bonar. 1985. "The Ethnic Elderly in a Dominant Culture Long-Term Care Facility." *Canadian Ethnic Studies* 15(3): 51–59.

MacLeod, L. 1980. *Wife Battering in Canada: The Vicious Circle*. Ottawa: Supply and Services Canada.

Marshall, V., ed. 1987. *Aging in Canada*. 2nd ed. Toronto: Fitzhenry and Whiteside.

Marx, K. 1965. *Capital*. New York: Modern Library.

Matthews, A. 1980. "Women and Widowhood." In V. Marshall, ed., *Aging in Canada*. Toronto: Fitzhenry and Whiteside.

Matthews, R. 1983. *The Creation of Regional Dependency*. Toronto: University of Toronto Press.

Matza, D. 1964. *Delinquency and Drift*. New York: John Wiley.

Mayo, E. 1945. *The Social Problems of An Industrial Civilization*. Cambridge, Mass.: Harvard University Press.

McClelland, D. 1971. "The Achievement Motive in Economic Growth." In P. Kilby, ed., *Entrepreneurship and Economic Development*. New York: Free Press.

McKie, D.C. et al. 1983. *Divorce: Law and the Family in Canada*. Ottawa: Supply and Services Canada.

McVey, W. 1987. "The Study of Population." In M. Rosenberg et al., eds., *An Introduction to Sociology*. 2nd ed. Toronto: Methuen.

Meadows, D. et al. 1972. *The Limits to Growth: A Report on the Club of Rome's Project on the Predicament of Mankind*. New York: Signet.

Meissner, M. 1971. "The Long Arm of the Job: A Study of Work and Leisure." In W. E. Mann, ed., *Canada: A Sociological Profile*. 2nd ed. Toronto: Copp Clark.

Merton, R. 1968. *Social Theory and Social Structure*. New York: Free Press.

Messinger, H. and B. Powell. 1987. "The Implications of Canada's Aging Society on Social Expenditures." In V. Marshall, ed., *Aging in Canada*. 2nd ed. Toronto: Fitzhenry and Whiteside.

Miller, S. and F. Reissman, eds. 1968. *Social Class and Social Policy*. New York: Basic Books.

Mills, C. W. 1956. *The Power Elite*. New York: Oxford University Press.

Morris, J. 1969. "Professor Malthus and His Essay." In K. Kammeyer, ed., *Population Studies*. Chicago: Rand McNally.

Moyer, S. 1980. *Diversion from the Juvenile Justice System and Its Impact on Children*. Ottawa: Supply and Services Canada.

Myles, John and M. Boyd. 1988. "Population Aging and the Elderly." In D. Forcese and S. Richer, eds., *Social Issues*. 2nd ed. Scarborough: Prentice-Hall.

Nagler, M. 1975. *Natives Without A Home*. Toronto: Longmans.

Naidoo, J. 1981. "The South Asian Experience of Aging." In V. Ujimoto et al., *Asian Canadians: Regional Perspectives*. Halifax: CASA

Nass, G. 1978. *Marriage and the Family*. Reading, Mass.: Addison-Wesley.

National Council of Welfare. 1984. *Sixty Five and Over*. Ottawa: Ministry of Supply and Services.

Nett, E. 1983. "The Family." In R. Hagedorn, ed., *Sociology*. 2nd ed. Toronto: Holt, Rinehart and Winston.

Nettler, G. 1981. "A Critique of Labeling." In E. Rubington and M. Weinberg, eds., *The Study of Social Problems*. 3rd ed. New York: Oxford University Press.

Neugarten, B. 1976. "Grow Old Along With Me/The Best Is Yet To Be." In B. Hess, ed., *Growing Old in America*. New Brunswick, N. J.: Transaction Books.

Nishio, H. and H. Lauk. 1987. "Patterns of Labour Participation of Older Female Workers." In V. Marshall, ed., *Aging in Canada*. 2nd ed. Toronto: Fitzhenry and Whiteside.

Novak, M. 1988. *Aging and Society: A Canadian Perspective*. Toronto: Nelson Canada.

Odum, H. and H. Moore. 1938. *American Regionalism*. New York: H. Holt and Company.

Olsen, D. 1980. *The State Elite*. Toronto: McClelland and Stewart.

Ornstein, M. 1986. "Regionalism and Canadian Political Ideology." In R. Brym, ed., *Regionalism in Canada*. Toronto: Irwin.

Pammett, J. 1976. "Public Orientations to Regions and Provinces." In D. Bellamy et al., eds. *The Provincial Political Systems*. Toronto: Methuen.

Park, R. 1981. "Social Change and Disorganization." In E. Rubington and M. Weinberg, eds., *The Study of Social Problems.* 3rd ed. New York: Oxford University Press.

Peck, M. 1977. "Adolescent Suicide." In C. Hatton et al., eds., *Suicide: Assessment and Intervention.* New York: Appleton-Century Crofts.

Perroux, F. 1970. "Notes on the Concept of Growth Poles." In D. McKee, ed., *Regional Economics.* New York: Free Press.

Pitman, W. 1977. *Now is Not Too Late.* Metropolitan Police Force. Toronto.

Polsky, N. 1972. "On the Sociology of Pornography." In C. Boydell et al., *Deviant Behaviour and Societal Reaction.* Toronto: Holt, Rinehart and Winston.

Poplin, Dennis. *Social Problems.* Glenview, Ill.: Scott, Foresman & Co., 1978.

Population Reference Bureau. 1983. *World Population Data Sheet.* Washington, D.C.: U.S. Government Printing Office.

Porter, John. 1965. *The Vertical Mosaic: An Analysis of Social Class and Power in Canada.* Toronto: University of Toronto Press.

Porter, John. 1979. *The Measure of Canadian Society.* Toronto: Gage.

Porterfield, A. 1968. "The Problem of Suicide." In J. Gibbs, ed., *Suicide.* New York: Harper and Row.

Price, J. 1978. *Native Studies.* Toronto: McGraw-Hill Ryerson.

Quebec Police Commission. 1977. Commission of Inquiry on Organized Crime. *The Fight Against Organized Crime.* Montreal: Editeur Official du Quebec.

Quinney, R. 1974. *Critique of Legal Order.* Boston: Little Brown.

Ramcharan, S. 1982. *Racism: Nonwhites in Canada.* Toronto: Butterworths.

Ramey, J. 1976. "Communes, Group Marriage and the Upper Middle Class." In L. Larson, ed., *The Canadian Family in Comparative Perspective.* Scarborough: Prentice-Hall.

Rawlyk, G. ed. 1979. *The Atlantic Provinces and the Problems of Confederation.* St. John's, Nfld.: Breakwater Books.

Reasons, C. 1972. "Crime of the American Indian." In H. Bahr et al., eds., *Native Americans Today: Sociological Perspectives.* New York: Harper and Row.

Reisman, D. 1969. *The Lonely Crowd.* New Haven: Yale University Press.

Reitz, J. 1980. *The Survival of Ethnic Groups.* Toronto: McGraw-Hill Ryerson.

Richer, S. 1980. "Equality to Benefit from Schooling: The Issue of Educational Opportunity." In D. Forcese and S. Richer, eds., *Social Issues.* Scarborough: Prentice-Hall.

Richmond, A. 1972. *Ethnic Residential Segregation in Metropolitan Toronto.* Toronto: Institute for Behavioural Research, York University.

Rimm, D. and J. Masters. 1974. *Behaviour Therapy: Techniques and Empirical Findings.* New York: Academic Press.

Rinehart, J. 1987. *The Tyranny of Work: Alienation and the Labour Process.* 2nd ed. Toronto: Harcourt Brace Jovanovich.

Ritzer, G. and D. Walczak. 1986. *Working: Conflict and Change.* 3rd ed. Englewood Cliffs, N.J.: Prentice-Hall.

Roach, J. 1965. "Sociological Analysis and Poverty." *American Journal of Sociology* 71: 68–75.

Roadburg, A. 1985. *Aging, Retirement, Leisure and Work in Canada.* Toronto: Methuen.

Robertson, J. 1980. *Social Problems.* 2nd ed. New York: Random House.

Rombout, M. 1975. *Health Care Institutions and Canada's Elderly: 1971–2031.* Ottawa: Department of National Health and Welfare.

Rose, A. and W. Peterson, eds. 1965. *Older People and Their Social World.* Philadelphia: F. A. Davis.

Rubin, J. 1976. "The Sexless Older Years: A Socially Harmful Stereotype." In B. Hess, ed., *Growing Old in America.* New Brunswick, N.J.: Transaction Books.

Rubington, Earl and Martin Weinberg, eds. 1981. *The Study of Social Problems: Five Perspectives.* 3rd ed. New York: Oxford University Press.

Ryan, T., ed. 1972. *Poverty and the Child.* Toronto: McGraw-Hill Ryerson.

Ryerson, S. 1968. *Unequal Union.* Toronto: Progress Books.

Salamon, E. 1988. "Homosexuality: Sexual Stigma." In V. Sacco, ed., *Deviance: Conformity and Control in Canadian Society.* Scarborough: Prentice-Hall.

Sagarin, E. 1975. *Deviants and Deviance.* New York: Praeger.

Saghir, M. and E. Robins. 1973. *Male and Female Homosexuality.* Baltimore, M.D.: Williams and Wilkins.

Saunders, E. 1988. "Women and Canadian Society: The Sociological Frame." In D. Forcese and S. Richer, eds., *Social Issues.* 2nd ed. Scarborough: Prentice-Hall.

Scanzoni, J. 1976. *Sex Roles, Life Styles and Childbearing: Changing Patterns in Marriage and the Family.* New York: Free Press.

Scheff, T. 1984. *Being Mentally Ill: A Sociological Theory.* 2nd ed. Chicago: Aldine.

Schermerhorn, R. 1970. *Comparative Ethnic Relations.* New York: Random House.

Schlesinger, B. 1979. *Families: Canada.* Toronto: McGraw-Hill Ryerson.

Schlesinger, B. 1983. "Living in One-Parent Families: The Children's Perspective." In K. Ishwaran, ed., *The Canadian Family.* Toronto: Gage.

Schneidman, E. 1968. "Preventing Suicide." In J. Gibbs, ed., *Suicide.* New York: Harper and Row.

Schwenger, C. and J. Gross. 1980. "Institutional Care and Institutionalization of the Elderly in Canada." In V. Marshall, ed., *Aging in Canada*. Toronto: Fitzhenry and Whiteside.

Schwutz, M. 1974. *Politics and Territory: The Sociology of Regional Persistence in Canada*. Montreal: McGill-Queen's University Press.

Scott, R. and E. Vaz. 1969. "A Perspective on Middle-Class Delinquency." *Canadian Journal of Economics and Political Science* 29: 112–18.

Scott, W. 1966. *Human Relations in Management*. Homewood, Ill.: R. D. Irwin.

Sellin, T. 1938. *Culture Conflict and Crime*. New York: Social Science Research Council.

Senate Committee on Poverty. 1971. *Report of the Senate Committee on Poverty*. Ottawa.

Silverman, R. and J. Teevan, eds. 1980. *Crime in Canadian Society*. 2nd ed. Toronto: Butterworths.

Simpson, G. and Yinger J. 1972. *Racial and Cultural Minorities*. New York: Harper and Row.

Snider, D. et al. 1980. "A Critical Perspective on Law in the Canadian State: Deliquency and Corporate Crime." In R. Ossenberg, ed., *Power and Change in Canada*. Toronto: McClelland and Stewart.

Srole, L. et al. 1978. *Mental Health in the Metropolis: The Midtown Manhattan Study*. 2nd ed. New York: Harper and Row.

St. Laurent, J. 1980. "Income Maintenance Programs and their Effect on Income Distribution." In J. Harp and J. Hofley, eds., *Structured Inequality in Canada*. Scarborough: Prentice-Hall.

Stamler, R. 1987. "Organized Crime." In R. Linden, ed., *Criminology: A Canadian Perspective*. Toronto: Holt, Rinehart and Winston.

Strauss, R. 1971. "Alcohol and Alcoholism." In R. Merton and R. Nisbet, eds., *Contemporary Social Problems*. 3rd ed. New York: Harcourt Brace Jovanovich.

Stebbins, R. 1983. "Deviance and Social Control." In M. Rosenberg et al., eds., *An Introduction to Sociology*. Toronto: Methuen.

Stebbins, R. 1988. *Deviance: Tolerable Differences*. Toronto: McGraw-Hill Ryerson.

Sullivan, T. et al. 1980. *Social Problems: Divergent Perspectives*. New York: John Wiley.

Susman, G. J. 1972. "Process Design, Automation and Worker Alienation." *Industrial Relations* 11: 34–45.

Sutherland, Edwin and D. R. Cressey. 1981. "Learning to Be Deviant." In E. Rubington and M. Weinberg, eds., *The Study of Social Problems*. New York: Oxford University Press.

Szasz, T. 1961. *The Myth of Mental Illness: Foundations in a Theory of Mental Illness*. New York: Harper and Row.

Szasz, T. 1974. *Ceremonial Chemistry*. Garden City, N.Y.: Doubleday.

Talbot, J. 1984. *The Chronic Mental Patient: Five Years Later*. New York: Harcourt Brace Jovanovich.

Thio, A. 1983. *Deviant Behaviour*. 2nd ed. New York: Harper and Row.

Thrasher, F. 1927. *The Gang*. Chicago: University of Chicago Press.

Toffler, A. 1980. "The Strategy of Social Futurism." In A. Toffler, ed., *The Futurists*. New York: Random House.

Tumin, M. 1953. "Some Principles of Stratification: A Critical Analysis." *American Sociological Review* 18: 7–21.

Turk, A. 1969. *Criminality and Legal Order*. Chicago: Rand McNally.

Ujimoto, V. 1987. "The Ethnic Dimension of Aging in Canada." In V. Marshall, ed., *Aging in Canada*. 2nd ed. Toronto: Fitzhenry and Whiteside.

Vaillant, G. et al. 1970. "Treatment Patterns for Mood-Altering Drugs." *New England Journal of Medicine* 282: 481–86.

Vallee, F. et al. 1969. "The Viability of French Groupings Outside Quebec." In M. Wade, ed., *Regionalism in the Canadian Community*. Toronto: University of Toronto Press.

Van Stolk, M. 1972. *The Battered Child in Canada*. Toronto: McClelland and Stewart.

Volkman, R. and D. Cressey. 1963. "Differential Association and the Rehabilitation of Drug Addicts." *American Journal of Sociology* 69: 129–42.

Ward, R. 1984. *The Aging Experience: An Introduction to Social Gerontology*. 2nd ed. Cambridge, Mass.: Harper and Row.

Weber, M. 1958. *The Protestant Ethic and the Spirit of Capitalism*. New York: Scribners.

Westley W. et al. 1971. *The Emerging Worker*. Montreal: McGill-Queen's University Press.

White, T. 1984. "Industrial, Work and Organizational Sociology in Canada." In S. D. Berkowitz, ed., *Models and Myths in Canadian Sociology*. Toronto: Butterworths.

Whitehurst, R. 1975. "Alternate Life Styles and Canadian Pluralism." In S. Parvez Wakil, ed., *Marriage, Family and Society*. Toronto: Butterworths.

Whitehurst, R. 1978. "Violence in the Family." In S. Ballantine and L. Cargan, eds., *Sociological Foot Prints*. New York: Houghton Mifflin.

Whyte, William. 1943. *Street Corner Society*. Chicago: University of Chicago Press.

Wilensky, H. 1966. "Work as a Social Problem." In H. Becker, ed., *Social Problems*. New York: Wiley.

Williams, J. et al. 1972. "Mental Health and Illness in Canada." In C. Boydell et al., eds., *Deviant Behaviour and Societal Reaction*. Toronto: Holt, Rinehart and Winston.

Winks, R. 1971. *The Blacks in Canada.* Montreal: McGill-Queen's University Press.

Woodcock, G. 1981. *The Meeting of Time and Space: Regionalism in Canadian Literature.* Edmonton: NeWest.

Wyatt, J. 1982. "Implications of Multiculturalism for Curriculum." In S. Shapson et al., eds., *Bilingualism and Multiculturalism in Canadian Education.* Vancouver: Centre for the Study of Curriculum and Instruction, University of British Columbia.

Index